Religion in a Changing Workplace

Religion in a Changing Workplace

ELAINE HOWARD ECKLUND, DENISE DANIELS,
AND CHRISTOPHER P. SCHEITLE

OXFORD
UNIVERSITY PRESS

OXFORD
UNIVERSITY PRESS

Oxford University Press is a department of the University of Oxford. It furthers
the University's objective of excellence in research, scholarship, and education
by publishing worldwide. Oxford is a registered trade mark of Oxford University
Press in the UK and certain other countries.

Published in the United States of America by Oxford University Press
198 Madison Avenue, New York, NY 10016, United States of America.

© Oxford University Press 2024

CIP data is on file at the Library of Congress

ISBN 978–0–19–767501–4 (pbk.)
ISBN 978–0–19–767500–7 (hbk.)

DOI: 10.1093/oso/9780197675007.001.0001

Paperback printed by Marquis Book Printing, Canada
Hardback printed by Bridgeport National Bindery, Inc., United States of America

For teaching about work, Penny Edgell, Harry Heintz,
Jeff Smith, and Robert Wuthnow—EHE

For my friends and mentors, Terry Mitchell, Jeff Van Duzer,
Alec Hill, and Al Erisman—DD

For my sociology mentors, Michael Kearl
and Roger Finke—CPS

Contents

Acknowledgments

Thank you, in particular, to Laura Achenbaum, Deidra Coleman, and Hayley Hemstreet, without whose organizational skills this book would not exist. In addition, we are very grateful for those who provided support, feedback, analysis, and input at every stage of research and writing, including Moses Biney, Dan Bolger, Di Di, Jauhara Ferguson, Jacqui Frost, Kerby Goff, Bradley Johnson, Laura Johnson, Brenton Kalinowski, Simranjit Steel, Bianca Mabute-Louie, Sharan Kaur Mehta, Oneya Okuwobi, Esmeralda Sánchez Salazar, and Rachel Schneider. We also acknowledge Rose Kantorczyk, Shannon Klein, Michael McDowell, Alex Nuyda, Shifa Rahman, Connor Rothschild, and Lindsey Schirn for their help with research for the book. We are grateful to our advisory board members for their feedback in early stages of this project: Melissa Alfaro, Katherine Leary Alsdorf, Katelyn Beaty, Luke Bobo, Jim Hackett, David Miller, Richard Mouw, Jerry Park, Alice Rhee, and Mark Roberts. Thank you also to our network advisers: Fernando Cascante, Kevin Dougherty, Kevin Dudley, Michael Emerson, Al Erisman, John Fontana, Brian Gagnon, Kaitlin Hasseler, Greg Jones, Chris Lowney, Gerardo Marti, Mia Mends, Will Messenger, Mitch Neubert, Cathy Nunnally, Steven Purcell, Shirley Roels, Amy Sherman, Laura Sorrell, Michael Stallard, Fernando Tamara, and John Witvliet. We are grateful for Heather Wax's editing and the guidance she provided. Special thanks to our editors, Theo Calderara and Cynthia Read, and everyone at Oxford University Press. We are most grateful for the support of our families.

This publication was made possible through the support of two grants from Lilly Endowment Inc. ("Faith at Work: An Empirical Study," #201-0021, Elaine Howard Ecklund PI, Denise Daniels Co-PI; and "The Impact of COVID-19 and Racism on Faith at Work," #2020-1655, Elaine Howard Ecklund PI, Denise Daniels Co-PI). The opinions expressed in this publication are those of the authors and do not necessarily reflect the views of Lilly Endowment Inc.

1

The Double-Edged Sword of Religion in a Changing Workplace

Brenda's Story

Brenda[1] is an oncologist and a Christian who loves her job. She operates her own medical practice, performs surgery, runs clinical trials, and leads national studies. She also attends church regularly, is involved in Christian ministries, and takes her children to Sunday services. She is one of only a couple of Black female surgeons in her city, she told us, and said she wants others to see that "I am doing what God has called me to do and that God has a purpose for all of us."

Brenda felt a "spiritual calling" to her work, she said, and derives great fulfillment from helping people with very serious and sensitive issues. Being able to connect with her patients spiritually is very important to her, and she feels lucky that her workplace gives her a lot of freedom to express her faith with them. "I pray, or sometimes I pray with them. I'm fortunate, I'm at . . . a Catholic hospital, where praying is fine. And so, it's nice, being able to do that," she shared. "I have patients' families who say, 'We want to pray for you and with you.'" Yet, if patients ask her to "stop with all the God stuff," she said, she does. Brenda previously worked in what she called "a secular hospital," where conversations about faith were discouraged for fear of pushing unwanted religion onto patients. She respected those rules but felt incredibly stifled by them.

She thinks that she is a better doctor, surgeon, and confidante to her colleagues and patients because she is a Christian. Her faith, she believes, is vital to helping her not only cope with but also thrive in her work. There are "days when I have to tell people really bad stuff," she said of her cancer patients, and she finds comfort in the theological perspective that "God gives me a lot of things that I can do to help, but there are times where it's just—it's His way. And there's nothing else that I can do. . . . And so, we have to rest that His plan is bigger than ours."

Religion in a Changing Workplace. Elaine Howard Ecklund, Denise Daniels, and Christopher P. Scheitle, Oxford University Press. © Oxford University Press 2024. DOI: 10.1093/oso/9780197675007.003.0001

Brenda's expression of her faith at work is deeply influenced by how she understands being a Christian. It is also influenced by her social location: that she comes from a largely Black church tradition and there are not many Black female surgeons at her level. Her profession and industry also have an impact. Medicine is a particular type of relational work where we find it's more common for faith to be expressed in the course of interactions with others at work, particularly patients. Her ability to express her faith openly in the workplace is also affected by her organizational rank—that she is the leader of her team, and that she can choose, as she sometimes does, "to start meetings with prayer." Additionally, how Brenda expresses faith at work is influenced by the culture of the organization she works in (a Catholic hospital) and the region of the country where she works (where there is a highly religious population).

This is a book about a new way of looking at religion in the US workplace, which was already changing before the recent global pandemic transformed it even more. We approach this work as social scientists, considering not only how individual but also group characteristics and differences have an impact on expressions of faith in the workplace. We show how the expression of faith at work is shaped by a person's religious identity, as we might expect, but also by their racial and gender identities and their profession, industry, organizational role, and rank. And we show why these personal and organizational identities matter if our goal as scholars and workplace leaders is to foster healthy workplaces, healthy workers, and healthy religious tolerance and pluralism in our society more broadly.

The Problems and Possibilities of Religion at Work

Work is a major part of most people's lives. For many, it is the place where they spend the most hours of the day and find romantic partners, best friends, and childcare. It is also where many find purpose in their lives. Scholars have long argued that, particularly for professionals, work has replaced nearly all domains (even sometimes family life) in its importance for creating meaning, social rules, social identities, and social codes that were previously created by religion, as Robert Wuthnow writes in *God and Mammon in America*, his important mid-1990s study of religion at work.[2] For some, work even takes on a religionlike devotion. In *Work Pray Code*, for example, Carolyn Chen shows how, even in Silicon Valley, religion is still relevant to work, particularly as work becomes a replacement for traditional religious practice, a trend that she thinks has potentially negative societal consequences.[3]

As people spend more and more time at work, the line between our work lives and personal lives has blurred. Religious employees in the United States—in all types of occupations and sectors—feel more comfortable expressing their faith in the workplace and less comfortable leaving their faith behind when they go to work. A majority of Americans are affiliated with a religious tradition,[4] and many feel their religious faith is an essential part of who they are—associated with the deepest values they hold, the relationships they forge, the actions they take, and the decisions they make. For many people, religion helps them find meaning in the world, cope with stress, handle challenges, and get through the day. For others who are not religious in a traditional sense, spirituality is still a meaningful part of their identity and relationships. Most religious individuals, and many nonreligious people too, feel that not expressing their beliefs at work would be an affront to their core identity and that concealing their faith would be hiding a crucial aspect of who they are. "I think that sharing what is true about one's self is important," said a senior communications specialist at a major university who also works part-time at her Episcopalian church,[5] "and it's sad that we have somehow bought [into] the idea that we're supposed to segregate pieces of ourselves."

Our research shows that expressing faith at work doesn't necessarily mean praying or talking about faith. More often, for most workers, it means seeking out meaningful relationships, working in a way that is consistent with their faith, sometimes although not always making decisions in alignment with their faith-driven values, trying to effect positive change in the workplace, and reflecting on their faith commitments in times of stress or challenge. Research also shows that there are positive outcomes for employees when they can bring their faith and other aspects of their personal identity to the workplace. Burnout is reduced,[6] constructive conflict resolution behaviors increase,[7] and happiness and productivity often improve.[8] Faith can also help workers cope with difficult work situations. Organizations like Microsoft, Facebook, Ernst & Young, and Topgolf[9] have taken notice, and are now stressing the idea of workers bringing their "whole person" to work.

Yet allowing employees to express their faith at work can get complicated, and many managers and organizations are struggling with how to address faith in the workplace. Religion can be divisive, even more so as US workplaces have become increasingly diverse due to recent immigration trends. Christianity is still by far the most popular religion in the United States, but the share of other religious groups has tripled since the 1970s. A growing number of Muslims, Hindus, and Buddhists from various traditions of these faiths are now in US workplaces. Perhaps the largest growth is among the nonreligious. In addition, workplaces are becoming more racially and ethnically diverse, and many racial and ethnic minority groups in the United States are much more religious than white Americans.[10] At the same time, the percentage of Americans who identify as having no religion has increased dramatically, from 5 percent of the population in 1972 to nearly 30 percent in 2021.[11] This percentage is even higher among young adults. Many of these nonreligious individuals do not want to celebrate religious holidays or talk about faith at work. Another group of nonreligious workers, while they are often deeply cynical of what they call "institutional religion,"[12] see spiritual practices as important, especially when coping with the stresses of their jobs.[13] In her book The Mindful Elite,[14] sociologist Jaime Kucinskas shows how meditation and other spiritual practices went from fringe to so mainstream that they are now found in workplaces around the world.

At the same time, as US workplaces have become more religiously and racially diverse, some scholars have identified religion as a missing dimension of diversity initiatives at work. Talking about religion at work has long been considered taboo, and it is rarely discussed alongside other types of diversity as a part of workplace diversity programs—though major US firms, like Google, Target, and Goldman Sachs,[15] are beginning to recognize the importance of religious inclusion and diversity as a part of their corporate initiatives. Using data from fifteen countries and one thousand companies, a recent McKinsey report on diversity and why it matters concluded that "the relationship between diversity on executive teams and the likelihood of financial outperformance has strengthened over time."[16] Many of the nation's top business leaders are starting to acknowledge that diverse perspectives benefit an organization, and including religious perspectives.

Even when business leaders are well intentioned, faith at work can be a double-edged sword. On the one hand, our research shows that having room for religion and spirituality can benefit individuals at work. Welcoming faith into the workplace can make work feel more meaningful to employees, help them work better with others, and lead them to be more ethical, loyal, and motivated. At the same time, open expressions of faith or open discussions about faith in the workplace—by both those who are religious and those who are not—can marginalize others and make workers who do not share the majority faith perspective feel uncomfortable, discriminated against, or ostracized. Thus, managers and other workplace leaders worry about how to ensure that religious employees are not offended or alienated and that they do not offend or alienate others. These competing demands play out against a legal backdrop designed to ensure equal opportunities for workers regardless of their religious tradition or lack thereof. While religious accommodations for legitimate expressions of faith are legally mandated, it is often unclear to organizational leaders what counts as a legitimate expression of faith and how best to accommodate such expressions.

Our Distinctive Approach and Argument

As social scientists, we are interested in how individuals think and behave, as well as how group-level and organizational-level factors have an impact on the thoughts and behaviors of individuals and can change society. Social scientists know that groups and organizations have distinctive logics, norms, customs, dynamics, cultural features, and interaction patterns, and we can look at how these influence and shape how faith is expressed in the workplace. While many workplaces are secular, some are faith-based, like the Catholic hospital where Brenda works, while others are run by founders or managers with religious beliefs that permeate the organization. What it means for Brenda to express her faith in the workplace may differ greatly from what it means for someone who is in a different profession to do so, and how faith can be expressed in a healthcare setting or nonprofit environment might be different from what expressions of faith are appropriate in a corporate, for-profit setting.

We also find that social factors—namely the religious tradition one identifies with or was born into, but also gender, race, sexuality, and the intersection of these—shape the experiences, capacities, and norms of individuals at work, including those related to expressions of religion. Someone who is at the top of their organizational hierarchy faces different opportunities and prohibitions for expressing their faith in the workplace when compared to someone in an entry-level or service role. Women or members of minority faiths—even if they are at the top of their organizational structure—might not feel they are able to express their faith in the workplace in the same way as men or members of the dominant faith tradition.

Here we take a distinctive and comprehensive approach to examining religion at work, looking at the broader social and cultural forces that shape how faith plays out in different types of workplaces for different types of individuals and groups. We bring together nearly fifty years of collective experience exploring how religion operates in workplaces. Elaine, a sociologist, has studied the relationship between religion and science, technology, and medicine, with a focus on scientific and medical workplaces. Denise is a management scholar who focuses on leadership development, gender equity, and vocation in the corporate world. Chris, a sociologist, has examined issues of religious identity, expression, and discrimination at work. To explore the contemporary faith-at-work landscape, we use data we collected from 2018 to 2022, as well as insights from hundreds of empirical studies investigating religion in the workplace. All of our research was conducted during a time of upheaval in the United States, amid deep polarization, protests and calls for racial justice, and a pandemic that changed how people relate to their jobs. As a result, we collected data that deals specifically with these issues. We conducted focus groups on faith in the workplace with workers and religious leaders. We surveyed more than fifteen thousand Americans and had one-on-one conversations with hundreds of people across the country, from all sectors of the economy and from various faith traditions, including those without a faith tradition.[17]

Our work addresses three questions: First, what kind of logics surround religion at work? In other words, what reasoning and criteria do individuals and organizations use to determine the place of faith in the workplace? Second, how do individual social factors and group identities intersect with organizational culture and practice to shape the ways workers express their faith in the workplace? Third, as scholars who care deeply about the public implications and practical uses of our social scientific research, how might organizational leaders and individual workers utilize our social science findings to foster intelligent engagement of faith in different kinds of workplaces in a way that supports healthy societal religious pluralism?

In what follows we share what we have learned from our broad and deep study of religion in the US workplace. You will meet a cast of characters who show how workers are grappling with the ways their faith can, should, or already does impact their work, and how fostering faith within work organizations, if done in a diligent and thoughtful way, can bring positive possibilities. There is Ben, a criminal investigator who is part of a largely Black church;[18] Josie, a young evangelical Christian engineer;[19] Lorena, a Hispanic Catholic who works in elder care;[20] Ron, a school custodian and Baptist[21] who says his faith led him to his current job; Aamna, a gas station owner and Muslim[22] who draws from her faith at work; and many others who give voice to the original data from our large-scale national surveys and in-depth interviews with workers across the country. We examine how those of different religious traditions, genders, occupations, social classes, and racial groups bring faith to the workplace, drawing especially on the voices of women and people of color, who have often been left out of literature concerning faith at work, workplace success, and workplace spirituality. If you are interested in learning more about how we conducted our research, details appear in Appendix A at the end of the book.

We also provide guidance to workplace leaders on ways they can or should attend to the religious lives and faith commitments of their employees. At times, this means helping religious employees identify ways to express their faith without violating laws or company policies. At other times, it means working to better understand how faith might motivate employees and finding ways to engage their religious sensibilities, encouraging them to apply the values of their faith at work. It also means recognizing the ways individuals and groups experience religious discrimination in the workplace and implementing policies and expectations to help avoid those outcomes.

Structure of the Book

Religion in a Changing Workplace is divided into four parts. We start by looking at expressing faith at work—how workers do it and how they think about it—and argue that, even though organizations and organizational leaders often fear overt expressions of religion in the workplace because they worry those from different faith traditions might feel marginalized, faith can be expressed at work in ways that benefit both employees and organizations. Workers are often aware of the potential difficulties that can arise from engaging with others about faith in the workplace and they take pains to navigate this context with sensitivity, finding creative ways of expressing faith without harming or creating conflict with others. In the second section of the book, we address how workers use faith to find meaning, purpose, and calling in their work and how employers and organizational leaders can cultivate this sense of meaning and purpose for everyone in a way that contributes to positive outcomes for workplaces and workers. Employees who search for meaning in their work and view their work as a calling tend to do better work, but this experience of meaning is a double-edged sword, leading many to accept rather than try to change unfair or unreasonable work conditions. The third section addresses organizational policies and discrimination, helping managers integrate religion into the workplace in ways that meet the needs of their employees while avoiding tension, alienation, and disadvantage. In the fourth section, we look at the future of faith at work, focusing on how family life, work, and religion come together, and how work and faith expression changed during the pandemic. We also discuss strategies leaders can utilize to support religious expression while protecting and honoring the identities of both religious and nonreligious workers as an essential part of creating work environments that foster pluralism and inclusion more broadly.

Notes

1. F@W_ST137, Black, Woman, 43, Physician, Christian, conducted September 23, 2019.
2. The topic has become prevalent enough among scholars for Springer to publish about ten years ago the *Handbook of Faith and Spirituality in the Workplace: Emerging Research and Practice.* Springer, 2013; Wuthnow, Robert. 1994. *God and Mammon in America.* New York: The Free Press.
3. See Chen, Carolyn. 2022. *Work, Pray, Code: When Work Becomes Religion in Silicon Valley.* Princeton, NJ: Princeton University Press. It is worth noting that while Chen does identify the strong desire for religious meaning that many in Silicon Valley express, she also writes at length about some of the problematic ways that the workplace has replaced religion and spirituality, with many organizations in the tech industry operating "like the most extreme of religious organizations—cults" (p. 200). In many ways this book is a follow-up to Wuthnow's earlier *God and Mammon in America*, a tour de force on the subject.
4. Cox, Daniel, and Robert P. Jones. 2017. "America's Changing Religious Identity." PRRI. https://www.prri.org/research/american-religious-landscape-christian-religiously-unaffiliated/.
5. F@W_ST07, White, Woman, 49, Senior Communications Specialist, Episcopal, conducted October 31, 2018.
6. Grandey, Alicia, Su Chuen Foo, Markus Groth, and Robyn E. Goodwin. 2012. "Free to Be You and Me: A Climate of Authenticity Alleviates Burnout from Emotional Labor." *Journal of Occupational Health Psychology* 17: 1–14.
7. Fotohabadi, Mark, and Louise Kelly. 2018. "Making Conflict Work: Authentic Leadership and Reactive and Reflective Management Styles." *Journal of General Management* 43: 70–78.
8. Sabat, Isaac E., Alex P. Lindsey, Kristen P. Jones, Eden B. King, Carolyn Winslow, Ashley Membere, and Nicholas A. Smith. 2019. "Stigma Expression Outcome and Boundary Conditions: A Meta-analysis." *Journal of Business and Psychology* 35: 171–86.
9. Hastwell, Claire. 2019. "How the Best Companies Ensure People Can Bring Their Whole Selves to Work." Great Place to Work. September 13. https://www.greatplacetowork.com/resources/blog/4-ideas-to-encourage-people-to-bring-their-whole-self-to-work; Topgolf Blog. 2013. "The Freedom to Be Your Whole Self at Work." *Topgolf.* July 3. https://topgolf.com/blog/post/2013/07/the-freedom-to-be-your-whole-self-at-work/.
10. Dougherty, Kevin D., and Michael O. Emerson. 2018. "The Changing Complexion of American Congregations." *Journal for the Scientific Study of Religion* 57: 24–38.
11. General Social Survey, 1972–2021. Accessed at GSS Data Explorer | NORC at the University of Chicago.

12. Chen, *Work, Pray, Code*.
13. Baker, Joseph O'Brian, and Buster Smith. 2009. "None Too Simple: Examining Issues of Religious Nonbelief and Nonbelonging in the United States." *Journal for the Scientific Study of Religion* 48(4): 719–33
14. Kucinkas, Jaime. 2018. *The Mindful Elite: Mobilizing from the Inside Out*. New York: Oxford University Press.
15. Religious Freedom and Business Foundation. 2020. "Corporate Religious Equity, Diversity, and Inclusion (REDI) Index." https://religiousfreedomandbusiness.org/redi.
16. Dixon-Fyle, Suniatu, Kevin Dolan, Dame Vivian Hunt, and Sara Prince. May 19, 2020. *Diversity Wins: How Inclusion Matters*. Report Published by McKinsey & Company. See https://www.mckinsey.com/featured-insights/diversity-and-inclusion/diversity-wins-how-inclusion-matters, accessed January 5, 2020.
17. We conducted our main survey on faith at work in the fall of 2018 and winter 2019, which consisted of a nationally representative sample of 13,270 individuals. We followed up with a supplemental survey on faith at work in the fall of 2021, which consisted of a nationally representative sample of 2,486 individuals. We identify which survey our findings come from in endnotes.
18. F@W_ST49, Black, Man, 38, Criminal Investigator, Evangelical, conducted February 6, 2019.
19. F@W_ST31, White, Woman, 25, Civil Engineer, Christian, conducted December 19, 2018.
20. F@W_ST143, Hispanic, Woman, 57, Elder Caregiver, Catholic, conducted October 8, 2019.
21. F@W_ST44, White, Man, 31, Custodian, Baptist, conducted January 30, 2019.
22. F@W_ST105, Asian, Woman, 52, Gas Station Owner, Muslim, conducted July 29, 2019.

2

Leaders Fear Faith Expression

We need to start by being honest about fears, including our own. Religion in the workplace is indeed a double-edged sword. People understand writing a book about trying to avoid religious discrimination in the workplace; leaders and companies do not want to get sued, and many want to fight for equitable workplaces, including religious equity. But discussing actually *expressing* faith in the workplace can seem to some like we are devoting a lot of time and energy to something that is not actually a major issue facing workplaces today—and perhaps something that should not be happening at all.

We want to be clear here. Authenticity matters. On the one hand, research shows that when people are able to be fully authentic at work, they are more committed, motivated, and likely to act in ways that support their organizations. And, under certain conditions, expressing faith at work is part of being authentic at work; it helps workers be more likely to flourish personally and advocate for themselves in their workplaces.[1] Our own national survey of workers finds, for instance, that individuals who display or wear items at work that represent their faith or spirituality are more likely to say they are very satisfied with their job.[2] If we look at individuals' level of agreement with the statement "At work, I display or wear items that represent my faith or spirituality," in conjunction with their level of agreement with the statement "Overall, I am very satisfied with my current job," we find that 48 percent of those who strongly agree that they display their faith at work strongly agree that they are very satisfied with their jobs. In comparison, only 36 percent of those who strongly disagree that they display their faith at work have a strong sense of satisfaction with their jobs. Similarly, individuals who say that they feel comfortable talking about their faith at work are more likely to say that they feel a strong sense of commitment to the organization they work for.[3] If we compare individuals' level of agreement with the statement "I feel comfortable talking about my faith at work," with their level of agreement with the statement "I feel a strong sense of commitment to the organization I work for," we find that 61 percent of those who strongly agree that they feel comfortable talking about their faith at work also strongly agree that they feel a

Religion in a Changing Workplace. Elaine Howard Ecklund, Denise Daniels, and Christopher P. Scheitle, Oxford University Press. © Oxford University Press 2024. DOI: 10.1093/oso/9780197675007.003.0002

strong sense of commitment to their work organization. Only 39 percent of those who do not feel comfortable talking about their faith at work express a strong sense of commitment to the organization they work for.

On the other hand, while some organizational leaders know faith is central to identity for many of their employees, they often feel work is not the right place to express faith. Expressions of faith, they believe, are a kind of personal fulfillment that should happen outside of work. They worry that any reference to faith in the workplace may lead to conflict, ostracism, or a lawsuit. In our interviews we found that organizational leaders and workers themselves particularly fear overt expressions of faith because of the potential for marginalization and conflict and that leaders respond by trying to suppress all expressions of faith in the workplace or by separating faith from the workplace, subtly or explicitly encouraging their employees to keep their faith private. This leads many workers to perceive their workplaces as indifferent or even hostile toward their faith or spirituality.

Notably, when we asked workers whether the organization they work for "cares about the spiritual well-being of its employees," about 16 percent said that they strongly agree while an almost equal 11 percent strongly disagreed. This suggests that workplaces are taking very different approaches to faith at work, with some being quite unreceptive (the strongly-disagree responses) and others being welcoming (the strongly-agree responses). But the most popular response among the workers we surveyed is, "Neither agree nor disagree," suggesting that employees have no basis for knowing how their organization thinks about or views their spiritual lives.[4] Many organizations, it seems, are taking a nothing-to-see-here approach to faith in the workplace.

Marginalization

The potential problem with expressing faith at work is that marginalization may occur when one worker's faith comes in conflict with another person's faith and when expressions of faith challenge the explicit or implicit goals of the organization. Workers and organizational leaders both worry that expressions of faith at work will lead to the marginalization of those who have a faith perspective different from the majority. Indeed, there is evidence that workers whose religion is in the minority within their workplace are more likely to fear expressing their faith given their minority status. For instance, we asked workers in our survey whether they conceal their religious beliefs at work for fear of others' perceptions. As seen in Figure 2.1, 29 percent of Muslims, 51 percent of Hindus, 28 percent of Buddhists, and 19 percent of Jews agreed that they conceal their faith out of fear. This compares to only 9 percent of evangelical Protestants, 15 percent of other Protestants, and 13 percent of Catholics.[5]

This theme came up in our interviews with workers as well. A Jewish survey statistician explained,[6] "I feel kind of uncomfortable when people tell me to 'Have a blessed day,' right, which feels very Christian, to me. That's not . . . a way that we tend to talk, and [*laughs*] it makes me a little uncomfortable. So, that expression of faith in the workplace, when it's on the bottom of an email signature or something like that, I feel distinctly put off. . . . I guess it feels a little evangelical to me, that I'm doing something wrong by having a different faith." A Muslim who manages a real estate firm[7] said that when people question his faith at work, "I just keep it personal. Whatever you believe is what you believe, and I'm not here to offend people. . . . Christians shouldn't offend other folks about their beliefs or push their beliefs on other people." In short, when one feels different from others in their organization,

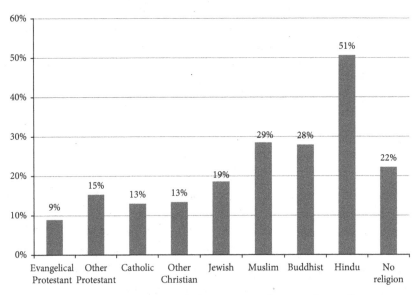

Figure 2.1 Percentage agreeing with the statement "I conceal my religious beliefs at work for fear of others' perceptions."

Faith at Work Survey 2021. Percentages represent the "strongly agree" and "somewhat agree" responses.

they are reluctant to bring their whole selves to work, but especially aspects of their faith.

Conflict

Another reason workers sometimes advocate keeping faith out of the workplace is that they believe it has the potential to cause conflict. This fear of conflict is often related to talking openly about one's faith, something evangelical Christians are particularly likely to do. Lorena,[8] who is Catholic and works in eldercare, is one worker who feels strongly that people shouldn't talk about their faith in the workplace. When people engage in conversations about faith at work, it often leads to problems, she said. "I think we shouldn't express our faith. Nobody cares how we feel and what we think except God. . . . I think we shouldn't talk about religion at work because that's when the problems arise," she told us. "I'm going to defend what I think and they will defend what they think, their way of being, their religion." She was wary of the potential for conflict with those she deemed "fanatics," often evangelical Christians, in terms of their faith. "I prefer to remain in silence," she said, "but there are some persons who are fanatics. They worship God with a strong fanaticism and that's when you say, 'Well, extremes are bad too.' Fanaticism is bad in any aspect." Lorena was not the only worker we spoke with who thought that any overt expression of faith in workplaces might lead to fanaticism.

Some workers told us about their uncomfortable experiences with multiple religious perspectives being expressed at work. "I think that that's where a lot of conflict comes from, in the workplace, is the clashing of different religions," an evangelical Christian nurse[9] said. And a sales account manager who does not practice a religion now but was raised Catholic[10] told us she feels "like as long as it doesn't interfere with how people relate to each other or get their job done, there shouldn't be a problem," but she has "found in other jobs that I've had, not this one, but [religion] can cause a lot of conflict . . . when you have people that are very different. People get really easily offended if they feel like their faith is being criticized or questioned, and I think it's probably best in the workplace to only bring it up under certain circumstances," which she thinks are quite limited.

Some workers censor themselves from talking about their faith beliefs in the workplace because they don't want others to take offense. An evangelical

Christian who works in IT tech support[11] decided to place a full personal moratorium on discussing religion at work so as not to cause hard feelings. "I don't really speak about religion . . . so much in our work because I'm not trying to offend someone," he said. "Because I know, now, in the world, if you say something about some religion . . . it's a very sensitive topic in public, so I rather choose not to say anything about it in public."

But a number of evangelical Christians also indicated discomfort with expressing their faith at work because they feel that due to changing norms and guidelines they might be sanctioned for talking about their faith. For example, Ben, a Black evangelical Christian who works as a criminal investigator,[12] said he could not keep up with the cultural changes governing religious expression, so he keeps his faith to himself at work. "As far as my opinion on faith expressing, just in general, I think that we live in a time where it's very unsafe to . . . let people know who you are because you don't know what's acceptable and what's not acceptable. And it changes from day to day, and so, you may think it is just you sharing your life, or you sharing your person with somebody, it could actually be punitive, or it can be consequential," he said. "My faith is not necessarily a protected [*laughs*] faith, and so I think that, as a result, people who have my faith kind of—we just have to put our heads down and try to keep a low profile because, at any time, somebody could get offended. And then you have to be on the defensive, and you have to justify why you're not all of these labels that are being placed and all of these prejudices that are placed upon us." Ben makes an important point about being in the majority faith versus the minority faith, which means he needs to keep a low profile.

Separation

We also heard from a number of workers who feel that expressions of faith should be very limited or not appear at all in the workplace. In our national survey, about 25 percent of workers *disagreed* when asked if they "feel comfortable talking about [their] faith at work."[13] A state trooper who said he regularly attends a Baptist church[14] told us, for example, that he does not express his faith at work or see a role for faith in the workplace, though he doesn't mind if others privately express their faith at work. "I keep it separate," he said. "It really doesn't compel me to try to change anything in my workplace. I'm kinda like, 'Live and let live,' with work. And I don't hold court on anybody that wants to say grace or pray or . . . they wanna sit there and take off for Sunday and go with their family to church. I have no issues with it." People like this state trooper feel that while faith is personally important to them, they should largely keep it private.

"If you want to express faith, do it! Just do it on your own time," a Muslim CEO of a technology company[15] told us, expressing an attitude we found to be prevalent among some organizational leaders. "If they need a prayer closet, great! Just don't make a big deal out of it." To him, faith is a personal matter. "If you need time off to go say your prayers, I have a space you can go do it. I have no problem with that, but you don't need to flaunt your faith in somebody else's face. . . . You know, if somebody wants . . . to sit in the break room and talk about it, that's their personal business. But in the official capacity I shouldn't be telling anybody that I am from a certain faith and this is what it says and this is what it doesn't. No, to me that would be wrong."

Nonreligious workers, in particular, tend to think discussions of religion should be kept out of the workplace. Among those we surveyed, only 8 percent of individuals who identified as having no religion (compared to 27 percent of all workers) said they feel motivated to talk about faith or spirituality with people at work.[16] "I mean, if somebody wants to have, say, a prayer before we eat, or say a prayer before they start work, that kind of stuff, that's fine. But on the whole, when they're out on the mill floor and they're doing their job, you know, the foremost thing to be on their mind is being safe and keeping their teammates safe," said an electrical engineer who works at a steel mill and was raised Catholic but no longer considers himself religious.[17] "Religion shouldn't play a role in any of that. . . . Religion is for after work or at home."

An appreciable minority of workers who said religion is an important part of their lives also expressed the feeling that faith should be kept out of the workplace. For example, an evangelical Christian we spoke with, who works as both a pastor and truck driver,[18] was firm in his belief that talking about faith does not belong at work. "The purpose of the workplace is to make money. . . . The church is the place to worship and express your faith," he said. As he sees it, there are "a lot of faiths that are intolerant . . . of any other faith, so you're opening up Pandora's Box" when you start to talk about faith in the workplace. We also spoke with a Jewish social worker[19] who told us that she works with many Christian coworkers and goes to great lengths to avoid telling others at work that she does not celebrate Christmas because she feels like they might judge her. In her sense of things, "Personally, from anybody's religion, I don't necessarily believe it belongs in the workplace," she said. "If it makes you a better person, wonderful. . . . Let everybody have their say, at home, in their own, private. But when you're at work, that's a work environment." Many of the people who raised concerns about expressing faith at work did so because of their fears that expressions of faith could lead to marginalization or conflict between people with different beliefs *and* because— like the Jewish woman quoted above—they had actual experiences that supported their fears.

While we are attentive to ways some types of faith expression might create difficulty in a pluralistic work environment, our survey research and interviews revealed that there are also many healthy and positive ways of expressing faith beliefs and values in the workplace. In the following chapters, we explore the range of ways that people express their faith at work and the organizational benefits that can result, while being honest about the downsides of expressing faith at work.

The Bottom Line

- Some workers and organizational leaders fear that expressions of faith will lead to marginalization and conflict in the workplace.
- Marginalization may occur when one worker's faith comes in conflict with another worker's faith or expression of faith in the workplace.
- Fear of conflict is often related to talking openly about one's faith, something evangelical Christians are particularly likely to do.
- Workers and organizational leaders often respond by encouraging themselves and others to privatize their faith at work or to completely separate faith from work.
- The better way is thoughtful, nuanced support, not suppression, of faith at work.

Notes

1. Selver, Prem. 2013. "Spiritual Values in Leadership and the Effects on Organizational Performance: A Literature Review." *University of Northern British Columbia.* https://doi.org/10.24124/2013/bpgub1588
2. Cross-tabulation's design-based F-test $p < .001$. Note that this does not seem to be simply due to religious individuals being more satisfied with their job. Even if we limit the analysis to the most religious workers (i.e., those who say they are "very religious"), we find a positive and statistically significant association between displaying faith items at work and job satisfaction.

3. Cross-tabulation's design-based F-test $p < .001$. Note that this does not seem to be simply due to religious individuals expressing more commitment to their organization. Even if we limit the analysis to the most religious workers (i.e., those who say they are "very religious"), we find a positive and statistically significant association.

4. Faith at Work Supplemental Survey. 11 percent of workers strongly disagree, 9 percent somewhat agree, 44 percent neither agree nor disagree, 19 percent somewhat agree, and 15 percent strongly agree.

5. Faith at Work Supplemental Survey. Evangelical Protestants identified as individuals who said that they were Protestant or "other Christian" and attend an evangelical congregation. Because of the religious composition of the United States, workers who are Muslim, Jewish, Hindu, and from other non-Christian groups are often in the minority. However, we note that each workplace has its own religious composition, so in some specific organizations it could be that Christians (and especially evangelical Christians) are in the minority.

6. F@W_ST155, White, Woman, 41, Survey Statistician, Jewish, conducted November 1, 2019.

7. F@W_ST186, Black, Man, 54, Organizational Manager in Real Estate, Muslim, conducted December 19, 2019.

8. F@W_ST143, Hispanic, Woman, 57, Elder Caregiver, Catholic, conducted October 8, 2019.

9. F@W_ST86, White, Woman, 21, Nurse, Evangelical, conducted June 13, 2019.

10. F@W_ST08, White, Woman, 50, Sales Account Manager, Nonpracticing Catholic, conducted November 1, 2018.

11. F@W_ST83, Black, Man, 20, IT Tech Support, Evangelical, conducted June 11, 2019.

12. F@W_ST49, Black, Man, 38, Criminal Investigator, Evangelical, conducted February 6, 2019.

13. Faith at Work Main Survey. Note that those who said this statement was "not applicable" to them are excluded from the calculation of the percentages. If they are included in the percentages, then 18 percent of workers disagree.

14. F@W_ST194, White, Man, 58, State Trooper, Baptist, conducted February 25, 2020.

15. F@W_ST106, Asian, Man, 71, CEO of a Fiber Electric Company, Muslim, conducted July 31, 2019.

16. Faith at Work Main Survey. These percentages exclude those who said that the question was "not applicable" to them. If we include that response in the calculations, then about 4 percent of those who do not identify with a religion agree that they feel motivated to talk about their faith/spirituality in the workplace, compared to 22 percent of all workers.

17. F@W_ST02, White, Man, 54, Electrical Engineer, Catholic, conducted October 16, 2018.

18. F@W_ST48, White, Man, 39, Truck Driver/Pastor, Evangelical, conducted February 5, 2019.

19. F@W_ST112, White, Woman, 49, Social Services, Jewish, conducted August 8, 2019.

3

Expressing Faith at Work

Josie[1] is a civil engineer who attends a nondenominational Christian church she is hesitant to classify as evangelical since that "term is pretty loaded these days," she said. Her work focuses on water design at a firm that is often hired by municipalities. She conducts calculations to determine "how water behaves in a city water system," she explained, then develops drawings, plans, and models to make recommendations. "Lots of emails," she said jokingly as she described the main tasks of her day. She said she left a job she felt served God—building water systems for communities in Uganda—for her current one, which she sees as less connected to her faith.

She does still express her faith at work, however. Josie told us she will "take breaks and take my big Bible into the conference room. Everyone sees me reading it, and then . . . one day I was having a rough day and a verse came to mind and so I wrote it on a Post-it Note and put it up on my computer and haven't taken it down." She believes people at work "are afraid to swear around me since I am [known as a Christian]," she shared, "even though I swear sometimes too." Her faith, she feels, helps her when she experiences conflict with others in the workplace. "When I take time to pray about that and examine myself, my motives, I feel like I'm able to apologize when necessary or maybe stand up for myself when I need to," she said. "I feel like I'm kind of backed up by my faith in that way because . . . I'm learning not to put my worth in what my boss or my coworkers think of me but to put it in God and I think that gives me a lot more confidence to stand up for myself when I need to." But, she said, she is "pretty careful to evaluate where my coworkers are at with their [own approach to] faith, and that definitely affects how I talk about it to them." She expressed some frustration with her boss, who is a Seventh-day Adventist, because "he's happy to talk about his faith in a practical way, but I've never gotten him to engage on a deeper level about what his faith means."

Research suggests that individual and workplace factors both shape religious expression at work. When management scholars Ericka R. Lawrence and James E. King looked at the determinants of religious expression in the

Religion in a Changing Workplace. Elaine Howard Ecklund, Denise Daniels, and Christopher P. Scheitle, Oxford University Press. © Oxford University Press 2024. DOI: 10.1093/oso/9780197675007.003.0003

workplace, they found that individual religiosity, as well as organizational culture and the congruence between the values of the company and those of the worker, influence the likelihood of religious expression.[2] They suggest that organizational cultures that workers perceive to be more accepting of religion will result in more religious expression, and employees who perceive their values as congruent with the values of their organization are more likely to express their religion at work. Other researchers have found that disclosing religious identity at work depends on a number of factors both personal (such as religion and religiosity, job rank, and ethnicity) and organizational—specifically, the size of the organization and the workplace's dominant religion.[3] Employees in smaller organizations and those who are members of the organization's dominant religious tradition are more likely to express their religion in the workplace. Here we examine more closely the factors that influence whether workers express their faith in the workplace and how they do so, who is more likely to express their religion at work, what kinds of religious expression are most common, and what factors shape these decisions. In the end we argue that organizational leaders need to help create norms and cultures that foster a healthy expression of religion at work that honors religious pluralism rather than, while such policies are certainly important, just focusing on policies and procedures that minimize discrimination.

Who Expresses Faith at Work?

Like past research, we found that religiosity is linked with workplace religious expression. In our main survey, 45 percent of workers who describe themselves as very religious agreed that they "display or wear items that represent [their] faith or spirituality" at work. This drops to 24 percent among workers who are moderately religious, 13 percent among those who are slightly religious, and 7 percent among those who say they are not at all religious.[4]

Our survey also finds racial differences in workplace religious expression. For instance, when we asked workers whether they "feel motivated to talk about [their] faith or spirituality with people at work," 36 percent of Black workers, 26 percent of white workers, and 18 percent of Asian workers agreed with this statement. Even after accounting for other factors, like religiosity and religious tradition, Black workers are still more likely than white workers to say they feel motivated to talk to others about their faith while at work.[5]

We also find that individuals who work in smaller organizations are more likely to display or wear items that represent their faith or spirituality in the workplace. In the smallest organizations (those with only 1 to 9 employees), 34 percent of workers display such faith items. This percentage declines as organizations get larger. For instance, in organizations with 55 to 99 employees, 27 percent of workers display such faith items, compared with 22 percent in organizations with 100 to 499 employees.[6] We find a similar organizational size effect for the question asking whether workers feel motivated to talk about their faith with others at work. This suggests that something about the size of an organization facilitates or restricts religious expression, or perhaps that those who are interested in talking about their faith are more likely to self-select into smaller organizations. Based on our research we think it is because workers in smaller organizations are more likely to know each other and to know whether it's safe to display their faith at work.

Religious expression among workers also differs somewhat by industry, according to our findings. Unsurprisingly, as seen in Figure 3.1, workers who describe their work as in the religion sector are more likely than those in any other industry to say they express their faith at work, with 71 percent saying they feel motivated to talk about their religion in the workplace. When we look at other industries, the differences in worker motivation to discuss faith at work are more modest. At the higher end are workers in caretaking (28 percent), farming (28 percent), and construction (26 percent), and at the lower end are workers in the arts (17 percent), computer (17 percent), legal (16 percent), and science (13 percent) sectors. Even when we account for other factors—including religiosity, religious tradition, race, gender, organizational size, and position in the organization—industry-level differences remain: Workers in the tech, legal, and scientific industries are less likely to say they feel motivated to talk about their faith at work than are workers in the healthcare and religion sectors.[7] We think there is something unique to the cultural logic of these sectors, that these professions (like science and technology work) are perceived as secular, draw people who are more likely to be secular, and are perceived by religious people as being more hostile to expressions of faith.

Other research supports this idea. Elaine and her colleagues have spent the past twenty years studying how religion shows up in scientific workplaces; they find that, under certain conditions, the scientific environment can be openly hostile toward religion and expressions of faith, and some individuals we spoke with discussed this.[8] Scientists in the United States are less religious

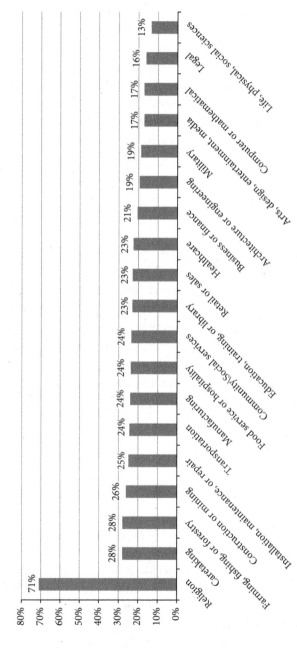

Figure 3.1 Percentage of workers agreeing that "At work, I display or wear items that represent my faith or spirituality," by industry

Data: Faith at Work Main Survey. Percentages represent combine "somewhat" and "strongly agree" responses and exclude those who said "not applicable." "Not applicable" response not included in calculations.

than the general population, and research suggests the culture of science can create an environment that makes religious individuals feel like outsiders who are discriminated against because of their faith. A Christian who manages a scientific lab,[9] for example, said she thinks there are "a few people in the laboratory who I know go to church regularly and are Christian, [Muslim], Catholic, or whatever. But they just—you don't cop to it in the lab." She said, "People just make comments about, 'Oh, that's so dumb. Christians are this, Christians are that.' Or like, 'Anyone who believes in God is stupid.' It's not directed at a specific person, but I can imagine, especially the friends in the lab that I have that I know are very religious, I'm sure it stings, a little bit." While she isn't necessarily afraid to express her own faith in the workplace, after hearing how her coworkers speak about people of faith, she is tentative about expressing her religion at work.

How Do People Express Faith at Work?

Our research shows that expressing faith at work can take various forms and differ among individual workers. Some workers we spoke with express their faith at work in overt ways. Like Josie, they might speak with coworkers about their religious tradition or discuss their faith with clients. Some wear religious symbols, observe religious practices during the workday, offer to pray with others, take time off to observe religious holidays, or tell others about religious services in which they participate.[10]

Verbal Expression

In our survey, 22 percent of US workers said they are motivated to talk about their faith or spirituality with people at work, and we find that the desire to talk about religion in the workplace varies by religious tradition. As seen in Figure 3.2, 52 percent of workers who are evangelical Protestant say they are motivated to talk about their faith with people at work, a much higher percentage than in any other religious tradition. After evangelical Christians, Muslims are the most motivated to talk about their faith with other workers, with 29 percent saying they have a desire to do so. While a higher average level of religiosity among evangelicals compared with members of other religious traditions might partly explain why evangelicals are much more likely than

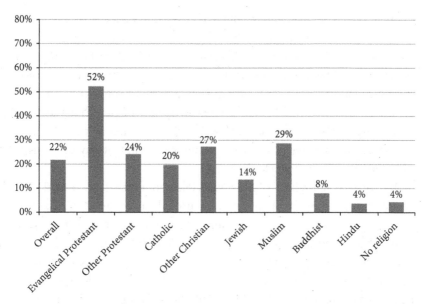

Figure 3.2 Percentage agreeing that "I feel motivated to talk about my faith or spirituality with people at work," by religious tradition

Data: Faith at Work Main Survey. Percentages represent responses for "somewhat agree" and "strongly agree." "Not applicable" response coded as "strongly disagree."

workers of other faiths to express a desire to talk about their faith at work, it is not the whole picture.[11] When we control for religiosity, race, gender, organizational size, position in organization, and industry, we still find that evangelical Protestants are significantly more likely to say they feel motivated to talk about their faith at work than are members of any other religious tradition. We believe that the difference is due to differences in religious tradition. Evangelical Protestantism uniquely motivates adherents to talk with others about their religion, often to try to convert others to their faith. Muslims may feel compelled to talk about their faith for different reasons. When Chris conducted interviews with mosque leaders about fears of violence against their congregations, Muslim leaders often expressed feeling a need to represent or be ambassadors for their faith.[12] We suspect that this feeling could drive Muslims to talk about their faith in the workplace as well.

Several workers we spoke with described to us how they shared their faith as a way to directly or indirectly create opportunities to evangelize to others. "A lady I had worked with for a number of years . . . we were working on our computers. She kept looking up, and she's like, 'Can I talk to you for a minute?' This woman was basically like, 'I want to be a Christian' . . . and I led her to Christ, outside the back of the building," shared Marla, a corporate trainer[13] in Georgia who attends a largely Black Pentecostal church. This coworker, said Marla, "saw enough from me to say, you know what? I know, if anybody has an answer to what I'm feeling, it's gonna be [you]. And that blessed my heart so much." A Christian who owns a logging company[14] told us, "As we're talking to foresters, as we're talking to landowners, I end up sharing . . . why I believe what I believe. And then . . . in that way, opening the subject to be able to witness to them."

More often when religious individuals talk about their faith at work, they are not trying to convert others but rather provide some sort of spiritual support to their coworkers, a type of faith expression they think can make an organization a more caring place for workers. "A lot of times I'll bring up different Scriptures that I've heard and that I've read that have been meaningful to me, or I'll point people to that as a source of encouragement for them," said a tax accountant[15] who is Catholic. "A lot of times they're not really Christians, or they're not practicing, but if it comes up in conversation and it seems like I'm being led in that direction," she said she will talk to them about her faith. "I don't just, like, get my Bible out and start thumping it at people!" she assured us.

"I guess I deeply feel that I need to talk about my faith at work to some extent because I care about my coworkers, and I think if I truly care about them then that concern has to extend to their spirituality, not just things besides that," said Josie,[16] the civil engineer we met earlier. She knows her five coworkers well and they mean a lot to her, she said, but she is also aware that she is the most religious among them, and that the small size of her office means there is very little room for tension. She has struggled with how to express care for her colleagues via her faith without "bugging them," she said. We found that workers who overtly express their faith at work often worried a lot about how their faith expression might impact others.

A number of workers we interviewed talk about their faith at work in more subtle ways. Rather than directly engaging in conversations about faith topics, they passively signal their religiosity to others. A program manager we spoke with in Illinois, who described himself as a Black Baptist,[17] said signaling that he is a Christian is a way to show his faith in case others want to talk about it with him. He spoke to us at length about the ways he lets his coworkers know that his faith is important to him. Sometimes he'll intentionally use religious language. "I personally will say, 'Oh, OK, well that's just a blessing.' . . . I try to express it in a way where it shows that I realize God is in control of all this, so it's just a blessing to me that this person crossed my path or I labor to work with that person," he told us. He will also purposely mention his church or his faith as a routine part of office small talk. "In conversation, I don't shy back if somebody says, 'Oh, what'd you do this weekend?' I have no issues saying, 'Oh, we had a wonderful service at church on Sunday,'" he said. "If you ask, I'm going to tell you what I did. I'm not going to go, 'OK, well, I guess I better not talk about church, I'll talk about something else.'"

A communications specialist[18] who is deeply involved in her Episcopal church also signals her faith at work by talking about her church activities. "I talk about when I'm preaching on a particular Sunday or I talk about some church thing that's going on," she said. "I was always talking about some retreat I was going on or some class I was teaching or taking, and it's met with varying degrees of interest. Some people are like, 'Oh, tell me more about that,' or, 'Tell me what subject your sermon's going to be this week.'"

Praying

Particularly among the Protestants and Catholics we interviewed, prayer is a common way workers express their faith to offer emotional support to colleagues or customers, show they care for coworkers, or cope with stressful situations. At times, these workers might directly offer to pray with a coworker, but more often they might let someone know that they were praying for them. (While many Muslim workers also engage in prayer at work, they told us such prayers are generally a specific spiritual practice rather than something they do with or for others outside their faith.) Those who pray for others at work are not typically focused on praying about the tasks of the workplace. It was rare for us to hear about workers praying for performance outcomes or about professional challenges that others faced. More often, prayer was performed as a signal of care, concern, or compassion for the personal lives of coworkers or clients. The examples they shared of what they prayed about were almost always related to personal topics. While workers we spoke with believed these prayers were sincerely offered to God, they also often had the intention or effect of cultivating a stronger relationship between themselves and the people in their prayers. Offering to pray for someone else seemed to reinforce a sense of vulnerability on the part of the person praying and being prayed for—which ultimately resulted in a greater sense of connection between them.

"Maybe they're dealing with an illness in the family, and once I find out about that, I might offer to pray for them.... Or they're struggling because of a coworker or because of some situation outside.... Sometimes, it's family, and I would offer—offer them advice.... I would, again, both offer prayer and sometimes offer guidance or encourage them to seek God's help," said an evangelical delivery driver.[19] An evangelical Christian who works as a UPS manager[20] told us he uses prayer to care for others in the workplace and, "There are people who know who I am and know enough about God that, hey, they can ask for prayer." He told us about a woman he worked with whose husband died on a cruise they had planned for a year and "by the time she got back to work, she was still a mess," he said. "I was able to leave my area and go and console her and pray with her."

Even though praying for others is considered an overt expression of faith, most people who described engaging in this practice did so with quite a bit of sensitivity for how the person they were praying for might feel about being the subject of a prayer. An evangelical Christian massage therapist,[21] for example, told us, "I have offered prayer, to pray for clients who are struggling through major things. And that doesn't mean I always pray for them there on the spot, although I have done that, on rare occasions, when someone was in a situation where I felt like this might help them.... I'll occasionally text them and say, 'I've been praying for you. I'm just thinking about you.'" For one client who is Catholic, she wrote the prayer on a piece of paper and handed it to her when their appointment was done, saying, "I've been praying for you, and this is what I've been praying." She said she tries to "use discernment, to know whether or not I should even offer it ... [if] I should just pray silently but not tell them I'm praying for them, or if I should pray openly, or hand them a piece of paper. And probably the biggest expression of my faith would be prayer, in whatever form it takes, like that."

Symbols

Other workers signal their faith overtly yet nonverbally in the workplace through the way they dress or objects they keep around them. While, as we saw earlier in this chapter, there is a very large gap between evangelical Protestants and members of other religious traditions with regard to talking about their religion in the workplace, the differences across religious traditions are much smaller when we look at such visual displays of religion. As we see in Figure 3.3, about 15 percent of all US workers say they wear or display religious items at work. Evangelical Protestants do engage in such visual displays of religion at a relatively high rate (28 percent), yet Muslim workers are as likely to wear or display religious items (28 percent). Catholic workers are not far behind (23 percent), nor are Jewish (19 percent) and Buddhist (19 percent) workers. In short, visual displays of faith are generally shared across religious traditions. There are still qualitative differences in these displays, however. Some traditions, for instance, may lead individuals to wear certain clothing items while others might lead individuals to display religious images or text in their workspace.

The religious workers we interviewed talked about this way of expressing faith in the workplace. Some keep Bible verses or prayer mats near their workspaces; some display religion-based artwork. An assistant professor of English who is a nondenominational Christian[22] told us, "I have Bible verses up in my office and I also have tattoos that are religious in nature, that can

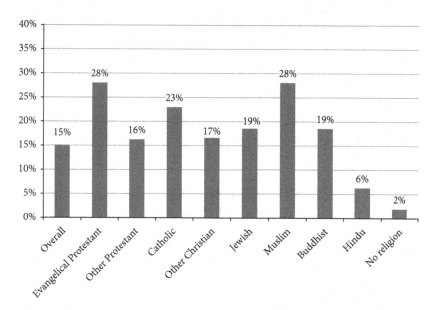

Figure 3.3 Percentage agreeing that "At work, I display or wear items that represent my faith or spirituality," by religious tradition

Data: Faith at Work Main Survey. Percentages represent responses for "somewhat agree" and "strongly agree." "Not applicable" response coded as "strongly disagree."

be visible depending on . . . if I'm wearing a sleeve or if I'm wearing a short, my ankle is out or something." A Muslim case manager[23] told us about the necklace she wears that says "Allah" in Arabic, and about a number of religious objects she keeps on her desk and in her office. "My mom went to Hajj in Mecca so it's like the little Kaaba, which is like a holy stone in the center of Mecca everyone walks around, so I have that. It's a replica that she bought while she was in Saudi Arabia. And then prayer beads I have on my desk. And then a little prayer rug that she bought for me. That's in my office," she said. A Jewish freelance writer and EMT[24] discussed how she "dress[es] very modestly, according to certain rules," which include covering her hair because of her religion. "I wear either a snood or a wrap or a wig," she said.

The Push to Subtlety Can Marginalize

While subtle expressions of faith make many organizational leaders more comfortable, largely because they tend to lead to fewer problems in the workplace than more overt expressions of faith can cause, they can also be the result of workers feeling too scared or uncomfortable to express their faith otherwise. A consultant who was raised Episcopalian but now considers himself nonreligious[25] described how he sees workplaces sometimes overcensoring religious individuals in order to prevent offending others. "It's a little bit like the peanut-free school, you know what I mean? There's obviously a small number of kids that have a big problem, we need . . . to be sensitive to them," he told us. "But I think there sometimes is a tendency to basically bully the hell out of everyone else for one person's viewpoint." Yet ultimately, he said, "people need to learn to get along and accommodate each other."

We encountered some workers who said they only express their faith at work in private or secretive ways because they are afraid they would be judged as different if they expressed their faith more overtly. This is particularly consequential for workers who belong to a minority religious tradition, who are more likely to feel or fear being religiously marginalized in a workplace setting. George Cunningham,[26] a Texas A&M University researcher, collected data from 260 managers across the United States about religious beliefs, policies, and practices in the workplace and found that when employees are religiously similar to their colleagues, they are more likely to fit into the workplace and be satisfied with their jobs. Employees who think their religious beliefs make them a little bit "different" are less likely to fit in and are less satisfied with their jobs. "Clearly, consistent, fair, and legal accommodations of religious and spiritual requests are needed," he concluded at the end of the study.

> "Perhaps more substantively, however, is the need for people to feel valued in the workplace, irrespective of their religious beliefs. Therein rests the importance of an organization's diversity mindset. When differences among people are seen as assets to the organization, when there is a focus on understanding the way in which people vary, when there is a realization that workforce diversity can bring positive outcomes to the organization, and when there is an understanding of how to realize said benefits, then people who may differ from the typical majority are likely to have positive experiences in that context."

Protecting Practitioners of Minority Religions

In most industries and geographic regions of the United States, with some notable exceptions, Christians are a majority. In our interviews, Christians sometimes said they are afraid to express their faith in the workplace. A Catholic woman who[27] has a picture of the pope and a necklace with a picture of Jesus on her desk, for example, said that, "For some reason I feel, because I'm Christian, it's OK [for others] to mock me more. I'm starting to feel in the workforce that they are trying to do diversity but at somebody else's expense. And for some reason it's the Christians, to be at our expense."

One study led by Brent Lyons, a professor of organization studies, found that Christian workers who felt that their organizations required them to distance themselves from their religious identity experienced a number of negative outcomes at work. These workers rated themselves lower on job satisfaction and personal well-being, and reported a higher likelihood of turnover compared with those in organizations who were more supportive of diverse opinions and beliefs. Conversely, those who felt their workplaces were more supportive of various religious identities at work were more likely to openly talk about their faith in the workplace and were more satisfied at work than those who did not share their religion in the workplace.[28] Lyons and his colleagues conclude that when employees feel comfortable bringing their social identities to work—including their religious identities—they are less stressed and more committed to their organizations.

There may be times, though, when religious expression in the workplace leads to conflict, hard feelings, or discrimination, especially for those who are members of a minority religion or are not religious. "I don't want my orientation, my religious orientation, to be off-putting to someone else or to make them feel that this is not the place for them," said an Episcopalian teacher and librarian[29] we interviewed. When an organization prioritizes one religion over another in the workplace, creating an environment that doesn't recognize the traditions and practices of all religions or make all employees feel like they can share their faith in the workplace, it can lead to negative employee outcomes. For example, if an organization acknowledges and celebrates only Christian holidays, it may inadvertently lead those who are not Christian to hide religious aspects of their identity that don't match what they perceive to be the values of the workplace—resulting in higher stress and reduced commitment to the organization.

More often than not, Christian, Muslim, Jewish, and nonreligious workers talked about feeling they have to be careful in how they express their beliefs at work, due to fear of mistreatment or judgment. Members of minority religions feel most pushed to express their faith in more subtle ways. "One of my best service managers is Muslim. . . . He prays five times a day. It doesn't interfere with his work, but some people just don't like that," said a Catholic facilities director[30] we interviewed.

A social worker[31] who converted to Islam said she expresses her faith at work when she feels comfortable, by "kind of educating people more" about aspects of Islam, such as religious holidays or practices of observant Muslims, but she is wary of expressing her faith in the workplace. Her job involves helping recently incarcerated individuals receive employment training, obtain a GED, and find a place to live, and "I rely on people to volunteer to come to my class and like to come back," she said, "and I hear a lot of racist and other things [from the clients I work with]. . . . I feel like if I came in in hijab, nobody would come to my class. Nobody would come back, or they wouldn't like me anymore . . . so, like, I feel like I can't do that if I wanted to."

Aamna, the Muslim gas station owner[32] we introduced in chapter 1, told us that she often feels marginalized by customers because of her faith: "What I sometimes feel is that expressing faith when you're a Christian is easier than expressing faith when you are a Hindu or a Muslim or any other kind, belonging to another minority, because people are used to the Christian faith, so they will talk about Jesus Christ or they talk about Christmas or, you know, greetings in a religious way much easier than people of other faith. Like being a Muslim is harder because of so much . . . negative talk about Muslims, so you can't say *As-salaam alaikum* [peace be upon you] to anybody."

Martha[33] told us she no longer displays anything that says "Islam" in her personal workspace because of the tremendous "heat" she received from her coworkers and managers when she initially did. She said she believes people ought to be able to express their faith in the workplace "without retribution from anyone or judgment from anyone. Everyone should be allowed to worship and follow whatever faith they choose. That's not always possible. In my case it was not. I had to be very careful. . . . I was learning Arabic. I could not have any of the really beautiful Arabic calligraphy anywhere around my desk. The most I would do is maybe find a stupid meme or something on Facebook or something like that that would say something about how to do the right thing."

Pluralism, Not Privatization

We have found through years of research that employees can express their faith at work in ways that both respect coworkers with different belief systems and foster a sense of community and belonging in the workplace.[34] In some cases, talking about faith at work can help workers develop tolerance and respect for diversity. Legal scholar John Inazu and pastor Timothy Keller write in their book *Uncommon Ground: Living Faithfully in a World of Difference*—about how Christians can engage with and respect those with different beliefs—that

> "too often, the fact of pluralism is obscured, at least in the United States, with idealized visions of 'one nation, indivisible' and the pursuit of a 'more perfect union.' But our actual existence is often characterized more by difference and disagreement than by unity. Americans, like citizens of many nations today, lack agreement about the purpose of our country, the nature of the common good, and the meaning of human flourishing. These differences affect not only what we think but also *how* we think about and see the world."[35]

Workers we spoke with told us that it is important for them to see an appreciation for diversity and an environment of communal learning in their workplace. "I'm fortunate that I work for a company that is really focused on inclusion and allowing people to bring their full self to work. . . . Our company is very focused on being inclusive and really allowing us to be the best people that we can be, whether it's a religion, it's a sexual orientation, it's race, all those things. We want people to feel comfortable that they can be who they are here, when they are here, that they can be their whole self, or they don't have to pretend to be someone else," a Catholic man[36] told us. We found that when organizational leaders allow for curiosity and nonjudgmental discussions of religion and nonreligion among workers, workplaces become more inclusive and welcoming spaces. An evangelical woman who works in management[37] told us she feels faith should be expressed in the workplace "because it helps everybody understanding where everyone's coming from, and if we're able to openly make communication about that then I feel like there's more understanding overall. Suppressing it, I feel like, makes more secrets and more enemies than anything." A Muslim who works as a pharmaceutical assistant in Kentucky[38] told us that her Christian colleagues are all very open about their faith and are interested in her religion. This openness has fostered camaraderie, understanding, and an educational work environment. "I think I've taught them more about the things that I do and what I do in my religion. . . . And I think they've actually taught me a lot, too, because sometimes they'll ask me questions that I have no idea of the answer to," she said. "So, then, we'll sit there and we'll Google it and we'll learn something." She said she feels like "they want to learn. . . . They don't want me to just bottle that part of me up."

A Muslim social worker[39] said her faith motivates her to appreciate the religious diversity of her work environment. She told us that some of her best friends are her coworkers and they have discussions at work about their faith. "I have Catholic, Buddhist, those from different denominations of [Protestants] among my friends and some of them are atheist and agnostic so it's very diverse and we always have conversations about what we believe in. So I think I've just been lucky to have people around me that teach me and I can learn from it [and] I can teach," she said. A Jewish man who works as a consultant in the Midwest[40] thinks there should be some boundaries with regard to expressions of faith in the workplace—for example, he worries that having something like morning prayer as part of a workplace regimen could lead to problems—but he also believes that expressing faith in the workplace can do enormous good, helping workers learn more about those who are different from them and supporting efforts toward healthy pluralism and diversity. "You can do a lot to make people understand diversity—there are a diversity of cultures and religions out there—and you can sort of do a lot to educate," he said. "And in a very educational way almost, I have had that conversation about . . . what does your Christmas look like? . . . Or what's your Easter look like? Here's what my Passover looks like. Let's compare, right. So, I think in terms of learning and understanding traditions, that's an OK conversation to have." An evangelical Christian engineer[41] also spoke about expressing faith at work as a way to embrace religious pluralism. "I am one that I seek out additional perspectives. While I identify myself as a Christian, I have an aunt who is a Buddhist and I have friends who are Hindu and I appreciate those perspectives," he said. "I appreciate different ways of looking at problems and challenges and life in general, and as long as it's respectful, I think it's fine. I don't see an issue with it . . . as long as you're able to get your job done."

Workplaces are one of the spaces in society where people must interact—and work together—with others who disagree with them on faith and other matters. Expressions of religion in the workplace, in respectful and appropriate ways, can help workers better tolerate and even cultivate understanding and appreciation of differences in ways that serve the broader goals of workplaces.

We also found that it is nearly impossible to have a completely faith-free workplace. The employees for whom faith is important will often find each other and ways to express their faith. Marla, the Evangelical corporate trainer whom we introduced at the beginning of the chapter,[42] told us about her workplace's policies for expressing faith and how employees circumnavigate them. Christians in her workplace, she said, "can make some people uncomfortable. So, we have to just be mindful of that. But . . . we have one guy now who works in our building, and he is a strong Christian believer. He organizes our . . . prayer meeting. . . . You kind of just have to hear about it . . . word of mouth, and they'll get together and pray for our company. And then, if you ask him, he'll add you to a distribution list. And he sent out a daily devotional, every day, via email. I think that that's wonderful."

We think it would be beneficial for organizational leaders to be explicit about which forms of religious expression are appropriate in the work environment and to ensure that any guidance is applied uniformly and in a way that values workers of all faiths (including those who have no faith).

Organizational leaders should also be aware that when it comes to talking with others about their faith, evangelical Christians are uniquely motivated or compelled, and organizations must decide how they will handle this. It might be helpful for organizational leaders to meet with employees to discuss how they can maintain the types of religious expression that are important to their identity, while staying consistent with the organization's goals, values, and culture. It's incredibly important to recognize that the voices of those who are nonreligious are also a piece of religious diversity and pluralism, and whatever organizational leaders do they must take into account the growing number of nonreligious individuals.

Younger workers, in particular, seem to be wrestling with how faith should be expressed in the workplace. They were likely to say they want training from their faith communities or work organizations on how to express their faith in diverse, pluralistic work environments while valuing respect for others. A twenty-three-year-old Catholic engineer, for example, said he wants people to be better equipped to have "a rational conversation"[43] with those of different religions in ways that encourage openness and curiosity. These younger workers are not looking for additional policies on what can or cannot be communicated about faith at work (and, indeed, a policy that endeavored to restrict what people could say or do at work with respect to religion would run the risk of violating federal discrimination law). Rather, they seek clear norms and values regarding religious expression communicated by their organizations and those who lead them.

The Bottom Line

- Workers express their faith at work in different ways, some of which are overt, like talking about their faith, praying, or signaling their faith via religious symbols or clothing.
- Evangelical Christians are the most overt in talking about their faith.
- Organizational leaders need to ensure that overt expressions of faith are encouraged in ways that respect all employees, regardless of their religious perspective.
- When there is no marginalization, expressions and discussions of faith at work can lead to happier and more productive workers, deeper relationships at work, and more inclusive workplaces.

Notes

1. F@W_ST31, White, Woman, 25, Civil Engineer, Christian, conducted December 19, 2018.
2. Lawrence, Ericka R., and James E. King Jr. 2008. "Determinants of Religious Expression in the Workplace." *Culture and Religion: An Interdisciplinary Journal* 9(3): 251–65.
3. Charoensap-Kelly, Piyawan, Colleen L. Mestayer, and G. Brandon Knight. 2020. "To Come Out or Not to Come Out: Minority Religious Identity Self-Disclosure in the United States Workplace." *Management Communication Quarterly* 34(2): 213–50.
4. Faith at Work Main Survey. Overall design-based F p < .001; Note that these percentages are calculated excluding those who say that the question concerning displaying or wearing items is not applicable to them. However, even if we include this response we still see the same strong association between religiosity and agreement with displaying religious items at work.
5. Faith at Work Main Survey. If we estimate an ordinary least squares regression model predicting agreement with the statement "I feel motivated to talk about my faith or spirituality with people at work," we find a statistically significant difference between white and Black workers even after controlling for religiosity, religious tradition, gender, organizational size, and position in organization.
6. Faith at Work Main Survey. Cross-tabulation's design-based F-test p < .001; Note that these percentages are calculated excluding those who say that the question concerning displaying or wearing items is not applicable to them. The organizational size question asked individuals to report "how many people work at the location where you work." Note that the organizational size effect remains statistically significant even when controlling for other factors like worker religiosity, religious tradition, gender, race, and position in organization.
7. This is based on an ordinary least squares regression model predicting agreement with the statement "I feel motivated to talk about my faith or spirituality with people at work." The not-applicable response is coded as "strongly disagree." Other controls in the model include religiosity, religious tradition, race, gender, organizational size, and position in the organization. Note that workers could identify their organization as being in multiple industries, so there is no reference or comparison category. Rather, all industries are included as dichotomous indicators representing whether the individual selected it as one of the industries representing the organization they work for.
8. See, for example, Scheitle, Christopher P., and Elaine Howard Ecklund. 2018. "Perceptions of Religious Discrimination among U.S. Scientists." *Journal for the Scientific Study of Religion* 57(1): 139–55.
9. F@W_ST91, White, Woman, 24, Lab Manager, Methodist/Mainline, conducted June 27, 2019.
10. Scheitle, Christopher P., and Elaine Howard Ecklund. 2017. "Examining the Effects of Exposure to Religion in the Workplace on Perceptions of Religious Discrimination." *Review of Religious Research* 59(1): 1–20.
11. If we conduct an ordinary least squares regression model predicting agreement with this outcome while controlling for religiosity, race, gender, organizational size, position in organization, and industry, we still find that every religious tradition is significantly less likely to agree that they feel motivated to talk about their faith at work when compared to evangelical Protestants.
12. Scheitle, Christopher P., and Jeffery T. Ulmer. 2018. "Profane Concerns in Sacred Spaces: The Challenges and Consequences of Implementing Security Measures in Religious Congregations." *Journal of Applied Security Research* 13(1): 29–44.
13. F@W_ST17, Black, Woman, 40, Corporate Trainer, Evangelical/Assemblies of God, conducted November 27, 2018.
14. F@W_ST33, White, Man, 48, Co-Owner of Logging Company, Evangelical/Mennonite, conducted January 8, 2019.
15. F@W_ST03, White, Woman, 50, Income Tax Preparer, Roman Catholic, conducted October 23, 2018.
16. F@W_ST31, White, Woman, 25, Civil Engineer, Christian, conducted December 19, 2018.
17. F@W_ST09, Black, Man, 50, Program Manager, Black Protestant/Baptist, conducted November 2, 2018.
18. F@W_ST07, White, Woman, 49, Senior Communication Specialist, Mainline/Episcopal, conducted November 2, 2018.
19. F@W_ST100, Hispanic, Man, 65, Delivery Driver, Evangelical, conducted July 15, 2019.

20. F@W_ST193, Black, Man, 45, UPS Operations Manager, Evangelical/Baptist, conducted January 31, 2020.
21. F@W_ST123, White, Woman, 50, Massage Therapist, Evangelical, conducted September 2, 2019.
22. F@W_ST102, Black, Woman, 32, Assistant Professor of English, Nondenominational Christian, conducted July 17, 2019.
23. F@W_ST119, Black, Woman, 26, Case Manager, Muslim, conducted August 28, 2019.
24. F@W_ST122, White, Woman, 34, Freelance Writer and EMT, Jewish, conducted August 30, 2019.
25. F@W_ST01, White, Man, 59, Self-Employed Consultant, Episcopalian/Catholic, conducted October 16, 2018.
26. Cunningham, George B. 2010. "The Influence of Religious Personal Identity on the Relationships among Religious Dissimilarity, Value Dissimilarity, and Job Satisfaction." *Social Justice Research* 23: 60–76.
27. F@W_ ST169, Latina, Woman, 45, Information Systems Analyst, Catholic, conducted December 5, 2019.
28. Lyons, Brent, Jennifer Wessel, Sonia Ghumman, Annie Marie Ryan, and Sooyeol Kim. 2014. "Applying Models of Employee Identity Management across Cultures: Christianity in the USA and South Korea." *Journal of Organizational Behavior* 35: 678–704.
29. F@W_ST103, White, Woman, 52, Teacher and Librarian, Episcopalian, conducted July 18, 2019.
30. F@W_ST61, White, Man, 43, Facilities Director, Catholic, conducted March 1, 2019.
31. F@W_ST107, White, Woman, 26, Instructor at a Nonprofit, Muslim, conducted August 1, 2019.
32. F@W_ST105, Asian, Woman, 52, Gas Station Owner, Muslim, conducted July 29, 2019.
33. F@W_ST111, Caucasian, Woman, 63, Retired (Sales), Muslim, conducted August 7, 2019.
34. Ecklund, Elaine Howard, Denise Daniels, Daniel Bolger, and Laura Johnson. 2020. "A Nationally Representative Survey of Faith and Work: Demographic Subgroup Differences around Calling and Conflict." *Religions* 11(6): 287: 1–18; Ecklund, Elaine Howard, Denise Daniels, and Rachel C. Schneider. 2020. "From Secular to Sacred: Bringing Work to Church." *Religions* 11(9): 442.
35. See Keller, Timothy, and John Inazu, editors. 2020. *Uncommon Ground: Living Faithfully in a World of Difference.* Nashville: Thomas Nelson Books, xv.
36. F@W_ST184, White, Man, 50, Industrial Sales, Catholic, conducted December 18, 2019.
37. F@W_ST92, White, Woman, 32, Property Management Assistant, Evangelical, conducted July 2, 2019.
38. F@W_ST191, Arab, Woman, 21, Pharmacy Assistant, Muslim, conducted January 23, 2020.
39. F@W_ST119, Black, Woman, 26, Case Manager, Muslim, conducted August 28, 2019.
40. F@W_ST108, White, Man, 52, Consultant, Jewish, conducted August 2, 2019.
41. F@W_ST15, White, Man, 32, Engineering Consultant, Evangelical, conducted November 20, 2018.
42. F@W_ST17, Black, Woman, 40, Corporate Trainer, Evangelical/Assemblies of God, conducted November 27, 2018.
43. F@W_ST72, White, Man, 23, Engineer, Catholic, conducted May 29, 2019.

4

The Double-Edged Sword of Being Called to Work

Krista[1] is an evangelical Christian and marine biologist whose work as a high-level researcher is hard in many ways. There is the science itself, in which she tries to understand and implement difficult molecular heating processes. She sometimes spends two weeks to a month out at sea, away from her family and friends. There is also the competitive culture of science, the relational structures and power hierarchies she has to navigate, plus the profession's approach to religion.[2] Some of the professors she has worked with throughout her career have been so terrific that they inspired her and helped her realize that "I would love to be in a role where I can share what I'm passionate about with others and help students possibly find what they are passionate about, to have opportunities to mentor students at a very important time in their lives." But she notices too that other scientists who lead large research groups often seem to care more about themselves than the next generation of scientists. Sometimes—because of her faith—she feels belittled by those at work.

Krista says viewing her scientific work as a "calling" compels her to sometimes act against the prevailing norm of self-interest she commonly encounters in science. "I think that all truth is from God and, as a scientist, I try to understand and reveal the truth of how the world works, and so, in that sense, my calling is a spiritual calling," she said. This feeling of being spiritually called to her work helps her overcome some of its challenges, gives her a higher purpose, keeps her motivated to do the best science she can, and leads her to think strategically about how to help others through her work. "Calling is everything," she said. "I wouldn't stay if I didn't feel called."

What Is Calling?

Psychologist Amy Wrzesniewski and her colleagues studied people's relationships to their work and divided how people understand their work

Religion in a Changing Workplace. Elaine Howard Ecklund, Denise Daniels, and Christopher P. Scheitle, Oxford University Press. © Oxford University Press 2024. DOI: 10.1093/oso/9780197675007.003.0004

into three categories: job, career, and calling. People who view their work as a "job" see their work as a product of necessity and a provider of financial rewards; those who see themselves as having a "career" have personal investment in their work and a desire to advance within their occupational structure. In contrast, those who view their work as a "calling" do their job because it is personally fulfilling *and* because they can make a difference in the world, as opposed to seeing monetary gain or status advancement as the principal motivation for doing the work.

Consider the classic story of the three bricklayers architect Sir Christopher Wren is said to have observed working to rebuild St. Paul's Cathedral after a great fire leveled London in 1666. The story goes that he saw one crouched, another working slowly, and the third standing tall, working hard and fast. Wren asked them all, "What are you doing?" to which the first replied, "I'm a bricklayer. I'm working hard laying bricks to feed my family." The second responded, "I'm a builder. I'm building a wall." The third bricklayer, who would become a great leader in the effort, replied, "I'm a cathedral builder. I'm building a great cathedral to the Almighty."[3] Research shows that many workers—even those whose jobs might appear mundane to the outside observer—are able to construct a larger sense of meaning and purpose from their work, sometimes even a sacred sense that God has used their gifts and placed them in their particular job for a specific purpose. In other words, they feel "called" to their work.

But what does that mean, exactly? Can anyone be "called," and can every job be a calling? Is calling, which has been seen as a specifically Christian concept, even relevant to those who are part of other religious traditions or no tradition? Does feeling called contribute to the feeling that work is meaningful and purposeful, or lead people to do better or more beneficial work? Are there conditions in which it can actually be maladaptive for individuals and organizations when workers feel called to their work?

The idea of calling has roots in European Christian history.[4] In the Middle Ages, the term was used to talk about men and women who felt called by God to move away from the daily activities of common people and toward a life of prayer and dedication to God as monks and nuns. The Protestant Reformation of the sixteenth century changed the notion of calling, at least for Protestants, shaping its modern-day meaning. Instead of a calling to the monastery, German theologian Martin Luther taught that all people had a calling from God that was to be lived out in their ordinary lives—as spouses in marriage, as parents to their children, as neighbors in their communities, *and in their daily labor,* whether paid or unpaid. It was not only clergy who could feel spiritually called to their work. Everyday people in everyday work could feel called too.

The idea of calling as commonly discussed in the social sciences originates from German social theorist Max Weber's concept of *beruf* (translated as calling or vocation). According to Weber, religious calling derives not just from a Protestant but also from a specifically Calvinist worldview. The belief of predestination in Calvinism—that the fate of your soul is already determined by God regardless of your own actions—led believers to feel that the only way to know they were bound for heaven was to be as pious and hardworking as possible. In this view, work has a divine purpose, and wholehearted devotion to their work became one way that Christians saw themselves glorifying God and demonstrating the surety of their own salvation. Sociologist Robert Wuthnow writes, "The faithful were thus challenged to live dutiful, responsible lives before God by working diligently in their occupations, rather than regarding such work as a necessary evil, and to consider it as important as time spent in prayer, serving the church, or preparing for life in heaven."[5] This, in turn, resulted in behavior that manifested as a religiously dedicated work ethic, an ethic that Weber argued proliferated into culture more broadly. He defined calling as "a task set by God" and considered the process of following one's calling as acceptance of a worldly task imbued with divine significance. A person served God and proved they were chosen by God to be called to the work they were doing by the amount of monetary success they had in the work as well as the social significance of the work, a concept that became known as the "Protestant work ethic."[6]

In this way, calling was generally linked to work for pay in capitalist systems. Weber suggested that the spirit of capitalism arose—at least in part—from the ways that Protestant Christians understood the sanctity of their work. In his conception, the post–Protestant Reformation view of a spiritual calling was that "the only way of living acceptably to God was not to surpass worldly morality in monastic asceticism, but solely through the fulfillment of the obligations imposed upon the individual by his position in the world,"[7] or by his work. According to sociologist Robert Wuthnow in his book *God and Mammon in America,* Protestant Christianity provided boundaries on work as well; one was not just called to work but called to family and community.[8] The understanding of calling that emerged in our modern day, however, is more linked to individual rather than community pursuits *and* monetary rather than voluntary terms, which can lead to the idea that higher-paid, higher-prestige jobs are more worthy of a sense of calling than are lower-paid and lower-prestige jobs.

Calling is often discussed today with no reference to a specific religious history, and there is no widely agreed-upon definition of what a modern-day spiritual calling might entail. Business scholars Mitchell Neubert and Katie Halbesleben define it as "a summons from God to approach work with a sense of purpose and a pursuit of excellence in work practices."[9] Some organizational psychologists think the idea of calling can be viewed more broadly as a sense of higher purpose in work, and many workers do not necessarily perceive calling as having divine origins.[10] In this vein, psychologists Bryan Dik and Ryan Duffy[11] define calling as "a transcendent summons, experienced as originating beyond the self, to approach a particular life role in a manner oriented toward demonstrating or deriving a sense of purpose or meaningfulness that holds other-oriented values and goals as primary sources of motivation." They find that workers with this sense of calling are more likely to commit to their careers and put more effort into their work. Scholars have referred to this neoclassical conception of calling as "the secular reimagining of the classic formulation anticipated by Weber, a view of calling that retains the core elements of destiny, duty, and discovery" but "does not presume or require an explicit belief in a divine Caller."[12]

Who Is Called to Work?

About one in five American workers agree with the statement, "I see my work as a spiritual calling,"[13] and most of those who see their work in this way link it to religious sensibilities and practices. While seeing work as a spiritual calling is not exclusively tied to a single religious tradition or to being religious at all,[14] a person must have the language of calling—often provided by faith—to feel called to their work. We do find notable differences across religious traditions, however, as seen in Figure 4.1. According to our national survey, feeling called to work is most common among evangelicals and Muslims. About 38 percent of evangelical Protestant workers and 32 percent of Muslim workers describe their work as a spiritual calling, while only 18 percent of Catholic workers and 16 percent of Jewish workers said they see their work this way. Perhaps unsurprisingly, those *without* a religious identity are the least likely to see their work as a spiritual calling. These differences seem to be heavily tied to differences in religious practice—the

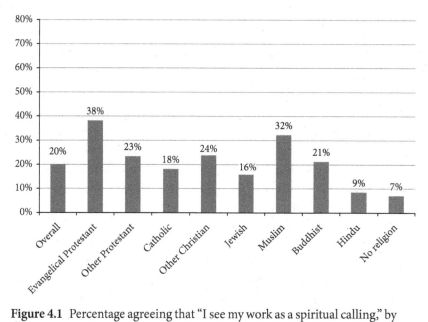

Figure 4.1 Percentage agreeing that "I see my work as a spiritual calling," by religious tradition

Data: Faith at Work Main Survey. Question: "I see my work as a spiritual calling." Percentages represent responses for "somewhat agree" and "strongly agree."

result of evangelical Christians and Muslims in the United States being the most likely to practice their religion and feeling the most strongly about the role of religion in their lives. If we look at self-reported religiosity apart from a person's specific religious tradition, we find that 43 percent of those who describe themselves as very religious feel called to their work compared with 22 percent of those who say they are moderately religious, 14 percent of those who are slightly religious, and 8 percent of those who say they are not religious at all.

Business management and administration scholars Abbas J. Ali and Abdullah Al-Owaihan note that Muslims experience calling differently than Christians, with the Islamic work ethic related to *zakat*, a Muslim finance term referring to the obligation that an individual has to donate a proportion of wealth to charity in order to help the needy. They say that while both the Protestant work ethic (PWE) and Islamic work ethic (IWE) "place an emphasis on work involvement and work as a divine calling, [the] IWE encompasses dimensions that are not explicitly addressed in PWE. In particular, there is an emphasis in IWE on intention, rather than outcome, as a measure of morality."[15] A man we spoke with who is part of a Black Muslim tradition[16] told us he does *not* feel called to the specific work he does as a real estate agent, but because he is Muslim he does feel "called" *to want to* help coworkers succeed in their work and to feel differently about his work than how he thinks non-Muslims might. A Muslim woman who feels called to her work as an optometry assistant[17] said that this feeling is expressed through the type of work she does and her intention to help non-Muslims change their perspective on Islam. "Since I work in the health field it's kind of a given that you're helping people, for one," she said. "Especially since I wear the scarf, for me being around non-Muslims or just wearing a scarf and being around people in general, they might have a conception about what person wears the scarf but when they see someone or meet me, that changes their perspective." A Muslim pharmacy technician[18] who talked to us about her work said she "wouldn't say it's much of a spiritual calling," but when asked about the idea of zakat responded enthusiastically, "Yeah!" and went on to say that zakat resonates deeply with her as a framework through which to understand her work: "I think that there is something like that, to be giving back to the community, which I could see that as being something spiritual."

A number of Jewish workers we interviewed invoked the idea of *tikkun olam*, describing a calling to improve society, alleviate suffering, care for others, and help those in need. "We're supposed to be in partnership with God to repair the world," explained an Orthodox Jewish primary school teacher.[19] A retired Jewish lawyer who worked as a civil service attorney[20] referenced tikkun olam when talking about his work, saying, "The law is the best suited for that because you're trying to do right, you're trying to correct wrongs, you're trying to fix the world."

The "Purpose" and "Meaning" of Calling

When workers feel called to their work, it is generally positive. Workers who view their work as a calling—*regardless of organizational position or salary*—have higher levels of life and work satisfaction than those who do not feel called to their work.[21] Our national survey shows that 53 percent of those who feel called to their work strongly agree that they are "very satisfied" with their current job compared with 39 percent of those who do not feel called.[22]

Our interviews with a variety of workers also reveal that a sense of calling provides workers with a sense of higher purpose in their work, especially when facing work that is either extremely challenging or mundane. Brenda,[23] the oncologist we met in the first chapter, talked about having to tell patients that there was little more that medicine could do to help them. Teachers talked about dealing with the bureaucracy of state educational systems. Medical service workers talked about mopping floors and handling bodily waste. Ben the criminal investigator[24] spoke of dealing with "a lot of broken people." All these workers and many others said they are able to get through the difficult or mundane day-to-day aspects of their jobs because they feel spiritually called to their work. Psychologist Richard Treadgold, who conducted research on "transcendent vocations"—by which he means work to which one feels called—found that having a sense of calling was correlated with better coping with work problems, as well as overall lower stress and depression rates, in the people he studied.[25]

Our national survey found that those who feel called to their work are much more likely than those who do not feel called to say that their faith or spirituality helps them "experience meaning and purpose in [their] daily work tasks" (61 percent among those who agree they feel called compared with 13 percent who do not). Even if we limit this comparison to those who describe themselves as very religious, workers who feel called to their work are still more likely than those who do not feel called to say that their faith or spirituality helps them find meaning in their daily work tasks (83 percent vs. 50 percent).[26] In our research, we identified four approaches that people of faith use to find meaning and purpose in their work. These four approaches can be conceptualized in a two-by-two table. One axis reflects the kind of purpose they find—intrinsic (meaning inherent to the work itself) versus extrinsic (experienced through what the work provides or allows for, like the ability to pay bills). The other axis identifies the location of the audience they see the work serving—proximal (meaning those closest to the workplace, like the worker, colleagues, and customers) versus distal (people farther away from the work, like the worker's family, broader society, or their faith community).

When you cross these two dimensions, you get something like Figure 4.2, with four quadrants. While each quadrant represents a different way that workers identify meaning and purpose in their work, these quadrants are not mutually exclusive. That is, someone who finds meaning and purpose in their work because their work seems important and their skills are being put to good use (intrinsic/proximal) might *also* find their work meaningful because it provides them with the means to pay their mortgage or tithe to

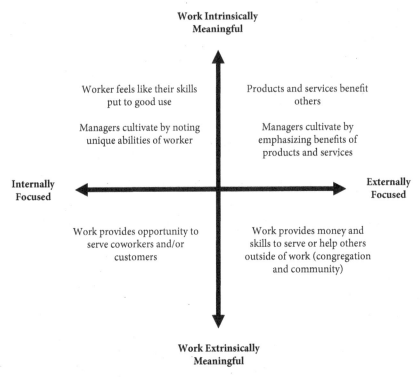

Figure 4.2 Four Quadrants of Making Meaning from Work

their church (extrinsic/distal). To the extent that people can locate their own workplace experiences on this figure, the more likely they are to experience meaning in their work.

Intrinsic/Proximal: Work Is a Chance to Use Gifts and Opportunities Provided by God

Workers with an intrinsic/proximal orientation (upper left quadrant) find meaning at work due to the nature of the work itself, as well as a focus on their own talents being used to serve others within the workplace. A common response among workers who fit this orientation is that they feel they are meant to do the work they do and were guided to it by God. They believe the skills used to do their job are gifts from God, they were given the opportunity to do their job as a blessing from God, or they have a sense that they were "made to do this work." We found that workers who experience meaning due to the nature of their work *and* have opportunities to exercise their skills through their work are more likely to say that they are called to their work.

"We should pray and really ask God, 'What is our purpose, how does our secular job line up to what God has for our life?' and I really do believe that I've been really good with numbers and math ever since I was in high school," said an evangelical man who works in human resources[27] and considers his work to be a spiritual calling. He emphasized the process of seeking out purpose or calling through prayer. Brian,[28] a facilities director for a property management company and a committed Catholic who views his work as a calling, truly believes that God led him to his current role. He does not describe his job as a passion, lucrative, or intellectually stimulating, nor does he think the tasks he performs are all that important, but he feels God has led him there to influence lives and build relationships with the team he leads. He told us, "Obviously being a boss in a workplace is like . . . God led us to do this. . . . I found my spiritual calling. I don't even know how to explain it. It's just, I'm in the right spot. I know I'm in the right spot and I feel like I could influence people; not influence them by pushing my will on them, but, if they're having a tough time or whatever, [I could say] 'There's other stuff out there for you other than what you've chosen to do, right?'" A correction officer in his sixties[29] told us he is still working because he has "the utmost respect for the people that I work for, the people that I work with, and I just really enjoy my job. I feel like I'm doing the job that God made me to do." He believes God gave him a special ability "to work with difficult people, to have a clear head when things are going really bad," he said, and in the most stressful moments to "think and act and work clearly. And I keep working at it until this day because I am good at it and I believe the Lord built me to do it, and I am doing the Lord's work."

An evangelical engineer from the Midwest[30] we interviewed said he feels "like I was called to be in this profession. . . . As corny as it sounds, this is what I'm good at. This is where I feel like I've been placed . . . where I feel like my journey has been heading." He told us his faith "provides grounding" for his work and allows him to be a voice of reason and morality in his workplace when faced with ethical dilemmas, noting that "it's been drilled into me since I was a little kid to always do the right thing regardless of the pressures that people in a position of influence may be putting [on] you." Research finds that those who feel called to their work have higher intrinsic motivation at work, and often hold themselves to a higher standard with respect to their attitude and performance. In our national survey, we asked workers how much they agreed with the statement, "Even if it does not benefit me, I always act with integrity at work." We expect that most people will agree with such a statement in a survey, given it is socially desirable to do so, and that is indeed what we found. Yet those who feel called to their work are more likely than those who do not feel called to agree that they always act with integrity (84 percent vs. 73 percent). We also found that 59 percent of those who see their job as a spiritual calling "feel a strong sense of commitment to the organization" for which they work, while only 37 percent of those who do not feel such a calling said they feel a strong sense of commitment to their organization.

Intrinsic/Distal: Calling as Service to the Common Good

When workers have an intrinsic/distal orientation (upper right quadrant) they find meaning in the nature of the work, but the goals being met by the work are beyond the boundaries of the workplace. Responses that fit this category often came from workers who see their work as holding value because the goods or services it produces benefit others or contribute to the common good in some way. Such responses sometimes overlap with the idea of receiving gifts from God (again, these are not mutually exclusive ways of finding meaning, and responses can be located in multiple quadrants), but the emphasis is more strongly placed on how their work meets needs beyond the workplace or themselves.

For example, one evangelical woman who works as an engineer designing city water systems[31] and sees her work as a calling focuses on how she can ensure her community is supplied with safe water. Another evangelical woman who works in political fundraising[32] sees her work as helping on a national scale. "I do think it is a spiritual calling for me. I love politics and I think there's a need for politics and I do feel like the work I'm doing is helping to change the world, and I know half the population doesn't agree with me just because of the party I represent, but I do feel like the party that I represent helps Americans live better and their policies overall help change the lives of

Americans and I believe in that," she said. "I mean I do think it's my calling because not a lot of people want to do politics or work in fundraising but it's necessary."

Ben,[33] who works in the criminal justice system and whom we met in chapter 2, said his upbringing in the Black Protestant tradition helps him see his work as a calling, and viewing his work in this way helps him take the pain of others seriously. If he can "offer kindness or can offer hope or compassion without impeding justice, it goes a long way," he said. When talking about the victims of crimes he told us, "It's their entire world that's been traumatized, and so, just being mindful of that and really trying to see, OK, what extra thing can I do, for victims, to show them compassion and empathy, as they're dealing with the pain of being victimized?"

Extrinsic/Distal: Work as a Means to a Higher Calling

Workers with an extrinsic/distal orientation (lower right quadrant) find meaning at work that is extrinsic to the nature of the work itself and therefore not specifically related to the tasks of the job or the goods or services being provided. Individuals who discuss their work as meaningful in these terms focus on how the skills or resources they gain through their jobs allow them to achieve a higher purpose by serving others outside of the workplace, typically those with whom they have personal relationships, like their family or immediate religious community. "It's supportive of my spiritual calling.... It provides the funds so that I can do what I believe I need to do," an evangelical man who co-owns a logging company[34] said of his work. "It is to bring honor and glory to God, in any way possible. If that is witnessing to a neighbor, if that is helping someone who has financial, mental, spiritual difficulties, health issues, I see it to bring honor and glory to God."

Among the workers we spoke with, the most common example of working to achieve a higher calling is caring for family. As a Catholic engineer[35] told us, "My work is more of a calling to support my primary vocation, which is getting married and raising a family." A Jewish woman who works as an EMT and freelance writer[36] and feels her work is a calling explained, "The way we look at it is that your intentions matter a lot. ... If your intention is also to support your family, then it becomes a spiritual pursuit because your kids need to eat. Your kids need shoes. Your kids need school supplies. You need a roof over your head. There is no real separation of what you're calling spiritual, when you have the right intentions. So, as far as working to support my family, that's an overall yes." An evangelical Christian woman who works in marketing[37] replied to the idea of her work being a calling with a distal focus: "My job now pays the bills, it allows me flexibility, it allows me to work from home at times and just [the] ability to kind of have my family be my main ministry." She spoke about her previous job working at a women's shelter as a religious calling that helped to serve those in the community—consistent with an intrinsic approach to meaning. How workers find meaning in their work is a subjective and interpretive process, and an individual's perception of their work can change over time, even when they do not change jobs.

Several times in our interviews, workers talked about seeing their work as having a higher calling because they were able to use resources, skills, or money gained through work to serve their religious congregation. An evangelical Christian IT associate,[38] for example, told us, "Is the work that I do at this company a spiritual calling? No. Is learning what I learned from doing, maintaining those skills, and continuing those skills, do I see that as a spiritual calling? Well, it seems like it to me because I use those skills to help the ministry whenever and wherever possible. People from ministries will call for tech support. I just help them. I don't charge." An evangelical Christian who works as a program manager at a medical supplies company[39] talked about using skills he gained in the military for ministry. "Our gifts are for the church and we're allowed to use and strengthen them outside of the church, but the gifts themselves are to be able to build up the church," he said. In one interview, a Baptist man who works as a program manager in marketing said he "wouldn't say that I see the work that I do as a spiritual calling. I see it more as a means to strengthen my gifts to be used within the church. . . . I think it helps benefit what I can take and say, 'Ah, and I can apply this now when . . . I'm working through ministry.'" Josie[40] pursued an engineering degree so that she could do the work she felt called to: working for an organization digging wells to provide clean water in Africa. "I kind of figured I would get this heroic job," she said, "and serve God every day with my job and help poor people." Instead, she found herself working for a water utility in a US municipality. Now, she said, "The way I live out my faith is a lot more about how I'm involved in my church, how I treat my neighbors, how I treat my family . . . and also how I treat people at work. . . . I think I've realized that I don't necessarily have to—my job doesn't have to be . . . something that's labeled as Christian, or something that's directly serving the poor."

Extrinsic/Proximal: Work as a Location for Sharing One's Faith and Values

For those with an extrinsic/proximal orientation (lower left quadrant), the workplace is seen as a location for serving others, though the focus is not on the goods or services being provided by the work. Instead, serving is focused on those inside of the workplace, including coworkers, customers, clients, or students, and the primary sense of serving is through the opportunity to care for others or share one's faith. Workers with this orientation commonly spoke about serving as a role model in the workplace or seeing work as a place to promote their religious ideals, equating being a good Christian, Muslim, or Jew with expressing their religious values in the workplace. For example, Ben, the evangelical Christian who works as a criminal investigator,[41] told us, "I believe that I'm called, not only to stand up for the rights of those who have been harmed and those who have been wronged, but also to really make sure that I exude some very Judeo-Christian values to people who might not otherwise experience them." An evangelical Christian who works as the CFO for a credit union[42] shared with us how he feels called to create a good work environment for his employees, saying, "As a manager I try to be a good moral example, and it's more than just the religious background—but you want to make it an ethical place to work, treat people fairly, support them in their career, whatever direction they're going, or however they're growing or learning, support them."

The Complications of Calling

While workers who experience a sense of calling have a stronger sense of meaning and purpose in their work, are more committed to their career and organization, and have higher job satisfaction than those who do not feel called to their work, it is important to acknowledge that most individuals *do not* feel called to their work. The majority of people we surveyed—four out of five—did *not* view their work as a calling. Sometimes, there are structural or cultural factors that restrict a person's ability to pursue a calling, while other times financial factors are at play. "I've always thought that, you know, maybe at some point in my career, more than likely later in my career, once my children are out and gone and off the payroll, and we're set for retirement, that I would take some time at the end of my career to maybe look at doing something more of what I want to do versus what I have to do," said one Catholic man in his fifties who works in industrial sales,[43] a job he doesn't see as a calling. Finally, sometimes people may not consider their work a calling simply because the term is not familiar given their religious location. For example, our survey showed that nonreligious and Hindu respondents were least likely to see their work as a spiritual calling. Often, however, when we interviewed these individuals, they talked about the meaning or purpose that their work provided them in ways that are consistent with our religious respondents' calling experiences.[44] For example, a Hindu man told us, "I wouldn't necessarily call it a spiritual calling. But I do choose to believe that whatever happens through me and people around me is part of a higher plan from God. So, you know, whatever it is that I'm doing, I feel that I am in this place because some Higher Power has deemed that this is the best thing for me to do, and I keep that mentality, and I keep that thought in the back of my head on a day-to-day basis."

Position versus Income

Much of the previous scholarly research on calling focused on individuals with higher incomes and occupational prestige. In sociologist D. Michael Lindsay's work *Faith in the Halls of Power*, he recounts how evangelicals transcended archaic and historical caricatures to make it into elite sectors of US society, where they have significant positions of power and often a sense of calling in their work.[45] In our national survey on faith at work, we found that those who occupy leadership positions at the top of their organizations are more likely to agree that their work is a spiritual calling than are those at the bottom of their organizations (26 percent vs. 16 percent).[46] On the other hand, we also found that workers who make less money are more likely to see their work as a calling compared with those who report higher incomes. For instance, workers with annual household incomes under $89,000 were more likely to see their work as a calling (22 percent) than were those with household incomes between $90,000 and $179,000 (18 percent) and those with household incomes of $180,000 or more (17 percent). In other words, while being at the top of an organization might foster a sense of calling among individuals—or individuals who feel called tend to move toward the top of an organization—earning a lot of money in itself *does not seem* to foster or attract such a calling and might actually be contradictory to feeling called.

These findings likely reflect the difference between those who work in for-profit settings (where a high organizational level is likely to correlate with a high income), and those who work in nonprofit settings (where a high organizational level is less likely to correlate with a high income, but employees are more likely to see their work as a calling). When we turn to our survey data and look at workers in different sectors, we find that about 14 percent of workers in the for-profit sector feel spiritually called to their work compared with 25 percent of those who work in the government sector and 36 percent of those in the nonprofit sector.[47]

There is research that can help us understand why those who work in the nonprofit sector experience higher levels of spiritual calling, specifically Edward Deci's work on the *overjustification effect*. Deci, an organizational psychologist, found that the more people are paid for a task they enjoy, the more they tend to minimize the intrinsic motivation for that task. "It appears that money—perhaps because of its connotation and use in our culture—may act as a stimulus which leads the subjects to a cognitive reevaluation of the activity from one which is intrinsically motivated to one which is motivated primarily by the expectation of financial rewards," he writes in one study. "In short, money may work to 'buy off' one's intrinsic motivation for an activity. And this decreased motivation appears (from the results of the field experiment) to be more than just a temporary phenomenon."[48] Think about the kinds of tasks that you might be willing to do when volunteering for a good cause that you would not be excited to do as part of a paid job. So, while it could be that individuals who follow their calling are more likely to find themselves in nonprofit jobs where their work centers around helping others and fulfilling a meaningful purpose, or that workers who make less money ascribe a sense of calling to their work to make up for lower compensation, it could also be that workers lose the feeling that their work is a calling the more money they make.

Those who see their work as a calling also tend to feel their work is important beyond making money[49]—thinking more about achieving personal fulfillment and making a difference in the world through their work. In our national faith at work study, 47 percent of those who feel called to their work strongly agreed that the "primary reason I work is to make money," compared with 68 percent of those who do not feel called to their work. In her research on the "passion principle"—the idea that Americans feel the need to follow their passion and choose jobs they find fascinating, intriguing, or fulfilling—sociologist Erin Cech notes how the concept of pursuing paid work one loves or feels called to can inadvertently foster structural and cultural inequalities. According to Cech, there are certain individuals who have the most agency to choose their work: those who are white, male, upper-class, and educated. Wealthy and middle-class workers, she found, are often more successful at launching into stable work in their passion areas. In contrast, working-class and first-generation workers are more likely to end up in jobs that are distant from their passions and education levels.[50] Additionally, the jobs that men and women feel passionate about tend to be differentiated by long processes of cultural socialization. As a result, women are more "naturally" passionate about care work—jobs that, generally speaking, tend to garner less pay and prestige.

Interestingly, we did find that members of marginalized groups are more likely to feel called to their work. For example, among racial and ethnic groups, workers identifying as Black are the most likely to say they see their work as a spiritual calling (31 percent, compared with 18 percent of white workers). Women are more likely than men to see their work as a spiritual calling (24 percent vs. 17 percent). This greater sense of calling among Black and female workers we surveyed remains even after accounting for differences in religiosity and spirituality.[51] While those in marginalized groups might have less agency or opportunity to pursue their calling, it is possible that ascribing a sense of calling to their work compensates for feeling marginalized in the workplace, being discriminated against at work, or doing lower-status work.

Calling as Relational Work

There is a relationship between the type of work one does and the likelihood of seeing one's work as a spiritual calling.[52] We found that those who are in deeply relational work are more likely to feel called to their work. We determined this in part by examining perceptions of calling by industry, as seen in Figure 4.3. Not surprisingly, those who say they work in "religion" are by far the most likely to feel spiritually called to their work, with 77 percent of workers we surveyed in that industry saying they see their work as a spiritual calling. We find significant variation beyond this outlier. Some industries have particularly low levels of workers who feel spiritually called to their work, such as manufacturing (11 percent) and retail sales (13 percent), while other industries—particularly those that involve relational work serving

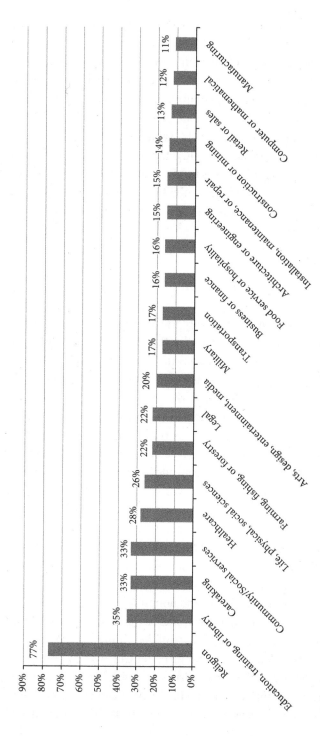

Figure 4.3 Percentage "somewhat" or "strongly" agreeing that "I see my work as a spiritual calling," by industry

Data: Faith at Work Main Survey. Question: "I see my work as a spiritual calling." Percentages represent responses for "somewhat agree" and "strongly agree." Industry question: "Which of the following categories best describes the industry you primarily work/worked in? Mark all that apply."

others—have comparatively high rates of workers who feel called, such as education (35 percent), caretaking (33 percent), community or social services (33 percent), and healthcare (28 percent). Many individuals we spoke with, especially those who are managers or hold organizational roles in which they interact frequently with others, think the relationships they have made through their work and the way they are able to lead and cultivate work for others gives meaning to their work and is evidence of the importance of their work as a calling. Based on our data and interviews, we think that working in sectors in which relating to others is the focus of the job creates a context for feelings of calling to occur *and* that individuals are more likely to feel called to jobs in these industries because relational work is perceived as more spiritual and meaningful.

Sacrificing for Calling

Researchers also find that because workers who feel called to their work have a high level of commitment to their jobs, they tend to be more likely to tolerate, endure, or ignore work situations that are unreasonable, inequitable, or even discriminatory. According to organizational ethics scholars Stuart Bunderson and Jeffrey Thompson, workers who feel called to their jobs are "more likely to see their work as a moral duty, to sacrifice pay, personal time, and comfort for their work." Thus, it becomes easier for organizations to exploit these employees, whether they do so intentionally or unintentionally. For example, if workers who feel called to their jobs are less likely to complain or leave, organizations can overwork and underpay them or get away with other unfair practices. Organizations can also take advantage of those who feel called to their work through what some call "mission-based gaslighting"[53]—using the mission of the organization to make employees feel guilty for asking for pay increases or more reasonable hours. This approach might be particularly effective in organizations that directly serve people (educational institutions, hospitals, and nonprofits, for example). A Catholic woman who is Asian American and works as a project manager for a nonprofit[54] told us, "I definitely feel more fulfilled in my work because of my faith, and vice versa. I feel like I'm being a better Christian by doing the work that I do." But, she added, the work is also "stressful, it's time consuming. And because we're a nonprofit, we don't get paid a ton of money. I could definitely make a lot more money elsewhere, but part of my faith is about giving back to the community our time, talent, and our treasure. . . . I'm salaried, so it doesn't matter how many hours I work, I can work overtime, I can stay really late, and I can still feel good about it, because I know it's what my faith calls me to do."

A nurse practitioner[55] we spoke with said that even though she is an agnostic and does not identify with any religious belief system, she sees herself as being called to her work and said, "Something I've realized working where I work is that, regardless of which religion my coworkers follow [or even] who does not identify as religious, we have a lot of the same core beliefs and motivations. Otherwise, we probably would not work in the setting in which we're overworked and underpaid." She works primarily with patients who are housing-insecure and have severe mental illness, she said, and even though the work is difficult, both physically and emotionally, she often works overtime for no extra pay because there are limited resources and her patients' needs are immediate. She feels called to continue this work, she said, because it helps others, and helping others provides her with a sense of greater purpose.

Our national survey shows us that when workers see their job as a spiritual calling, it can blind them to the difficulties *others* experience at work as well. They may be less able to empathize with those who feel stuck in their job due to money concerns, are unhappy or unfulfilled in their work, or are struggling to find a job. In our survey, 60 percent of those who view their work as a calling agreed that "anyone can find a good job if they try hard enough," while 49 percent of those who do not view their work as a calling agreed with the statement.

Calling Can Be Created

Workers we interviewed, particularly those who are part of religious communities, were attracted to work where their gifts and talents matched the demands of the job, where they could see the use of their skills mattering, and where others affirmed the use of their skills mattering. Workers who had jobs or careers they felt utilized their skills, talents, or interests particularly well often talked about a sense of calling, and part of experiencing that sense of calling, they said, is to "know thyself" and "to thine own self be true."[56] One person who explained that he was part of a Black church tradition[57] told us that his mother used to always say, "'The Lord gave you certain talents, and he didn't give everybody else certain talents. . . . He gave you those kinds of talents. You try to do the best you can with those talents.'" And Marla, the evangelical Christian who works as a corporate trainer in the South,[58] said that she is in her job because one of her core purposes "is just to help people" and "God has given me the gift to teach and to train, and so . . . being at this job, it allows me to do what I do well, which is train and educate."

Parker Palmer, a writer, teacher, and higher education activist, writes in his book *Let Your Life Speak* about finding one's true calling and vocation (a word commonly used interchangeably with "calling"), and concludes that "discovering vocation does not mean scrambling toward some prize just beyond my reach but accepting the treasure of true self I already possess." In other words, workers can be helped to find their calling by giving them opportunity and guidance to focus on who they are, realize their true self, and identify and apply their gifts and talents through their work.

We also find some evidence in our survey data that certain personality traits might foster or impede a sense of calling. Those who feel called to their work are more likely than those who do not feel called to strongly agree that they are extroverted (20 percent vs. 12 percent), likeable (39 percent vs. 23 percent), and emotionally stable (35 percent vs. 26 percent).[59] It could be that workers who have these personality traits are more likely to see their work as a calling, or that those who see their work as a calling are more satisfied and invested in their work and thus more likely to see themselves as extroverted, likeable, and emotionally stable.

It can be difficult to determine causation, and it helps to revisit some of the earlier findings on calling with this in mind. For example, in their work on calling, Duffy and colleagues hypothesized that "living a calling would predict career commitment, work meaning, and job satisfaction over time."[60] When they studied workers over time, however, they found that—contrary to their original assumptions—having career commitment, finding meaning in one's work, and having a sense of job satisfaction were actually causes of eventually feeling called to the work. There is a bit of "fake it until you feel it" here. Sometimes workers discerned *after* they had been doing a job for a while that they were "called" to that work because their circumstances allowed them to see the connection between their skills and talents and the demands of their current position or profession.[61] Other scholars have found similar patterns, documenting in their research that "professional identity, engagement in learning, and social support positively predict calling rather than the opposite."[62] These results are consistent with work that Robert Wuthnow did in the early 1990s, where he found that religion and religious values did not seem to influence the choices people made in pursuing a particular line of work; however, those who attended religious services regularly were more likely to experience meaning or value in their work, regardless of the type of work they did.[63] In short, calling can be cultivated.

We found some glimpses of this in our own data. Feeling a sense of calling to their work often took people time. A mainline Protestant Hispanic woman who works as a senior analyst for a natural gas company[64] told us in an interview that she was not initially interested in the industry, but a close friend encouraged her to apply for a temporary job at a natural gas call center, and when she did she "felt like it was God's hand moving me out of retail—where I didn't want to be—and giving me a new way or purpose to figure out what it was that I wanted to do with my life, or where I was supposed to be." Many workers who said they feel their job is a calling also feel that, when they look back, they had been on a path that led to their job even if they hadn't recognized it, or over time they came to realize their job or profession was somehow orchestrated by something greater than themselves. They expressed sentiments like, "My work at my company is 100 percent a spiritual calling," or "The way I came to this company can only be orchestrated by God."[65]

Our findings also suggest that there are ways to expand conceptions of calling, by considering the intrinsic/extrinsic and proximal/distal dimensions introduced earlier. Even when a job may not feel intrinsically meaningful, it might be viewed as means to a positive end that is extrinsic to the work itself. Similarly, focusing on the ways that one's work might serve others within the workplace (proximally) or beyond it (distally) could enhance a worker's sense of calling. It was striking that while the vast majority of our survey respondents did not view their work as a spiritual calling, many of those we interviewed would often conclude that their work was in fact a calling. Perhaps simply the opportunity we gave for them to talk about their work led to a more positive reappraisal of it. For example, a quality engineer who had an extrinsic/distal view of his job initially said that his work was not a calling. But after reflecting on it a while he concluded, "[My job] provides—well, it provides a means—we tithe, and so anything I do at work in turn helps my church or any other organizations we wish to give to, so I guess indirectly that's somewhat of a calling. Man, I never thought of that before."[66]

The Bottom Line

- People who feel called to their work are more likely to have a sense of purpose, commitment, and satisfaction in their jobs.
- Experiencing a calling at work is a beneficial component of work and something workplaces should endeavor to facilitate.
- Workplace leaders who both care about rectifying inequities in the workplace *and* want to foster the more positive aspects of calling should concentrate on creating environments where workers in all roles and at all levels have opportunities to experience feeling called to their work.
- If managers and workplace leaders do not want their employees to burn out—or find other places or ways to fulfill their calling—they need to provide fair and equitable working conditions. Organizations can help cultivate calling in lower-level positions by understanding how those at the bottom are faring, encouraging adaptive coping responses, and facilitating organizational changes that may increase meaning and motivation for those workers.
- Workers are more likely to experience a sense of calling when they believe their job resonates with their identity, taps into their sense of self, and serves needs beyond their own.
- Organizations can then also help cultivate a sense of calling in their workers by helping them identify their particular gifts and interests, and then putting them in roles in which these skills and propensities can be used to meet the needs of the workplace or serve others.
- When organizational leaders foster a sense of calling among their employees, while ensuring the organization fairly supports those who feel called to their work, it can benefit not only the individual workers but also make the organization a better place to work.

Notes

1. F@W_ST99, White/Hispanic, Woman, 23, PhD Student in Marine Biology, Evangelical Protestant, conducted July 12, 2019.
2. See Ecklund, Elaine Howard, and Anne E. Lincoln. 2016. *Failing Families, Failing Science: Work-Family Conflict in Academic Science*. New York: New York University Press.
3. It's hard to document a reference for this parable; most easily accessible sources are blogs. https://sacredstructures.org/mission/the-story-of-three-bricklayers-a-parable-about-the-power-of-purpose/; https://www.chancestochange.com/building-cathedrals-the-secret-of-meaningful-work/; https://www.lisanneswart.com/2019/11/30/from-the-short-stories-series-three-bricklayers/.

4. Beder, Sharon. 2000. *Selling the Work Ethic: From Puritan Pulpit to Corporate PR.* London: Zed Books; Dawson, J. 2005. "A History of Vocation: Tracing a Keyword of Work, Meaning, and Moral Purpose." *Adult Education Quarterly* 55(3): 220–31.
5. See Wuthnow, Robert. 1998. *God and Mammon in America.* New York: Free Press. Quote from page 92.
6. Weber, Max. 2006 (1930). *The Protestant Ethic and the Spirit of Capitalism.* New York: Routledge. See page 53 for quoted material; Collins, Randall. 1980. "Weber's Last Theory of Capitalism: A Systematization." *American Sociological Review* 45(6): 924–42.
7. See Weber, Max. 1930. *The Protestant Ethic and the Spirit of Capitalism.* New York: Scribners. See page 40 for quoted material.
8. Wuthnow, Robert. 1994. *God and Mammon in America.* New York: The Free Press.
9. See Neubert, Mitchell J., and Katie Halbesleben. 2015. "Called to Commitment: An Examination of Relationships between Spiritual Calling, Job Satisfaction, and Organizational Commitment." *Journal of Business Ethics* 132: 859–72. See page 860 for quoted material.
10. See Hall, Douglas T., and Dawn E. Chandler. 2005. "Psychological Success: When the Career Is a Calling." *Journal of Organizational Behavior* 26(2): 155–76. See also Duffy, Ryan D., and Bryan J. Dik. 2013. "Research on Calling: What Have We Learned and Where Are We Going?" *Journal of Vocational Behavior* 83(3): 428–36 regarding calling not necessarily needing divine origins.
11. Dik, Bryan. J., and Ryan D. Duffy. 2009. "Calling and Vocation at Work: Definitions and Prospects for Research and Practice." *Counseling Psychology* 37: 424–50. Quote is from page 427.
12. Thompson, Jeffery A., and J. Stuart Bunderson. 2019. "Research on work as a calling... and how to make it matter." *Annual Review of Organizational Psychology and Organizational Behavior* 6: 421–43.
13. Our Faith at Work Supplemental Survey asked individuals' level of agreement with the statement "I have been guided to my work by God or a higher power." We find that 28 percent of individuals somewhat or strongly agree with this statement. The correlation between this item and the statement "I see my work as a spiritual calling" is relatively high (r = .70), but not perfect. Indeed, we find that a sizable minority of individuals who do not see their work as a spiritual calling still feel like they have been guided by God to their work. For instance, 12 percent of those who disagree that their work is a spiritual calling still agree that they have been guided to their work by God. It is less common, though, for individuals to say that they feel called to their work but that they were not guided to their work by God. Specifically, only 5 percent of those who agree that they feel called disagree that they were guided to their work by God.
14. Duffy, Ryan D., Laura Reid, and Bryan J. Dik. 2010. "Spirituality, Religion, and Career Development: Implications for the Workplace." *Journal of Management, Spirituality and Religion* 7: 209–21.
15. See Ali, Abbas J., and Abdullah Al-Owaihan. 2008. "Islamic Work Ethic: A Critical Review." *Cross Cultural Management* 15(1): 5–19; see page 14 in particular.
16. F@W_ST186, Black, Man, 54, Organizational Manager/Real Estate, Muslim, conducted December 19, 2019.
17. F@W_ST152, Indian American, Woman, 27, Social Media Manager/Optometry Technician, Muslim, conducted October 23, 2019.
18. F@W_ST191, Middle Eastern/Arab, Woman, 21, Pharmacy Technician, Muslim, conducted January 23, 2020.
19. RUS_Mid SES Orthodox Synagogue Houston Int5, conducted October 17, 2013.
20. F@W_ST151, White, Man, 78, Retired Civil Service Attorney, Jewish, conducted October 23, 2019.
21. Wrzesniewski, Amy, Clark McCauley, Paul Rozin, and Barry Schwartz. 1997. "Jobs, Careers, and Callings: People's Relations to Their Work." *Journal of Research in Personality* 31(1): 21–33.
22. This cross-tabulation is statistically significant at p < .001 (design-based F test). This difference remains even if we look at only very religious individuals.
23. F@W_ST137, Black, Woman, 43, Physician, Christian, conducted September 23, 2019.
24. F@W_ST49, Black, Man, 38, Criminal Investigator, Evangelical, conducted February 6, 2019.
25. Allan, Blake A., Cassandra Batz-Barbarich, Haley M. Sterling, and Louis Tay. 2019. "Outcomes of Meaningful Work: A Meta-analysis." *Journal of Management Studies* 56(3): 500–528; Treadgold, Richard. 1999. "Transcendent Vocations: Their Relationship to Stress, Depression, and Clarity of Self-Concept." *Journal of Humanistic Psychology* 39(1): 81–105.
26. These cross-tabulations are statistically significant at p < .001 (design-based F test).

27. F@W_ST73, Black, Man, 31, Human Resources, Evangelical, conducted May 29, 2019.
28. F@W_ST61, White, Man, 43, Facilities Director, Catholic, conducted March 1, 2019.
29. F@W_ST11, White, Man, 63, Corrections Officer, Evangelical, conducted November 8, 2018.
30. F@W_ST16, White, Man, 32, Engineering Consultant, Evangelical, conducted November 26, 2018.
31. F@W_ST39, White, Woman, 39, Engineer, Evangelical, conducted January 16, 2019.
32. F@W_ST172, White, Woman, 26, Account Executive Political Fundraising, Evangelical, conducted December 9, 2019.
33. F@W_ST49, Black, Man, 38, Criminal Investigator, Evangelical, conducted February 6, 2019.
34. F@W_ST33, White, Man, 48, Co-owner of Logging Company, Evangelical, conducted January 8, 2019.
35. F@W_ST72, White, Man, 23, Engineer, Catholic, conducted May 29, 2019.
36. F@W_ST122, White, Woman, 34, Freelance Writer and EMT, Jewish, conducted August 30, 2019.
37. F@W_ST104, White, Woman, 31, Director of Partner Marketing, Evangelical, conducted July 25, 2019.
38. F@W_ST174, White, Man, 35, IT Associate, Evangelical, conducted December 10, 2019.
39. F@W_ST09, Black, Man, 50, Program Manager, Evangelical, conducted November 2, 2018.
40. F@W_ST31, White, Woman, 25, Civil Engineer, Christian, conducted December 19, 2018.
41. F@W_ST49, Black, Man, 38, Criminal Investigator, Evangelical, conducted February 6, 2019.
42. F@W_ST10, White, Man, 59, CFO for Credit Union, Evangelical, conducted November 6, 2018.
43. F@W_ST184, White, Man, 50, Industrial Sales, Catholic, conducted December 18, 2019.
44. F@Wsup_07, Asian_Man_34_Drug Safety_Hindu, conducted October 28, 2021.
45. Lindsay, D. Michael. 2008. *Faith in the Halls of Power: How Evangelicals Joined the American Elite.* New York: Oxford University Press.
46. Survey respondents were asked, "Think about the organization of job roles in your industry, where the leaders are at the top of the organization and employees are at the bottom of the organization. Would you say that you are toward the top of the organization, middle, or at the bottom?" The cross-tabulation of this question with the calling question is statistically significant at $p < .001$ (design-based F test).
47. Percentages represent those who somewhat and strongly agree with the statement "I see my work as a spiritual calling." The cross-tabulation indicates overall significant differences in agreement across work sector types (Design-based F test = 30.93, $p < .001$).
48. Deci, E. L. 1971. "Effects of Externally Mediated Rewards on Intrinsic Motivation." *Journal of Personality and Social Psychology* 18: 105–15; Deci, E. L., R. Koestner, and R. M. Ryan. 1999. "A Meta-analytic Review of Experiments Examining the Effects of Extrinsic Rewards on Intrinsic Motivation." *Psychological Bulletin* 125(6): 627–68.
49. This cross-tabulation is statistically significant at $p < .001$ (design-based F test).
50. See Cech, Erin. 2021. *The Trouble with Passion.* Oakland: University of California Press.
51. A logistic regression model predicting agreement with the spiritual calling statement while controlling for race, ethnicity, gender, religiosity, and spirituality finds that the odds of Black individuals agreeing that they feel called are 54 percent greater than the odds of white individuals. Similarly, the odds of women agreeing that they feel called are 32 percent greater than the odds for men.
52. Ecklund, Elaine Howard, Denise Daniels, Daniel Bolger, and Laura Johnson. 2020. "A Nationally Representative Survey of Faith and Work: Demographic Subgroup Differences around Calling and Conflict." *Religions* 11(6): 287, 1–18.
53. Tam, Ruth and Sylvie Douglis. "It's okay not to be passionate about your job." npr.org, February 1, 2022. https://www.npr.org/2022/01/31/1076978534/the-trouble-with-passion-when-it-comes-to-your-career.
54. F@W_ST180, Asian American, Woman, 31, Real Estate/Project Manager, Catholic, conducted December 16, 2019.
55. F@W_ST201, Asian American, Woman, 33, Family Nurse Practitioner, Agnostic, conducted May 6, 2021.
56. To "know thyself" is an ancient Greek aphorism, while "to thine own self be true" is referenced popularly from William Shakespeare's *Hamlet*. Both encourage practices of self-knowledge and self-understanding. See Best, Kenneth, "Know Thyself: The Philosophy of Self Knowledge." *UConn Today*, August 7, 2018. https://today.uconn.edu/2018/08/know-thyself-philosophy-self-knowledge/#

57. F@W_ST59, Black, Man, 49, Director of Operations/Technology Consultant, Evangelical, conducted February 26, 2019.

58. F@W_ST17, Black, Woman, 40, Corporate Trainer, Evangelical, conducted November 27, 2018.

59. Cross-tabulations of these personality traits with the calling measure show statistically significant differences (Design-based F tests, $p < .001$).

60. See page 605 of Duffy, Ryan D., Blake A. Allan, Kelsey L. Autin, and Richard P. Douglass. 2014. "Living a Calling and Work Well-Being: A Longitudinal Study." *Journal of Counseling Psychology* 61(4): 605–15.

61. Duffy et al. "Living a Calling and Work Well-Being."

62. Rosa, Anna Dalla, Michelangelo Vianello, and Pasquale Anselmi. 2019. "Longitudinal Predictors of the Development of a Calling: New Evidence for the A Posteriori Hypothesis." *Journal of Vocational Behavior* 114: 44–56.

63. Wuthnow, Robert. 1994. *God and Mammon in America*. New York: Free Press. See ch. 3 in particular.

64. F@W_ST30, Black but of Hispanic Heritage, Woman, 47, Senior Analyst for Natural Gas Marketing, Mainline, conducted December 18, 2018.

65. F@W_ST15, White, Woman, 47, Manager of Community Engagement, Evangelical, conducted November 20, 2018.

66. F@W_ST75, White, Man, 69, Reliability and Quality Engineer, conducted May 30, 2019.

5

The Why for How: Religion, Coping, and Meaning at Work

"I couldn't survive if I didn't have Jesus. There's no way," an evangelical woman who works as a kindergarten teacher told us as she was describing the stress and challenges of her job.[1] Workers we surveyed and interviewed in our Faith at Work study spoke of using their religious or spiritual beliefs and practices to cope with certain days, tasks, or even entire jobs that are stressful, difficult, unappealing, or painful. Sometimes the pain of work that needs to be coped with is defined by extreme stress and traumatic events (think about the medical personnel who sat with dying patients during the COVID-19 pandemic when patients' families were not allowed to see them). Sometimes the pain is the dullness or monotony of the work—as in many entry-level office jobs. Other times, workplace pain might be the result of physically demanding or even disgusting aspects of the job—consider field labor in the hot sun or cleaning bodily waste. And sometimes the pain results from a combination of factors. We are reminded of an episode of the sitcom *Everybody Loves Raymond*, when a character named Robert describes his job as a police officer as "just hours of boredom interrupted by moments of unbelievable horror."[2]

Religion and spirituality provide particularly powerful tools for coping with a variety of challenges and stresses in life, research shows, and while much of this research has examined coping with issues outside of work, the presence and importance of religious and spiritual coping has been demonstrated in the workplace as well.[3] We argue here that religion provides resources for coping at work, particularly if an individual's religious identity and community is central to their life. After all, to use religion or spirituality to cope with work, you must first have religious or spiritual language and practices within your coping toolkit.[4] Religion helps workers reframe their work in ways that develop a sense of meaning and purpose in their jobs and difficult workplace circumstances, and when an individual attaches meaning

Religion in a Changing Workplace. Elaine Howard Ecklund, Denise Daniels, and Christopher P. Scheitle,
Oxford University Press. © Oxford University Press 2024. DOI: 10.1093/oso/9780197675007.003.0005

and purpose to work that is hard or unappealing, it can significantly impact their short- and long-term well-being. As Friedrich Nietzsche wrote, "If we have our own why in life, we shall get along with almost any how." Religious practices and communities, including coworkers who are people of faith, can provide that "why," reducing the stress that workers experience in difficult workplace situations, including situations of discrimination.

Emphasizing religion as a coping mechanism for workers can have its drawbacks, however, because it puts the onus on workers to cope with the stress of their jobs rather than on the organization to reduce workplace stressors and hardships. Moreover, using religion to cope with difficult work experiences at the individual level can prevent workers from thinking about how to bring changes to systemic workplace problems. In our research it was unusual to find faith viewed as a resource for improving workplace situations so that there is less stress or difficulties for individual workers to cope with—and less need for religion or spirituality as a coping mechanism.

Using Religion to Reframe Work

Meaning and Purpose in Daily Tasks

Brother Lawrence was a monk who lived in a French monastery in the 1600s. He had what many would consider the incredibly mundane—and perhaps even demeaning—responsibility of washing the dishes. Lawrence did not feel called to the work of washing dishes, in particular, but he felt called to being a monk, and as a monk he viewed his everyday tasks through the lens of his faith and used this experience to develop spiritual practices that he wrote about in his now-famous book, *The Practice of the Presence of God.* According to Lawrence, "That our sanctification did not depend upon changing our works, but in doing that for GOD's sake, which we commonly do for our own."[5] Lawrence wrote that he found meaning and purpose in his work and even came to see the act of washing dishes as a spiritual practice, which he saw himself doing obediently out of a pure love of God. He did not think of his prayer time as separate from his work time, but rather his work washing dishes became an act of prayer.

It is natural for people to imbue work tasks with some meaning or a sense of fulfillment, even if such tasks do not on the surface appear particularly meaningful or fulfilling. Often, individuals find meaning and purpose in their work not because of the nature of their jobs but because it is a way for them to cope with that work.[6] Many religious individuals use their religion or spirituality to find that meaning. "This is a place where God wants me to be. . . . He reminds me all of the time," said a white evangelical woman who works as a Spanish teacher[7] and attends church services and Bible study regularly. This belief provides her with a sense of purpose and intention for her work that helps her find meaning in her daily activities.

Some workers we spoke with utilize faith to find meaning in even the most mundane tasks, using their religion or spirituality as a tool to positively reframe work that lacks obvious meaning. In one of our surveys, we asked workers whether they agreed with the statement "My faith or spirituality helps me experience meaning and purpose in my daily work tasks." As seen in Figure 5.1, 23 percent said they strongly agree with this statement, while another 19 percent somewhat agree.[8] Not surprisingly, we found that these workers are more likely to identify as religious or spiritual.

As we saw in the previous chapter, the ability to rely on one's faith to find meaning in daily work tasks is strengthened when work is already placed within a context of meaning (i.e., a calling). While those who do not feel called to their work often use religious resources to find meaning in and cope with their work—especially work that is difficult, stressful, or demeaning—such daily meaning-making is obviously easier when a person is employed in a job to which they feel called.

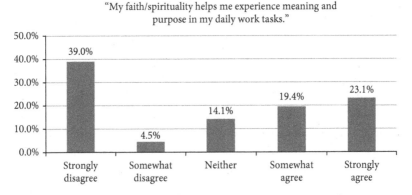

Figure 5.1 Faith or Spirituality Helps Experience Meaning at Work

Data: Faith at Work Main Survey. Note that the "strongly disagree" category includes those who responded "not applicable."

Meaningful Products and Impacts

We found that some workers find meaning and fulfillment at work based on how they view the products and services of their work. If workers believe that the end products or services their workplace provides are meaningful, they are better able to find meaning in their daily work tasks, even if those tasks may be tedious and seemingly unfulfilling. When we asked individuals whether they see "the end product or service" of their workplace as "highly meaningful,"[9] 40 percent of all workers said they strongly agree, while an additional 26 percent said they somewhat agree. The percentage of workers who feel this way is higher in some industries than others. We found that 82 percent of workers in education, for example, somewhat or strongly agree that the end product or service of their work is highly meaningful, compared with 57 percent of workers in retail. Still, a majority of workers see the products or services they are contributing to as highly meaningful, which suggests a common desire among workers to find meaning in the products or services they are helping to provide.

We found that workers are better able to use their faith or spirituality to find meaning in their daily work tasks if they see their workplace's products or services as meaningful. (Of course, it is also possible that those who use their faith or spirituality to find meaning and purpose in their daily work tasks are more able to see the products or services of their jobs as meaningful in some way.) Among very religious workers, we found that 78 percent of those who strongly agree that the end product or service of their work is meaningful also strongly agree that they use their faith or spirituality to make meaning out of their daily work tasks. Among those who strongly disagree that the end product or service of their work is meaningful, 43 percent strongly agree that they use their faith or spirituality to find meaning in their daily work. While many religious individuals still use their religion to find meaning in daily work tasks even if they do not see their work product as meaningful, it is easier for religious workers to tap into their religion's meaning-making ability when the work itself is seen within a larger context of meaning.

Regardless of how religious or spiritual an individual is, however, or what type of work they do, their ability to cope with their work by finding meaning in it is predictive of their wellbeing at work. Our survey data show that even after accounting for a wide variety of other factors, such as an individual's religiosity, employment status, race, gender, age, income, and organizational position, and their industry, the use of religion to find meaning in daily work tasks is associated with greater job satisfaction and more organizational commitment.[10]

Religion Supports People in Stressful Work

The workers we interviewed frequently spoke about the stress of their jobs. While there are several strategies for coping with stress related to work, religion and spirituality serve as a key resource for many individuals. As seen in Figure 5.2, a little more than half of the workers we surveyed agreed that they "turn to faith for support through stressful times" in their work life, with about 28 percent strongly agreeing with this statement.[11] For religious workers in the medical profession, in particular, faith can be a deep part of coping with high-stress situations. A Black evangelical nurse,[12] for example, told us, "When I have the person bleeding out on the table in the OR [operating room], yeah, I'm praying. I'm praying as I'm loading the sutures and getting the platelets ready and assisting anesthesia. . . . I'm absolutely praying for guidance and [for] this person and for the family, and I'm doing it as I work. So, I don't separate that. . . . I pray for guidance, I pray for clarity. I pray that I'll be able to make the correct decisions and I will make the decisions based on what's best."

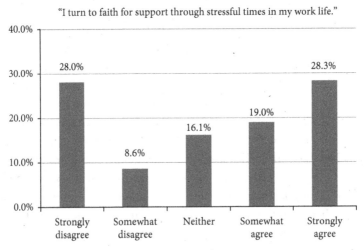

"I turn to faith for support through stressful times in my work life."

Figure 5.2 Turning to Faith for Support with Work Stress
Data: Faith at Work Supplemental Survey.

Unsurprisingly, very religious workers are the most likely to say they turn to faith in times of stress at work. Among those who describe themselves as very religious, 91 percent agreed that they turn to faith to cope with stress at work. Among those who see themselves as slightly religious, only 34 percent agreed that their faith helps them cope with work difficulties.[13] We take from this that religion has to be more than a light identity to be useful as a form of coping with the difficulties of work; it has to be taken seriously in terms of commitment and practices.

Larger tech firms, in particular, are beginning to recognize that religious practices like praying and meditating can help some employees cope with workplace stress. Companies like Google, Facebook, and Salesforce have all started to implement meditation rooms, breaks for prayer, and yoga classes, and a number of other companies are providing chaplain support in the workplace. Our survey results show that more than 35 percent of workers agree that they "benefit from praying or meditating privately at work,"[14] and we found that those who engage in prayer more frequently are more likely to say that faith helps them with stress at work—regardless of how religious they are.[15] The religious individuals we spoke with, however—especially those who are consistently part of a religious community—told us that religious practices like prayer, meditation, and reading a sacred text are particularly important in dealing with the stress of work. The Spanish teacher we introduced earlier[16] told us that her spiritual practices give her the ability to cope with some of the hard aspects of her job, like helping students who have behavior problems or do not have the support they need at home. In these times, she said, she tries to remember "the mantra 'worry less, pray more'—that when you start feeling overwhelmed just turn to prayer instead of trying to battle through; just taking a moment in prayer usually will help you with it."

Religion Supports People Experiencing Racial Discrimination

Religion is also a resource that some workers use to cope with discrimination at work, and we found that religious workers encountering discrimination lean strongly on their faith. Among the workers we surveyed, 14 percent agreed that their faith helps them cope with racial discrimination at work, 14 percent said their faith helps them cope with religious discrimination, and

12 percent said their faith helps them cope with sex/gender discrimination.[17] (While these percentages are relatively small, we would not expect them to be large since not everyone will say they have experienced workplace discrimination.) Interestingly, when we look at only those who said they experience discrimination "very often" due to their race or ethnicity, the percentage of those who say their faith helps them cope with racial discrimination rises from 14 percent to 44 percent. It jumps to 90 percent if we look at just those who are very religious. This shows that faith is an important resource for religious individuals when discrimination does occur.

A Muslim woman who owns and operates a convenience store[18] told us about a recent incident in which someone smashed one of the displays on her gas pumps with a hammer—an act she suspects was motivated by anti-Muslim hate. We asked her how she deals with situations like these, and she said, "I pray. That's all I do. I believe in staying on the right path. In Islam, the beginning of the Qur'an is about staying on the right path. Stay—no matter what comes in your way, you stay on the right path. So, we try to adhere to whatever the Qur'an has said. And when things happen like that, I could have easily said, 'OK, I hate all these people who do this, and I hate whoever is here.'... [But] there is no point having hatred for anybody, I think. If one thing happens, I will take it as an isolated incident and try to still deal fairly with everybody."

Previous social science research has shown that religion can be an especially important resource for people of color in coping with racial discrimination,[19] and we found the same. Some of those we talked with utilized faith to cope with racial discrimination at work with a submission to divine sovereignty, expressed through phrases like, "God has a plan."[20] An Asian American man who describes himself as a Christian[21] and works as an investment analyst, for example, told us that he believes he is treated differently and loses some opportunities at work because he is Asian. He is perceived as being "really good at math," he said, but not "as presentable in front of clients." His faith helps him cope with these situations, he explained, saying, "I know that God has placed me in my work, so I should not grumble or complain. I should be as the Bible says, 'content.' I believe that . . . God is sovereign, and He's placed me where He's placed me. It's made me who I am, and if I grumble or complain, which I do, I am complaining against God, not necessarily only against my situation or against a supervisor who potentially treats me a little bit unfairly or whatever. . . . The ideal thing for me is to be content with what the situation is."

Others we interviewed, particularly those who experienced anti-Black discrimination, explained that their faith gave them strength to persevere and continue working amid racism and the challenges of a hostile work environment. Religion can have buffering effects for individuals experiencing discrimination—providing social support and religious guidance to mitigate the adverse effects of discrimination on mental health outcomes,[22] for example—and faith can also function to affirm their worthiness and dignity when they feel their dignity and personhood are not being affirmed by others in the workplace. In some cases, individuals can exert agency via religion to cope with discrimination. Some of those we talked with said their faith helped them take the higher path: to forgive, turn the other cheek, and not react with anger when facing racial discrimination at work (where expressions of anger are often punishable). One Black respondent,[23] for instance, shared that his faith helps him "not to fly off the handles, and not to react as instinctively" when he experiences racial discrimination from his coworkers, and these incidents "don't affect him professionally," he said, because of his moderated reactions.

On occasion, faith provides religious individuals who experience racial discrimination in the workplace with strength and motivation to speak out and seek change. We found that some religious individuals are compelled by their faith to "stand up"[24] for themselves and others, and to talk openly about situations of racial discrimination at work. Their faith affirms that racism is morally wrong and empowers them to respond to it. The Black evangelical nurse introduced earlier[25] told us about one instance in which she was going to prepare a patient for surgery and someone stopped her because, she told us, they did not think someone of her race could be the head nurse, even though she was wearing a badge identifying her role. When faced with such experiences, it was important to her that she not react with hate or anger but that she stand up for herself. She saw her faith as a central resource for how she responded. An evangelical Hispanic woman who works in finance[26] shared her experience with discrimination, saying, "I felt like it's wrong. . . . I personally feel that God doesn't want us to be like that. We should all be united as one . . . and when I can, if I feel it's necessary . . . I will say something. . . . You know, you just get that feeling where I need to say somethin'. And that's when I feel like when God's tellin' me to say it, do it. . . . Bring it out in the open." Other workers similarly shared that their faith "does not make them a wimp or a carpet"[27] when experiencing racial discrimination. An evangelical Christian who works for the US government in homeland security,[28] for example, told us, "It is difficult being an African American woman in this field, so my faith allows me to step back sometimes and remove myself from the situation. And again, try to put myself in the other people's shoes and try to make positive change."

Religion Provides Alternative Coping Communities

Some workers we spoke to told us that having coworkers who share their faith, or at least an interest in faith, helps them cope with issues at work. "There are a few that are Christian, and so I think we can sort of garner strength with each other, in times of stress," a pediatrician[29] said about her coworkers, "and work can be pretty stressful." Talking about a mentor at work who shares her faith, Marla, the evangelical corporate trainer[30] we met earlier, told us, "I appreciate that I have been able to express my faith openly with her and that she has shared some of her personal spiritual struggles with me that I have learned from." She said "that by having that resource, that I know, to this day, if I am struggling with something, I know I can call her on the phone right now, about personal stuff or work stuff, and she will have a word from the Lord. . . . I just appreciate her for setting the example that she has."

An increasing number of organizations—including Alphabet (Google), Apple, Meta (Facebook), Target, Toyota, American Airlines, the US Department of Agriculture, and the Internal Revenue Service—support faith-based employee resource groups (often cultivated as a part of diversity, equity, and inclusion efforts within the organization), and there is good evidence that groups like these can help employees cope with challenges in the workplace, regardless of whether those challenges have a direct connection with religion. Our survey data show that a little more than 20 percent of workers "value participating with others in a faith/spiritual group or activity to help [them] better deal with work-related issues."[31] Our data also show that individuals participating in such work-related faith communities are more likely to say that their faith helps guide them through stressful times at work *regardless of their religiosity.*[32] In other words, being highly religious makes it more likely that an individual will use religion as a coping tool in the workplace, but participating in a faith-based work group makes it more likely a person will use religion as a coping mechanism regardless of how religious they personally are.

Communities of faith outside of the workplace, and the support they provide, can also help religious individuals cope at work. We asked workers if they agree with the statement "My faith community supports me in my work or career." Overall, 26 percent of workers said they agree with this statement, but among workers who attend religious services weekly or more, the percentage increases greatly, with 66 percent agreeing that their faith community supports them in their work or career.[33] Our work aligns with that of sociologist Carolyn Chen, in her study of tech workers in Silicon Valley, who argues that those who are deeply religious are sometimes able to "resist being swallowed up by work by plunging into their tight-knit, hermetic religious communities."[34]

When we looked specifically at how faith communities helped workers during the COVID-19 pandemic, we found that about half of workers we surveyed—48 percent—agreed that their faith community "looked for ways to support those who had increased demands on their time due to school or daycare closures," and about 60 percent agreed that their faith community "looked for ways to support" those whose physical or mental health were negatively affected by the pandemic. These percentages were higher among workers who were more active in a religious congregation during the pandemic, which reinforces the idea that religion's coping benefits are strongest or most available for those most connected to their faith beliefs and communities.[35] "If I was just feeling uneasy about something or the high stress levels during COVID," a Black Protestant woman who works in public health[36] told us, "Being able to talk to other individuals in the congregation or even just through prayer or even just through the messages that I heard was an encouragement to be able to still do the work that I do."

Yet while workers frequently look to their faith or spirituality to find meaning in work tasks, deal with stress at work, or cope with other workplace issues, our research shows that religious and spiritual leaders rarely address workplace matters or discuss how faith might be used to cope with difficult work situations. When we asked workers how often their "faith leader teaches about the meaning of work,"[37] only 9 percent said often or very often. Even among workers who attend religious services weekly or more, only 26 percent said their faith leader teaches about the meaning of work. When we asked workers, "How often do you talk with a faith leader about workplace issues?" only 2 percent said they do this often or very often and a strong majority—80 percent—said they *never* do this. Even among those attending religious services weekly or more, only 5 percent said they often talk with a faith leader about workplace issues and almost half say they never do it. Part of the problem might be that workers do not look to their faith leaders for counsel on challenges they face at work, perhaps because they assume workplace issues are outside of the leaders' domain, and faith leaders are therefore unaware of the need to address such issues. Yet our research over the years suggests it would be beneficial for faith leaders to engage their communities on issues related to work and to discuss how faith can help them cope in the workplace. By ignoring work-related topics, pastors and other spiritual leaders may be missing a significant way of connecting with those they lead.

A vast social science literature highlights the importance of religion as a coping resource, so we should not be surprised that many workers use their faith to find meaning in their work—even if mundane—and mitigate the impacts of workplace stress. To the extent that the nature of one's work must be mundane, stressful, or otherwise difficult, using one's faith to make that work a bit more pleasant or tolerable would seem to be a positive outcome. We must be careful, however, not to point to coping as an ultimate solution when actual alterations to one's workplace conditions could eliminate the need for coping in the first place.

German social theorist Karl Marx[38] felt that when workers used religion to cope with work, it led to worker exploitation. In his view, religion aids the economic system by giving comfort to workers who are oppressed and, as a result, prevents them from seeing the true nature of their condition and taking action to improve their circumstances. In a capitalist society, he believed, the meaning that religion provides at work encourages a complacent workforce. As he famously wrote, "Religion is the sigh of the oppressed creature, the heart of a heartless world, and the soul of soulless conditions. It is the opium of the people."[39]

We found some evidence supporting Marx's skepticism of religion as a motivator for structural change. Only rarely do workers appear to utilize religion to support structural changes in the workplace. This does not mean, however, that religion cannot be a powerful framework for workers advocating for such changes, as it has been for other social movements of the past—maybe most importantly for the US civil rights movement.[40] Yet the ability to frame workplace reforms as a religious movement likely cannot succeed on the efforts of individual workers laboring in isolation. Rather, such efforts may require more attention and organizational effort from leaders and organizations to be effective.

The Bottom Line

- Workers for whom religion is important in their lives use religion to find meaning in and cope with difficult work situations.
- Faith-based workplace communities such as employee resource groups are a helpful resource for a broad spectrum of workers who are experiencing stressful times at work.
- But when workers use religion to cope privately with workplace stress, organizations are often let off the hook for making work organizations more humane.
- Workplace organizational leaders can be supportive of faith-based ERGs and workplace chaplaincy programs while also proactively taking steps to remove sources of workplace stress and trauma when possible.

Notes

1. F@W_ST28, White, Woman, 56, Kindergarten Teacher, Evangelical, conducted December 12, 2018.
2. *Everybody Loves Raymond*. 1997. "Who's Handsome?" Season 1, episode 14. CBS Broadcasting.
3. Much of this work has focused on the role of religion and spirituality in coping with a variety of health problems, although some work has also looked at other adverse experiences, such as discrimination, criminal victimization, migration, and so on. While the focus is often on the positive aspects of religious and spiritual coping, it is worth noting that some research has identified negative coping strategies related to religion and spirituality. For some brief examples and overviews, see Wachholtz, Amy B., Michelle J. Pearce, and Harold Koenig. 2007. "Exploring the Relationship between Spirituality, Coping, and Pain." *Journal of Behavioral Medicine* 30(4): 311–18; Mattis, Jacqueline S. 2002. "Religion and Spirituality in the Meaning-Making and Coping Experiences of African American Women: A Qualitative Analysis." *Psychology of Women Quarterly* 26(4): 309–21; Pargament, Kenneth I. 2011. "Religion and Coping: The Current State of Knowledge." In S Folkman (Ed.), *The Oxford Handbook of Stress, Health, and Coping*. 269–88. Oxford, UK: Oxford University Press; Ní Raghallaigh, Muireann. 2011. "Religion in the Lives of Unaccompanied Minors: An Available and Compelling Coping Resource." *British Journal of Social Work* 41(3): 539–56; Koenig, Harold G., and David B. Larson. 2001. "Religion and Mental Health: Evidence for an Association." *International Review of Psychiatry* 13(2): 67–78; Peres, Julio F. P., Alexander Moreira-Almeida, Antonia Gladys Nasello, and Harold G. Koenig. 2007. "Spirituality and Resilience in Trauma Victims." *Journal of Religion and Health* 46(3): 343–50; Schnabel, Landon, and Scott Schieman. 2021. "Religion Protected Mental Health but Constrained Crisis Response during Crucial Early Days of the COVID-19 Pandemic." *Journal for the Scientific Study of Religion* 66(2): 530–43; Cummings, Jeremy P., and Kenneth I. Pargament. 2012. In Peter Hill and Bryan Dik (Eds.) "Religious Coping with Workplace Stress." *Psychology of Religion and Workplace Spirituality*. 157–77. Charlotte, NC: Information Age Publishing; Bakibinga, Pauline, Hege Forbech Vinje, and Maurice Mittelmark. 2014. "The Role of Religion in the Work Lives and Coping Strategies of Ugandan Nurses." *Journal of Religion and Health* 53(5): 1342–52; Pandey, Jatin, and Manjari Singh. 2019. "Positive Religious Coping as a Mechanism for Enhancing Job Satisfaction and Reducing Work-Family Conflict: A Moderated Mediation Analysis." *Journal of Management, Spirituality & Religion* 16(3): 314–38.
4. About 83 percent of those individuals identifying as very religious say they utilize their faith or spirituality to cope with daily work tasks, compared to 60 percent of those who are moderately

religious, 26 percent of those who are slightly religious, and 12 percent of those who are not at all religious. We find a similar pattern with spirituality. Seventy-five percent of those who say they are very spiritual use their faith or spirituality to cope with daily work tasks. This compares to 52 percent of those who are moderately spiritual, 18 percent of those who are slightly spiritual, and 4 percent who are not at all spiritual.

5. "That our sanctification did not depend upon changing our works, but in doing that for GOD's sake, which we commonly do for our own." *The Practice of the Presence of God.* "Fourth Conversation." p. 7.

6. Davidson, James C., and David P. Caddell. 1994. "Religion and the Meaning of Work." *Journal for the Scientific Study of Religion* 33: 135–47.

7. F@W_ST21, White, Woman, 25, Spanish Teacher, Evangelical, conducted December 3, 2018.

8. Faith at Work Main Survey. Note that this question offered a response of "not applicable." We coded these cases as strongly disagree for the purposes of this figure.

9. Faith at Work Main Survey. Full statement was, "The end product or services itself produced by my organization is highly meaningful to me." Similarly, the Faith at Work Supplemental Survey included a question asking for individuals' level of agreement with this statement: "The goods or services my organization provides have a positive impact on others in the world." Forty-five percent of individuals overall strongly agreed, 29 percent somewhat agreed, 15 percent neither agreed nor disagreed, 4 percent somewhat disagreed, and 7 percent strongly disagreed.

10. Faith at Work Main Survey. Ordinary least square regression models show that—independent of self-reported religiosity, employment status (i.e., full time, part time), race (white vs. non-white), gender, age, income, organizational position (i.e., bottom, middle, top), and industry working in—using faith/spirituality to experience meaning in daily work tasks was a statistically significant predictor of satisfaction and organizational commitment.

11. A separate question on the Faith at Work Main Survey asked individuals' level of agreement with the statement "My faith guides me through stressful times in my work-life." Twenty-eight percent strongly agreed, 20 percent somewhat agreed, 12 percent neither agreed nor disagreed, 3 percent somewhat disagreed, and 36 percent strongly disagreed. Note that the last percentage includes those who said the statement does not apply to them.

12. F@W_ST47, Black/Native American, Woman, 63, Executive Director of Non-profit/Nurse, Evangelical, conducted January 31, 2019.

13. Faith at Work Supplemental Survey. Percentages combine "agree" and "strongly agree" responses.

14. Faith at Work Main Survey. The full statement was, "I benefit from praying or meditating privately at work." Forty-five percent of respondents strongly disagreed, including those who said that the statement does not apply to them. Three percent somewhat disagreed, 16 percent neither agreed nor disagreed, 15 percent somewhat agreed, and 21 percent strongly agreed.

15. Faith at Work Main Survey. Ordinary least squares regression predicting agreement that faith helps with stress at work by prayer frequency while controlling for religiosity.

16. F@W_ST21, White, Woman, 25, Spanish Teacher, Evangelical, conducted December 3, 2018.

17. Faith at Work Supplemental Survey. Percentages combine "agree" and "strongly agree" responses.

18. F@WSUP_28, Asian-Indian, Woman, 55, Owner of Gas Station/Convenience Store, Muslim, conducted February 8, 2022.

19. See Bacchus, Denise N. A. 2008. "Coping with Work-Related Stress: A Study of the Use of Coping Resources among Professional Black Women." *Journal of Ethnic & Cultural Diversity in Social Work* 17(1): 60–81; Hall, J. Camille, Johnnie Hamilton-Mason, and Joyce E. Everett. 2012. "Black Women Talk about Workplace Stress and How They Cope." *Journal of Black Studies* 43(2): 207–26; Lee, Daniel B., Melissa K. Peckins, Alison L. Miller, Meredith O. Hope, Enrique W. Neblett, Shervin Assari, Jaime Muñoz-Velázquez, and Marc A. Zimmerman. 2021. "Pathways from Racial Discrimination to Cortisol/DHEA Imbalance: Protective Role of Religious Involvement." *Ethnicity & Health* 26(3): 413–30.

20. F@W_ST37, White Hispanic, Man, 43, High School ROTC Instructor, Evangelical, conducted January 10, 2019.

21. F@W_ST159, Asian/Chinese American, Man, 37, Investment Analyst, Evangelical, conducted February 26, 2019.

22. See Bierman, Alex. 2006. "Does Religion Buffer the Effects of Discrimination on Mental Health? Differing Effects by Race." *Journal for the Scientific Study of Religion* 45: 551–65; Ellison, Christopher G., Reed T. DeAngelis, and Metin Güven. 2017. "Does Religious Involvement Mitigate the Effects of Major Discrimination on the Mental Health of African Americans? Findings from the Nashville Stress and Health Study." *Religions* 8(9): 195.
23. F@W_ST43, Black, Male, 48, Graphic Artist, Evangelical, conducted January 29, 2019.
24. F@W_ST47, Black/Native American, Woman, 63, Executive Director of Non-profit/Nurse, Evangelical, conducted January 31, 2019.
25. F@W_ST47, Black/Native American, Woman, 63, Executive Director of Non-profit/Nurse, Evangelical, conducted January 31, 2019.
26. F@W_ST38, Hispanic, Woman, 51, Finance, Evangelical, conducted January 11, 2019.
27. F@W_ST47, Black/Native American, Woman, 63, Executive Director of Non-profit/Nurse, Evangelical, conducted January 31, 2019.
28. F@W_ST162, Black, Woman, 38, CIO for Homeland Security Agency, Evangelical, conducted November 22, 2019.
29. F@W_ST56, Asian, Woman, 35, Pediatrician, Evangelical, conducted February 20, 2019.
30. See F@W_ST17, Black, Woman, 40, Corporate Trainer, Evangelical/Assemblies of God, conducted November 27, 2018.
31. Faith at Work Main Survey. The statement was, "I value participating with others in a faith/spiritual group or activity to help me better deal with work-related issues." Fifty-six percent of respondents strongly disagreed with this statement, including those who said that it does not apply to them. Six percent somewhat disagreed, 17 percent neither agreed nor disagreed, 11 percent somewhat agreed, and 10 percent strongly agreed.
32. For instance, if we conduct an ordinary least squares regression predicting agreement with the statement that faith guides the individual through stressful times at work, we find that agreement with the value of participating in a faith group or activity connected to work is positively associated with this outcome even after controlling for religiosity. Another way to look at this is to only look at those who are very religious. Of those who are very religious, 96 percent of those who strongly agree that they value participating in a work-based faith group or activity say that they agree that their faith helps them in stressful times. This decreases to 75 percent among the very religious who strongly disagree that they value participating in a work-based faith group or activity.
33. Faith at Work Main Survey.
34. See page 47 of Chen, Carolyn. 2022. *Work Pray Code: When Work Becomes Religion in Silicon Valley.* Princeton, NJ: Princeton University Press.
35. Faith at Work Supplemental Survey. For instance, about 70 percent of those who said they attended religious services weekly or more during the pandemic (whether virtually or in person) agreed that their faith community attempted to help with mental health during the pandemic. This drops to between 30 and 40 percent of those who say they were attending sparsely (i.e., only once a year or less).
36. F@WSUP_12, Black, Woman, 47, Public Health Executive, Black Protestant, conducted November 12, 2021.
37. Faith at Work Main Survey.
38. Marx, Karl. 1978. "The German Ideology." In Robert C. Tucker (Ed.). *The Marx-Engels Reader*, 2nd ed. 146–200. New York: Norton.
39. Marx, Karl. 1970. *Critique of Hegel's "Philosophy of Right".* Cambridge: Cambridge University Press.
40. Morris, Aldon D. 1986. *The Origins of the Civil Rights Movement: Black Communities Organizing for Change.* New York: Free Press.

6

Faith and Ethics at Work

Most employees believe they act ethically in the workplace. Ninety-six percent of workers in our survey said they agree with the statement "Even if it does not benefit me, I always act with integrity at work." This percentage does not differ in any meaningful way between those who say they are very religious (95 percent) and those who say they are not at all religious (96 percent).[1] Most employees also care about "workplace ethics," the moral principles that govern a person's behavior at work.[2]

Moreover, social scientists find that the more religious a person is, the more they want to have their day-to-day ethical decisions shaped by their religious morality. And the importance of religion in an individual's life also impacts how much they care about their religious moral frameworks shaping workplace ethics.[3] Even if religious leaders are not explicitly discussing workplace ethics, they are often discussing ethics and morality more broadly within their congregations in ways individuals told us they draw on in the workplace. For example, in our survey research, a little more than 10 percent of workers overall said their faith leader often "discusses how we should behave at work,"[4] but those who are active in a faith community receive such messages more frequently. Among workers who attend religious services weekly or more, for instance, this percentage increases to 34 percent.

Simply being religious in the abstract or identifying with a religion might not be enough for a person to link religious morality to workplace ethics or to result in religiously influenced ethical behavior in the workplace. Rather, it matters whether a person's religious identity is *central* to how they think of themselves and whether their religious identity is *actually connected* in their minds to workplace ethics. The influence of religious role expectations in organizations is moderated in particular by "religious identity salience" and "religious motivational orientation." Management scholars Gary Weaver and Bradley Agle[5] looked at how religion influences ethical behavior in organizations and what they call "religious role expectations," the behaviors and beliefs that religious groups expect from their members. In their view, "The religious role expectations that, when internalized, constitute a person's

Religion in a Changing Workplace. Elaine Howard Ecklund, Denise Daniels, and Christopher P. Scheitle, Oxford University Press. © Oxford University Press 2024. DOI: 10.1093/oso/9780197675007.003.0006

religious self-identity create a potential for religiously influenced ethical behavior. But whether that behavior actually occurs reflects the salience of a person's religious self-identity, and also the individual's motivational orientation for being religious."

A worker who has a strong religious identity is more likely to behave according to their religion's ethical standards. "I operate with the highest ethical standards. I work with a lot of university researchers in my field. . . . I generate a lot of data that we then communicate to customers. There's a moral standard that I have," said a Jewish man[6] who works as a scientist for a fertilizer company and links his faith to the ethical standards he has for his work. "I could fudge things, to make our stuff look better than our competitors' stuff, or things like that, but I am not going to do that. . . . Ultimately, our customers are going to know if it works or if it doesn't work, so it doesn't make any sense to do that. And our customers, they're my friends. So there's a circular thing to this. And it all starts with, maybe it's religion or whatever. . . . You gotta have the moral high ground, to do good work. It's ethical work."

Robert Giacalone and Carole Jurkiewicz looked at the influence of personal spirituality on the perception of twenty-five ethically questionable business activities and found a significant relationship between ethics and spirituality. They also found that legally proscribed violations are not significantly related to spirituality, but for other unethical activities where the illegality is not clear—those related to personal integrity, situation-specific factors, and the natural environment (e.g., "exploitation of natural resources" and "pollution of air and water")—spirituality influences whether an individual views the practice as ethical or unethical. Giacalone and Jurkiewicz reason that "in more 'gray' areas where there is not a clear legal guidepost, one's degree of spirituality provided the moral framework from which to base a decision."[7]

Other research finds that religion matters most for situational ethics related to individual ethical choices. Psychologists Jesse Graham and Jonathan Haidt find that religion is highly correlated with what religious people see as more universal codes like in-group loyalty and respect for authority, as well as lifestyle issues like sexual "purity" and what many see as "sanctity of life."[8] Indeed our own research shows that people tend to link their religion to personal ethics. They say that religion prevents them from doing things like lying, cheating, and stealing. When they do link religion to large-scale organizational issues, they are more likely to connect religion to matters of life and sexuality (an organization's stance on abortion or same-sex marriage, for example), rather than corporate business responsibility (such as the organization's environmental practices or diversity programs).

For religious employees, however, workplaces can present ethical difficulties. As Weaver and Agle[9] explain, "Because people normally occupy multiple social positions, (spouse, parent, employee, and so on), each with its own unique set of role expectations, an individual's self-identity typically is multifaceted. The role expectations and corresponding self-identities attached to various social positions can conflict with each other." For example, a worker may be acting ethically according to the rules set out in the workplace, but those rules could be considered immoral by the individual's religious community. Nearly one-fifth of the workers we surveyed (about 21 percent) said that on at least some occasions at work they are expected to act in ways that contradict their religious beliefs.[10]

Among religious groups, Muslims (44 percent) and evangelical Protestants (34 percent) are most likely to say they are expected to act in ways that contradict their religious beliefs, as seen in Figure 6.1. Respondents told us that some of the things they have been asked to do go against their personal ethics

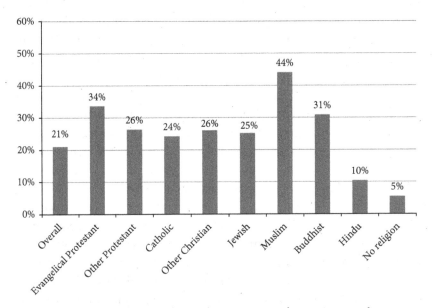

Figure 6.1 Percentage saying, "At work, I am expected to act in ways that contradict my religious beliefs."

Data: Faith at Work Main Survey. "Not applicable" response is coded as "never." Percentages represent combined "rarely," "sometimes," "often," and "very often" responses.

and at times even against the law. Workers told us about pressure they have experienced to cut corners, steal, misuse the property of others, or lie. In many cases, they struggled with what the right thing to do might be or how to do what they knew was right. A Christian woman who works in the academic office at a university,[11] for example, said, "There were times like that, that the faculty were trying to promote student success at the expense of policy, and some of those policies aren't just policy; they're actually law.... It usually had to do with [providing students more credits than they had earned] where I did feel it's going against my values, it's going against the law, and definitely that would be going against my faith as well because it's just fundamentally dishonest." An evangelical Christian barista[12] explained that the company she works for, "They ask us to wear certain shirts, like gay pride shirts and stuff like that, and that can make some people feel uncomfortable, because you kind of [laughs] don't really have a choice."

Our survey data suggest some differences across industries with respect to religious individuals feeling conflict between their work and their religious beliefs and expectations. To determine the industries in which religious workers face the most ethical difficulties, we tried to isolate that variable by looking at only workers who describe themselves as very religious (thus eliminating religiosity as a factor). In Figure 6.2, we see that the highest rate of religion-based ethical conflict is found among those working in the military. Forty-five percent of very religious individuals working in the military said they are expected to act in ways that contradict their religious beliefs. "The different jobs in the military, the infantry guys are the guys whose main purpose is to get close to and combat the enemy.... From my personal experience, most of those people in that realm, they're not too religious," said a man who has a leadership position in the army.[13] Religious individuals, he told us, may be more likely to be "a central unit or a peacekeeping unit. But they don't have to physically think a lot about that one thing, that they may take away the life of another human being." While we do not know all the specific roles the military workers we surveyed perform, the ethical conflicts many religious individuals in the military experience in their work is likely, at least in part, a function of the military's inherent connection to violence and war.

According to our findings, very religious workers in social services (38 percent), entertainment and media (37 percent), and the sciences (36 percent) also have relatively high rates of feeling like expectations at work conflict with their religious beliefs.[14] A Muslim man who works as an

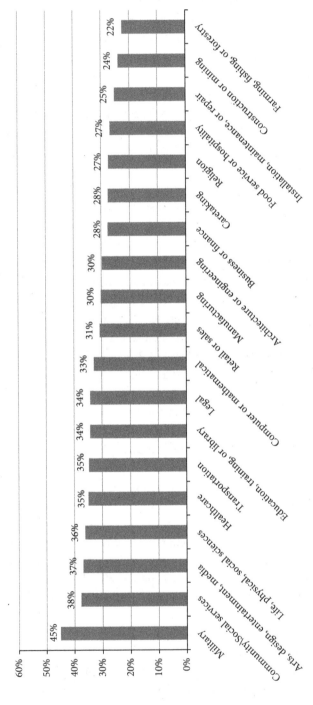

Figure 6.2 Among workers who are very religious, the percentage saying, "At work, I am expected to act in ways that contradict my religious beliefs," by industry

Data: Faith at Work Main Survey. Not applicable response is coded as "never." Percentages represent combined "rarely," "sometimes," "often," and "very often" responses. Sample limited to those who are very religious.

engineer for a company designing X-ray machines to find contaminants in food[15] said that he was told by his hiring manager during an interview for his job that he would need to handle pork products and said he was able to come to terms with this aspect of his job. "There are Muslim people who consider even handling it as something, they don't wanna do it," he said. "But in my case, I only believe ingesting it [would be problematic]. . . . So, I won't say that it's the most pleasant part of my job, but this is something that I deal with." A white, mainline Christian woman who works as a lab manager and supervises the use of animal models in science (which sometimes involves killing animals)[16] told us, punctuated by nervous laughter, about ways that work practices related to euthanizing animals were creating dissonance for her. "I don't think it's the best thing [laughs nervously] to become desensitized to killing of other mammals. And I definitely am desensitized, with the mice," she said. "I think, at first, it didn't really bother me, because I really bought into that, 'Oh, it's for the greater good and what we're doing really matters.' . . . Now it's made me very cynical. Just animal research, in general. It's made me question the worth of it." She is now training someone else to do this type of work. At the other end of the spectrum, highly religious workers in construction (24 percent) and farming (22 percent) are less likely than those in other industries to feel like work expectations conflict with their faith. It may be that in these industries there is less direct relationship between the tasks of the job and any perceived moral outcomes, perhaps because the job requirements are more concrete and objective, and not likely to be as bound up with human-centered concerns. In social services, entertainment, and science, on the other hand, more obvious friction may exist between the goods and services produced and the religious values the workers hold, simply because there are not likely to be as clear criteria for what constitutes good outcomes, and so these industries are more dependent on interpersonal judgments, which vary across people.

A number of the religious individuals we interviewed discussed the ways in which they evaluated the behaviors expected by their work organizations against those expected by their faith commitments. At times, religion-based ethics may be at odds with the expectations or practices of the profession, or with the prevailing norms or type of work done in the organization, or with secular ethical sensibilities expressed at work. In these circumstances, religion-based ethics may lead to conflict in workplaces. Such conflict may be good if it contributes to a more ethically healthy workplace, but it can also create tensions between groups of people who are using different standards of morality. We heard many stories from people who had experienced negative repercussions due to such conflicts.

Loyalty, Voice, Exit

Albert O. Hirschman's organizational theory of loyalty, voice, and exit can inform how we see people respond when workplace ethics conflict with the moral frameworks they get from their religion.[17] First, he explains that members remain *loyal* to an organization when their options in leaving the organization do not appear greater than those gained from staying. Second, members remain loyal if they believe they have an ability to bring change to the organization. Hirschman calls this belief possessing *voice*. Third, Hirschman argues that when people have few incentives to stay *and* they do not have voice, *exit* then becomes the most viable possibility.

Loyalty

Religious beliefs, commitments, and practices that employees bring to work influence their behavior and we found that some forms of religion result in less of a willingness to question authority. This can be quite positive if the workplace's ethical norms are positive and religion is used to reinforce positive ethical behaviors. Fostering faith-work integration in these circumstances may help contribute to a more ethically healthy workplace. However, when the prevailing norms in an organization are inequitable or destructive to some, and these norms are reinforced by a religious tradition perspective that values hierarchy and obedience to authority, the result is likely to be higher levels of unethical behavior.[18] Religious individuals—those most likely to draw on religious morality to resist or rebuke ethically questionable activities in their organizations—may be less likely than nonreligious workers to act to remedy those activities, given they are less likely to question authority or be disloyal.

Religious individuals will often need to determine whether their religious morals align well with the workplace ethics of their organization and, if there is misalignment, how to deal with it. For some, this means evaluating whether the moral codes and expectations of their religion outweigh the role expectations of their workplace or profession. According to sociologist

Robert Jackall, it is very hard for the ethical rules and moral codes of a religion to replace "occupational rules-in-use," or the codes of a given occupation, which tend to "gain ascendancy over more general ethical standards."[19] Ethical and unethical behaviors are often embedded and routinized in work organizations in ways that can make it difficult to enact outside ethical or moral standards.[20] Weaver explains that "a variety of rationalizing accounts can help actors overlook their initial qualms about such behavior, so that they become, in effect, morally disengaged rather than morally active" (350). For example, sociologists Michael Lindsay and Bradley Smith find that elite evangelicals often reinterpret workplace ethics in ways that help them align their religious values with their workplace values even if on the face of it these values seem to conflict.[21] "The thrust of the evangelical imperative— and that of many other religious traditions—is to make activities meaningful, to endow them with religious significance. But within this broad mandate, there is room for different forms of meaning-making. From the narratives evangelicalism provides, elite adherents are free to choose and customize according to personal disposition and professional context. This flexibility permits these leaders to understand fundamentals of the market's logic (such as profit maximization) as compatible with religious ends. By framing capitalistic behavior in ways commensurate with a moral and/or spiritual perspective, evangelical elites fulfill the integrative imperative required by their faith commitments," they write in one study. "Thus, for a significant number of these public leaders, the logic of religion in their self-accounting is not so much juxtaposed against the logics of their professions but infused into them" (743).

Ben,[22] the criminal investigator we introduced earlier, finds specific tasks that his job requires to be morally challenging and explained how he is able to frame these tasks in terms of the positive purpose of his work—to protect the vulnerable—as a way to justify these behaviors and align them with his religious perspective about what is right. "I think that, sometimes, there's certain language . . . that I have to use, because I'm reiterating something verbatim, that is uncomfortable. Certain times, there's things that involve pornography that I am required to be involved with, and that is uncomfortable," he told us. "I try to check myself [*laughs*], make sure that I'm not just using [my work] as a cover to indulge in something that I really want to do. So, there's a lot of introspection that goes on, ahead of time. . . . Just putting it in the appropriate context is helpful as well. . . . This is what this person said, and it's important that I relay what this person said, because it could hurt somebody, or somebody has been hurt by them. And I need to do this, because this is somebody's daughter that's been exploited, and I need to help."

Based on research, it seems that religious individuals are more likely to prioritize religious morality over workplace ethics when their commitment to and participation in their religious tradition is greater than their commitment to and participation in the workplace or profession where ethical challenges are occurring. Weaver and Agle believe that

> those with very little power or status, or little likelihood of gaining such, might be more likely than the average employee to attempt to invoke religiously-based values. The janitor, the line worker protected by a union contract, or the manager who is knowingly plateaued or who has opted out of the 'climb the ladder' contest, has fewer or less important commitments that are tied to a success ladder within the organization than does the manager oriented toward upward mobility. Persons with less important or fewer commitments based on an organizational role will be less likely to act on organizational role expectations when they conflict with role expectations based on other self-identities, including religious identities.[23]

Voice

In one of our surveys, we asked workers if they agreed with the statement "I express my view when I observe unfair work practices that conflict with my faith/spirituality." In some sense this is about how people respond to unfair situations that conflict in the most general and abstract way with morals that may come from religion or spirituality. Overall, 45 percent of workers said they speak up when there is such a conflict. When we look at the findings based on the religiosity of the workers, we find that the percentage of workers who speak up when they see unfair work practices that conflict with their faith is highest among those who say they are very religious (69 percent) and drops among those who say they are moderately religious (55 percent), slightly religious (39 percent), and not at all religious (28 percent).[24] This suggests that the more salient an individual's faith is to them, the more willing they are to risk the personal and professional consequences of challenging practices in the workplace that conflict with their faith or spirituality. It is worth noting that many people who do not have any religious identification (and therefore would self-describe as not at all religious) may have very strong humanistic values they draw from in making evaluations of workplace justice. Non-religious individuals may then speak out against the assumption that workplace ethics must be derived from religion.

If we consider only those who are very religious—that is, for whom religiously-based ethics may be the most salient—our survey data show that individuals at the top of their organization's hierarchy are more likely to say they express their view when they observe practices that conflict with their faith. Specifically, 76 percent of very religious individuals who self-identify as at the top of their organization agree that they speak out compared with 72 percent of those in the middle of their organization and 63 percent of those at the bottom. In other words, religious workers are more likely to speak out against workplace practices that conflict with their faith when they are in a position of power.[25]

Self-Advocacy

Many religious individuals we spoke with discussed drawing on their religion to ensure they stay honest and not cut obvious ethical corners in their work. In particular, they are likely to self-advocate in order to avoid personal behaviors that conflict with their religious beliefs (e.g., refusing to lie) and, in some cases, to stand up for their ethical principles. For example, when asked about instances when her faith has guided her in her job, Josie,[26] the Christian software engineer, told us about a time her faith compelled her not to participate in an activity she saw as unethical and to confront her supervisor. "One time we really needed to do this analysis . . . and we needed some software to do it, and we found this software online that could do it for us, but I found a note saying that it shouldn't be used for commercial purposes. I . . . kind of mentioned that to my boss, and he was like, 'Oh, it's fine, just use it,' and I was like, 'I really don't think that's OK.' [*laughs*] . . . I just told him 'No,'" she said. "And I told him that I would work with the IT person to find another way to do it."

A Christian man who works as a director of field operations at a fruit-packing company[27] told us about a time when he refused to act in a way he saw as unethical and how he relied on his faith to get him through the situation. "They told me to lie to him [the customer] to keep the business because they didn't want to lose the money that they would make from packing the fruit. And I refused to do it. And they threatened to fire me, and I told them that they would have to fire me because I was not going to be purposefully deceitful," he recalled. "I just knew that I was not going to step away from what my faith told me was right, that I was not to lie, and also, I knew or trusted God enough to believe that if they did fire me that He would provide something else for me," he said, adding, "And actually, two of the people involved—that threatened me—came up and apologized, and one of them said that they learned something about faith from that particular activity."

Advocating for Others

Religious workers we spoke to were most likely to intervene or speak up when unethical behavior affected someone for whom they were directly responsible. These workers would use their faith as a resource to step in and confront authority figures and structures, often based on a religious imperative to love and care for others. "Part of my faith is to help somebody. There was this girl who worked for us—she was drinking or on drugs or something. She came up to me. I didn't really know her, and she started talking to me, she's like acting real frantic. . . . One of the security guards down there told me, 'I think she needs help.' . . . And I went in and told my boss," a woman who works as an information systems analyst[28] told us. "Do you know what he did? . . . He was twisting it, making it worse because he wanted this girl out." This woman said she drew on her Catholic faith to defend the junior coworker in an effort to protect this employee from being fired. "I had to defend my case there and defend her and I got upset," she said. "So, my faith told me to stand up and say that I couldn't do it morally just because he wanted to get rid of her and he wanted someone else to come in and take her place." When her boss was telling her to lie about her coworker, she felt that he was telling her to go against her faith.

An evangelical Christian nurse[29] told us about a time her faith motivated her to report unethical practices at work. A resident, she said, was going to perform an invasive procedure on a patient in the ICU because he thought it could "be a teaching moment for the medical students." When the resident told the patient he was going to need to have this procedure, the patient "was lucid enough that [I heard him say] 'no,'" she said, yet the resident was going to do the procedure anyway. The nurse decided that it was her responsibility to go over the resident's head and tell the medical director that she thought the resident was not acting in the best interest of the patient. In the end, the medical director listened to her. She said that even though the resident was "ranting and raving," she felt that she did the right thing. "I'm a nurse, and I've taught nursing students, and I know you have to learn, but you don't have to learn at the expense of human beings. And if we lose sight of that, that's a problem," she said. "So, that's one time where I really took a strong stand and said, 'This is not right,' and I'm not gonna just sit back and say, 'Let it play out however it plays,' because [my patient] didn't have an advocate. . . . He had no family. . . . He had nobody to speak for him. And so, I always think about [the Bible and where it says] 'who will speak for me?'" referring to how Jesus stood up for the most vulnerable in society.

Making Systemic Changes

When facing ethical dilemmas at work, religious workers sometimes use higher-order religious morality to advocate for structural changes, focusing on using their *voice* to change the systems in order to minimize the likelihood that a given ethically charged situation will occur again in the future. But it is much less common for those we surveyed and interviewed to draw on their religion to voice their concerns in an effort to change the overall structure or practices of an organization than when they encounter a specific situation that violates their personal ethics. Some of those we interviewed did express specific concerns about how their job relates to broader society, and they wondered if the specific things they are regularly asked to do as part of their job or what their company produces really serves the greater good. Sometimes, especially if they were in a position of leadership, workers felt free to push back on workplace practices they felt conflicted with their faith. When they did use their voice to pursue change, however, they were most likely to try to change the decision making of their direct supervisor rather than the entire organization. "I try to be as honest as possible to be. I do, at times, cringe at the—I won't say the lies, but more so fibs . . . our sales folks say. . . . Because I'm like, 'Ah, we really don't do that, and I'm not sure if we should be saying that,'" a Muslim engineer[30] told us, explaining how his faith encourages him to resist what he sees as unethical practices within his company and guides his response. "It's not like I just keep it quiet," he said. "I do let them know and say, 'Hey, I wouldn't say as much that we can do such and such.'"

Ron,[31] the custodian we introduced earlier, previously worked as an office manager for a manufacturing firm, a job more typical of someone with his level of education. A Christian who attends services every Sunday and a deacon at his church, Ron told us that work is a place for him to express and live out his Christian faith, to the point that he was "run out of my previous job because I refused to do unethical things." He said he had noticed that one of his supervisors was harassing one of his female sales representatives, and out of a sense of Christian duty, he filed a report. He knew what the consequences might be and decided he had to pursue what he saw as "protecting the weak and pursuing justice." His workplace addressed the situation and dismissed the supervisor, he said, "but a pattern that I had seen in the company before I had become office manager was that if you filed a report, they usually work to try to find a reason to dismiss you within a month." After this, Ron noticed that people in the company seemed to be testing him, trying to figure out whether they were going to keep him or make him leave. He said that "within about a month . . . I was starting to be asked to do things . . . more frequently that were what I would consider unethical and not right. Be dishonest on paperwork or fudge numbers even on timesheets to try to cut employees down, and I refused." Because of his faith, Ron said he could not stand the pressure of being asked to act unethically. "I submitted my resignation, and I went in and met with [the CEO]," he said. "I handed it to the CEO and he turned and looked at me and said, 'You can't resign, you're fired.'"

Ron is a good example of someone who engaged in religiously motivated behavior reflecting self-advocacy (refusing to lie about numbers), other-advocacy (looking out for someone who was being harassed), and advocating for structural change (through reporting the harassing behavior to his supervisor). However, he ultimately felt a pressure campaign against him was building in the organization and he was not able to effect change in the workplace. At this point, he took the final step of tendering his resignation. In Hirschman's terms, when using his voice didn't work, Ron moved to exit.

Exit

Those we talked with seemed to make a distinction between occasional or situational conflicts like those we discussed above and times when an entire job, work organization, or industry is fundamentally at odds with what they view as religiously moral. For example, a Muslim pharmaceutical assistant[32] told us that she could never be a waitress "because if they wanted any alcoholic beverages or anything like that, I would have to serve it to them. And our religion says for me to give them any alcohol is considered a sin for me." Workers told us there were times when their entire job seemed to be so much in conflict with their religious identity and values, and they didn't think they would be able to change it, that they had to make a critical decision about whether to stay or leave the organization. When acting with integrity according to their faith put them in conflict with the goals of their organization, they almost always chose to leave the organization rather than try to stay and make changes by mobilizing others. Especially for those who are deeply religious, loyalty to the moral codes of their religious tradition often won out over loyalty to a work organization, which sometimes resulted in an exit from that organization. We did find that people who work for themselves or are part of the gig economy often feel freer to act on their religiously informed moral principles to leave a job than do those who are employees of an organization.

A Jewish woman who works as a freelance writer,[33] for instance, told us about an article in a magazine she worked for that, because of her religious ethics, "I was very uncomfortable with, and I was very uncomfortable being associated with that publication, even though I spoke to my rabbi, then, and he said it wasn't an issue. Everyone knows that individual writers are not representing the entire publication." Still, she felt it was better for her to not accept any more assignments from the publication and "to choose to kind of like let that relationship with that editor die a natural death," she said. A Black Christian man who does contract work as a graphic artist[34] told us, "I've kind of made a conscious choice not to take jobs that I feel would violate certain biblical principles, or things that I don't think would be honoring to God. . . . I've had offers to do logos for strip clubs and stuff, and I told them I can't do it. I've had people [ask] me to design logos for pot dispensaries, and I've told them . . . I can't do that. [laughs] Because, you know, the Bible has rules against . . . being intoxicated. I can't really promote that stuff. . . . God gave me these talents: What am I using them for? Would He be pleased with the things that I'm sort of promoting with my skills, or would He be displeased?"

Upselling is an interesting example of an organizational practice that can create internal conflict for workers in customer service.[35] Religious workers talked about how they sometimes brought their faith to bear in thinking through the conditions in which upselling would best serve the customer and the conditions in which it would not. For example, Darlene,[36] a human resources manager who attends a Black Baptist church, recalled her work for a telephone company in which her managers were encouraging her to upsell every customer. Darlene described this upselling as inappropriate, pushing people to buy things from the company they really did not need. She told us that her faith made her feel such actions were wrong and unethical for her on a personal level. "They would want you to push the products on everybody, and just push it, push it, push it. I'm not gonna do it," she said. "If I am on the phone with someone, seventy years old, and they're complainin' about their phone bill, and they want their phone bill to go down, and I'm tryin' to increase it. Mm-mm. That's not what they called for. So, no, I'm not doin' it. You can't write me up, because I've hit every point. You're just not happy, because I'm not making extra money for you." Eventually, she left the department to work in human resources, a job she feels allows her to work in a way that is more ethically consistent with her faith.

While most organizational leaders think that suggesting products that customers have not requested is part of doing good business, there are examples of how this practice can go wrong. Wells Fargo is a cautionary tale. In 2016, the company paid $185 million to settle a lawsuit charging that its customer service representatives had been inappropriately encouraged to sell to customers banking products they had not requested, and that over a five-year period it had opened millions of accounts without customer understanding or permission.[37] While the company blamed the problem on a small number of bad apples, the situation appeared to be more pervasive. Eventually thousands of employees were fired, and the CEO resigned over the situation. Afterward, many employees expressed their frustration over the pressure to meet ever-increasing new-account quotas. We have to wonder whether the outcome might have been different had company leaders been more responsive earlier to those who raised ethical concerns.

Organizational leaders can work to better understand how the faith commitments of their workers might be driving their ethical decision-making and how they evaluate the behaviors expected of them at work—or, better yet, tap into the moral teachings of religious traditions that can help lead to a more ethical workplace.

The Bottom Line

- Sometimes when organizational leaders foster the connection between religion and ethics at work, it can make the workplace a more ethically supportive environment.
- Under other conditions the loyalty to authority that religious traditions foster can make religious workers more reticent to address workplace practices they see as unethical.
- When religious workers do address what they see as unethical practices in the workplace, they most commonly use their faith perspective to address individual ethical behaviors rather than the ethics of the organization or job at large.
- When the perceived conflicts between organizational demands and religious moral frameworks become too much, many religious workers will exit the situation and leave the organization rather than try to change it.

Notes

1. Faith at Work Main Survey. We do find, though, that those who say they are "very religious" are a bit more likely to strongly agree with this statement (83 percent) compared to those who are not at all religious (73 percent). These percentages exclude those who said that this statement is not applicable to them.
2. This definition of "workplace ethics" is taken from Webster's Dictionary. See, in particular, https://www.merriam-webster.com/
3. Bader, Christopher D., and Roger Finke. 2010. "What Does God Require? Understanding Religious Context and Morality." In Steven Hitlin and Stephen Vaisey (Eds.). *Handbook of the Sociology of Morality*. 241–254. New York: Springer.
4. Faith at Work Main Survey. this percentage includes those saying "often" and "very often." Other possible responses were never (14 percent), rarely (7 percent), sometimes (15 percent), and "I do not have a faith leader" (54 percent). If we exclude those who say they do not have a faith leader, the percentage saying often or very often increases to 22 percent.
5. Weaver, Gary, and Bradley Agle. 2002. "Religiosity and Ethical Behavior in Organizations: A Symbolic Interactionist Perspective." *Academy of Management Review* 27(1): 77–97, 90.
6. F@W_ST166, White/Hispanic, Man, 46, Scientist in Research and Development for a Fertilizer Company, Jewish, conducted December 2, 2019.
7. Giacalone, R. A., Jurkiewicz, C. L. 2003. "Right from Wrong: The Influence of Spirituality on Perceptions of Unethical Business Activities." *Journal of Business Ethics* 46: 85–97. https://doi.org/10.1023/A:1024767511458.
8. Graham, Jesse, and Jonathan Haidt. 2010. "Beyond Beliefs: Religions Bind Individuals in Moral Communities." *Personality and Social Psychology Review* 14(1): 140–50.
9. Weaver and Agle, "Religiosity and Ethical Behavior in Organizations: A Symbolic Interactionist Perspective."
10. Faith at Work Main Survey. The full statement was, "At work, I am expected to act in ways that contradict my religious beliefs." Possible responses were never, rarely, sometimes, often, very often, or "I do not have religious beliefs." The percentages in the text represent the combined rarely, sometimes, often, and very often responses.

11. F@W_ST103, White, Woman, 57, Teacher and Librarian, Mainline, conducted July 18, 2019.
12. F@W_ST117, White, Woman, 20, Barista, Evangelical, conducted August 21, 2019.
13. F@W_ST196, Hispanic, Man, 58, Operation Officer, Non-Religious, conducted April 14, 2021.
14. The main ways people are expressing being uncomfortable with something as part of their work because of their religion are as follows: (1) teachers having to teach something they feel uncomfortable with, (2) people being asked to do something dishonest by a boss in all kinds of fields, and (3) people having to come in contact with pornography or strip clubs in some way (several people say this). In all of these examples, the religious aspect is usually not clearly stated by the respondent but it was the question asked.
15. F@W_ST115, Asian, Man, 53, Engineer, Muslim, conducted August 13, 2019.
16. F@W_ST91, White, Woman, 24, Lab Manager, Mainline, conducted June 27, 2019.
17. Hirschman, Albert O. 1970. *Exit, Voice, and Loyalty: Responses to Decline in Firms, Organizations, and States.* Cambridge, MA: Harvard University Press.
18. Weaver, Gary, and Jason Stansbury. 2014. "Religion in Organizations: Cognition and Behavior." *Research in the Sociology of Organizations* 41: 65–110.
19. Jackall, Robert. 2010. "Morality in Organizations." *Handbook of the Sociology of Morality* 203–209.
20. Weaver, Gary. 2006. "Virtue in Organizations: Moral Identity as a Foundation for Moral Agency." *Organization Studies* 27(30): 341–68.
21. Lindsay, D. Michael, and Bradley Smith. 2010. "Accounting by Faith: The Negotiated Logic of Elite Evangelicals' Workplace Decision-Making." *Journal of the American Academy of Religion* 78(3): 721–49.
22. F@W_ST49, Black, Man, 38, Criminal Investigator, Evangelical, conducted February 6, 2019.
23. Weaver, Gary R., and Bradley R. Agle. 2002. "Religiosity and Ethical Behavior in Organizations: A Symbolic Interactionist Perspective." *Academy of Management Review* 27(1): 77–97, 86.
24. Faith at Work Main Survey. Those who responded "not applicable" were coded as "strongly disagree." Design-based F for cross-tabulation = 109.40, $p < .001$.
25. The organizational position question asked, "Think about the organization of job roles in your industry, where the leaders are at the top of the organization and employees are at the bottom of the organization. Would you say that you are toward the top of the organization, middle, or at the bottom?" The cross-tabulation shows a significant difference in responses across organizational position (design-based $F = 2.81$, $p < .01$). The analysis is limited to those who said they are very religious N = 1,678. Those responding "not applicable" were coded as "strongly disagree" on the "express my view when I observe unfair work practices" question.
26. F@W_ST31, White, Woman, 25, Civil Engineer, Christian, conducted December 19, 2018.
27. F@W_ST58, White, Man, 63, Director of Field Operations, Evangelical, conducted February 22, 2019.
28. F@W_ST169, Latina, Woman, 45, Information Systems Analyst, Catholic, conducted December 5, 2019.
29. F@W_ST47, Black/Native American, Woman, 63, Executive Director of Non-profit/Nurse, Evangelical, conducted January 31, 2019.
30. F@W_ST148, South Asian, Man, 42, Technical Staff, Muslim, conducted October 17, 2019.
31. F@W_ST44, White, Man, 31, Custodian, Baptist, conducted January 30, 2019.
32. F@W_ST191, Middle Eastern/Arab, Woman, 21, Pharmacy Technician, Muslim, conducted January 23, 2020.
33. F@W_ST122, White, Woman, 34, Freelance Writer and EMT, Jewish, conducted August 30, 2019.
34. F@W_ST43, Black, Man, 48, Graphic Artist, Evangelical, conducted January 29, 2019.
35. Upselling is an attempt to convince a customer to purchase something additional or more costly. Merriam-Webster, s.v. upsell. https://www.merriam-webster.com/dictionary/upsell.
36. F@W_ST88, Black, Woman, 45, Human Resources, Baptist, conducted June 17, 2019.
37. For more about this example see Tayan, Brian. "The Wells Fargo Cross Selling Scandal" December 19, 2016, *Harvard Law School Forum on Corporate Governance*, https://corpgov.law.harvard.edu/2016/12/19/the-wells-fargo-cross-selling-scandal/.

7

Measuring and Managing Workplace Religious Discrimination

Martha,[1] a white Muslim convert who works as a salesperson in Louisiana for a company that sells industrial machinery, told us she regularly experienced overt religious discrimination at her workplace, which is predominantly white and quite Christian. After she converted, her colleagues relentlessly bullied her, she said. For example, it seemed to her like one of her coworkers began dressing to intimidate her: he wore a shirt with "a machine gun . . . and 'Infidel' on it. That was a play to intimidate me because I was very new to Islam, very excited about what I was learning, and it was ritual ridicule," she recalled. She was also subjected to negative comments from her employer. "My boss . . . she got up and talked a lot about me being Muslim now, and it was all negative from what I understand." After someone put up signs in the office attacking her newfound faith, Martha called in management, but they did nothing to help her; they actually harassed her more: "One of them said something about, 'I tried to see your point of view, but your point of view is stupid,' and it was one that said, 'It must be great coming to work and not having to do anything.' Just ugly stuff, really, really ugly stuff [related to my religion and my prayer schedule]." A Muslim woman[2] who works in social services in the Northeast said she hopes for a time when "women wearing the hijab wouldn't be denied employment or, you know, restricted." If she is applying for a job or chooses to wear a hijab to work, she said, she thinks that "there is a higher likelihood that you're not going to be hired."

Religious Discrimination Is Present and Pervasive

The organizational psychologist Frederick Herzberg, who became well-known for his work in business management, introduced a two-factor

Religion in a Changing Workplace. Elaine Howard Ecklund, Denise Daniels, and Christopher P. Scheitle, Oxford University Press. © Oxford University Press 2024. DOI: 10.1093/oso/9780197675007.003.0007

theory of worker satisfaction and productivity.[3] He argued that certain factors motivate people to do better work and other factors demotivate people. Motivators are positive factors that lead workers and organizations to flourish. These might be things like spaces for interpersonal relationships at work or creating good working conditions; employees may be more willing to engage in, lean into, and buy into the mission of the company if they feel safe there. Religious discrimination, on the other hand, *demotivates* workers, and preventing religious discrimination is a necessary but not entirely sufficient first step toward creating a workplace where individuals grow through their work and where overall organizational goals are met.

In most organizations in the United States, individuals are protected against religious discrimination by Title VII of the 1964 Civil Rights Act, the most far-reaching federal civil rights law in the country. The Equal Employment Opportunity Commission (EEOC) is responsible for enforcing this law and has created guidelines for helping workplaces understand what is and is not covered. Yet rarely do workplace leaders or workers openly discuss religious discrimination, how it relates to other kinds of discrimination, what can be done to rectify religious discrimination when it occurs, or better yet prevent it in the first place. Organizational scholar of diversity Diether Gebert and colleagues argue that indeed religion may be *the* "neglected dimension of diversity"[4] in workplaces, and thus religious discrimination might be generally overlooked as well. Moreover, religious discrimination issues can be challenging to address in pluralistic work environments, where individuals from multiple religious traditions and those with no religious tradition work side by side. In their review of workplace discrimination, management psychologist Sonia Ghumman and colleagues write that increased religious expression in the workplace can lead to religious discrimination toward workers of other faiths and may theoretically "be connected to the mistreatment of certain other protected groups"; one's "sincerely held religious beliefs" can sometimes conflict with workplace diversity policies that foreground respect for other groups, such as women, members of the LGBTQ+ community, and religious minorities.[5] It can be difficult, then, for employers to balance protections for the variety of people who make up their workplaces, since it may seem like the interests and needs of different groups may be at odds.

It was not uncommon for the workers we talked with in our Faith at Work study not to even know that religious discrimination—including treating people differently based on religion—is illegal for most types of workplaces under federal law. At the same time, little research had been done into how different groups perceive and experience religious discrimination in the workplace or how religious discrimination overlaps with other forms of discrimination. Yet between 1997—the first year the EEOC began to collect data on religiously based workplace discrimination—and 2018, reports of discrimination based on religion increased by 67 percent: from 1,709 to 2,859 reports. This growth is much larger than the changes seen in other types of discrimination, such as discrimination on the basis of sex (less than a half a percent increase) or national origin (about a 6 percent increase). What's more, our broader research indicates that religious discrimination at work is likely vastly underreported.

Here we set out to better understand what workers mean when they say they have been discriminated against due to their religion and how the frequency of religious discrimination varies across faith groups and other contexts in order to provide scholars and organizational leaders with better tools for understanding and eradicating religiously based workplace discrimination.

We fully recognize that religion has been and is utilized to justify explicitly or implicitly discriminatory attitudes toward others. For example, in their pioneering work sociologists Michael Emerson and Christian Smith notably found that white evangelical Protestants draw on a distinct religious-cultural "toolkit" when engaging issues of racial injustice, which can perpetuate systemic inequality.[6] However, the recent increase in public statements by white Christian leaders condemning racial injustice alongside vocal resistance to critical race theory and the public visibility of white Christian nationalism, as so powerfully noted by sociologists Andrew Whitehead and Samuel Perry, reignite empirical and theoretical questions about the evolving relationship between Christianity and racism in the United States.[7] In previous work alongside sociologist Sharan Kaur Mehta and religion scholar Rachel C. Schneider, Elaine has argued that these trends suggest that the tools white Christians sometimes use when engaging issues of racial inequality are dynamic, shaped by social conditions. Second, the value of Black lives can be legitimated through appeals to the *transcendent* value of all human life bestowed by God. However, this may produce notions of *spiritual equality* that risk overlooking and reinforcing *social inequality*, which could have critical implications for racial justice efforts.

In this chapter we are primarily concerned with how individuals understand religious discrimination rather than how they utilize religion to engage in other forms of discrimination, recognizing that these two dynamics cannot be easily separated. Organizational leaders need to be aware of the types of individuals who are most likely to face religious discrimination in the workplace and exactly how religious discrimination happens. They also need to be aware of the dynamics of religious discrimination in the geographic areas where their organizations operate; location can make a difference in how common religious discrimination is.[8] In addition, particular occupations, the types of people the occupations draw, and the norms of those occupations all might have an impact on how religion is viewed and treated in the workplace by those who are both religious and nonreligious.

Patterns of Religious Discrimination

When Chris and Elaine conducted a survey on experiences of religious discrimination among US adults, only 3 percent of respondents said they have been denied employment because of their religion, and only 4 percent said they have received an unfair work evaluation because of their religion (or nonreligion).[9] But these percentages increase significantly among certain religious minority groups, especially Jews and Muslims. Among Muslim adults, for instance, 18 percent reported being denied employment and 11 percent reported receiving an unfair work evaluation because of their faith. Among Jewish adults, 6 percent reported being denied employment and 7 percent reported receiving an unfair work evaluation due to their religion. When we asked individuals who reported an unfair evaluation at work due to their religion why they suspected this treatment was connected to their faith,[10] about 17 percent said they were directly told that they were being mistreated because of their religion, while 37 percent said their evidence was tied to "the person responsible [making] a religious slur/insult to me." But most of those we surveyed did not have such clear-cut evidence. Rather, the majority— 61 percent—said that their suspicions were tied to a perception that "the person responsible viewed [their] religion negatively."[11]

Being fired, denied employment, or receiving a poor evaluation based on religion are very specific and direct forms of religious discrimination and are largely focused on the actions of managers or supervisors. But the encounters that everyday workers have with religious discrimination often take other forms that are less severe or more subtle, do not originate from managers, and are much harder to pinpoint. Workers can encounter more interactional and everyday forms of harassment from coworkers in particular. With our Faith at Work survey, we intentionally cast a wider net, broadening the wording of our questions about religious discrimination to get a fuller picture of workers' experiences in the workplace. We asked individuals how often they have "felt that [they] have been treated unfairly in the context of [their] work" because of their "religion or non-religion." About a third (31 percent) of those we surveyed reported *at least some* experience with such unfair treatment due to their religion.[12]

Moreover, reports of unfair treatment due to religion were *much* higher among certain religious minority groups, as seen in Figure 7.1. Muslims (65 percent) and Jews (55 percent) have the highest rates by far of reporting at least some experience with religious discrimination at work. A significant minority of Hindus (41 percent), evangelical Protestants (38 percent), and the nonreligious (33 percent) have also experienced religious discrimination at work.

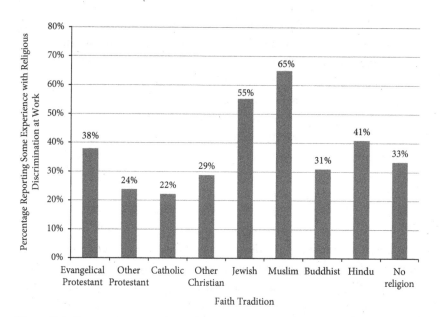

Figure 7.1 Percentage reporting at least some experience with unfair treatment at work due to their religion or nonreligion

Faith at Work survey. Question: "Throughout your lifetime, how often have you felt that you have been treated unfairly in the context of your work because of the following: Your religion or non-religion?" Percentages represent responses for "rarely," "sometimes," "often," and "very often."

Factors That Shape Religious Discrimination

When we look at the percentages in more detail, we see that—among religious minority groups—Muslim workers are much more likely than Jewish workers to say their experiences with religious discrimination occur "often" (about 9 percent vs. 2 percent) or "very often" (10 percent vs. 2 percent).[13] It did not surprise us that Muslims have faced greater religious discrimination in the workplace, given the warnings from some scholars of increased discrimination against Muslims since the September 11 attacks and that Muslims live in the context of US Islamophobia, an irrational fear that many Americans have of those who are Muslim.[14] It also does not surprise us that those from non-Christian faith traditions report experiencing greater workplace discrimination than Christians do given that Christian expressions of religion are more ingrained in the fabric of US culture.

When we compare Christian denominations, we see that evangelical Protestants are somewhat more likely to report experiencing at least some unfair treatment in the workplace due to religion (38 percent) than are other Protestants (24 percent), Catholics (22 percent), and other Christians (29 percent).[15] Evangelical Protestants are also more likely to report mistreatment at work due to their religious beliefs than are those who do not identify with a religion (33 percent).[16]

An individual's level of religiosity can also influence their experiences with religious discrimination. Our survey shows that an individual's intensity of religion—independent of their specific religious tradition—is positively associated with reports of experiencing discrimination due to their religion. In part, this is a function of the salience of a person's religious identity: when they are more religious, religion is more on their radar when thinking about how people interact with and treat them. That is, a person who thinks of herself as, say, "very Catholic" may be more likely to interpret certain experiences as being tied to her faith than would someone who sees herself as "nominally Catholic." In our survey, 30 percent of Catholics who said they are "very religious" reported having experienced religious discrimination at work compared with only 17 percent of Catholics who said they are "not at all religious." We see a similar pattern among Muslims we surveyed, though the overall percentages are much higher: 72 percent of Muslims who said they are very religious reported religious discrimination at work compared with about 55 percent of Muslims who said they are not religious at all.[17]

Those who see themselves as more religious are also more likely to express or practice their religion at work, which may lead to tensions in the workplace and hostility, harassment, or discrimination as a result. Indeed, our survey shows that 38 percent of individuals who strongly agree that they are motivated to talk about religion at work report some experience with religious discrimination at work. This compares to 25 percent of those who strongly disagree that they want to talk about religion at work reporting experiences of religious discrimination. More advanced analyses of our survey data show that both subjective religiosity and religious expression are associated with reports of religious discrimination even after controlling for the other. This means that, while a desire to express one's faith in the workplace does increase the risk of experiencing religious discrimination, such desires do not account for all of an individual's experiences with such discrimination.

Our survey indicates several other factors that also shape differences in experiences with religious discrimination. We found that women, non-white individuals, and older individuals are all *less* likely to say they have experienced religious discrimination at work compared with men, white individuals, and younger individuals. One possibility for this discrepancy is tied to the salience of identities. Issues of gender and gender discrimination, for instance, may be more salient for women than religious discrimination. This means that if a man and woman with the same religious identity and strength of religiosity experience the same sort of negative treatment, the woman may be more likely to attribute that experience to her gender than her religion, since gender discrimination is fairly common for women. The same explanation likely underlies the difference between white and non-white individuals, as race may be a more dominant identity for nonwhite individuals than is religion, impacting the lens through which they view their experiences and their attributions of discrimination. Age could be an issue of identity salience as well, but it could also reflect generational effects. That is, awareness of and conversations about discrimination appear to be more common among younger individuals, which in turn could make them more focused on issues of discrimination and potential biases driving their experiences and encounters.

Our data also show that reports of religious discrimination at work are more common among more highly educated individuals, although the differences are modest. Twenty-six percent of individuals with a high school education report ever experiencing religious discrimination at work, compared with 32 percent of those with a college education.[18] It is possible this difference could be a product of different work environments—jobs associated with higher education might have more secular norms or workforces and thus lend themselves to greater religious discrimination—or it could be a product of greater knowledge and empowerment among more educated individuals, making them more likely to recognize religious discrimination and label an experience as such.

Christians Perceive Religious Discrimination

Research on religious discrimination among Christian workers is limited, a fact probably attributable to their religious dominance in the United States, both numerically and culturally, and assumptions by scholars that those in the majority group are less likely to experience discrimination because of their relative power position. Yet several studies find that Christians can perceive religious discrimination in specific work contexts where they are particularly underrepresented or where the norms of the occupation are considered by occupational insiders or those in leadership to be different than the norms of the Christian faith.

Our interviews show how hostility and discrimination toward Christians can arise in the workplace, especially among those who observe religious holidays, display visible religious symbols, or have overlapping racial and religious identities.[19] A Latina Catholic[20] working as an information systems analyst described working a ten-hour shift on Good Friday. Upon leaving work, her manager called her cell phone to reprimand her, asking, in a harsh tone, "Why are you not at the office? You have a lot of work. [Your colleague] is complaining that you don't do enough work." When she reminded him that it was Good Friday, she was surprised by his response. "Your religion is not going to pay your food or rent or give you a promotion," he said. A white Catholic art teacher[21] described being ridiculed by a supervisor for observing Ash Wednesday, and a Latina evangelical[22] in finance told us her supervisor asked her to take down an angel Christmas decoration on her desk, though nonreligious decorations were deemed acceptable.

We found that religion-based verbal discrimination is quite common among Christians in workplaces and can include mocking and name-calling in addition to ridicule or teasing. When we spoke with Christian workers who had such experiences, they tended to link them to expressions of personal piety (e.g., not drinking alcohol, listening to Christian music, displays of religious symbols, or observing religious holidays) or to instances of moral conflict (e.g., not wanting to either break the rules, engage in behavior they thought was unethical because of their faith, or participate in workplace conversations seen as inappropriate). Many of these Christians felt that they were unfairly stereotyped by coworkers as judgmental, hypocritical, or "having the wrong thinking." Evangelical Christians were especially likely to say that coworkers stereotyped them as narrow minded or sanctimonious in ways that felt marginalizing. For example, the term "holy"—which might seem positive in certain kinds of contexts—can be applied in pejorative ways to Christians like Ben,[23] who attends a majority-Black congregation, expresses his faith openly in the workplace, and uses his faith to draw specific moral boundaries. A Hispanic evangelical woman[24] reported that coworkers at a past job would make fun of her and say, "'Oh, there's the hallelujah, or the sanctimonious person." A white evangelical nurse[25] told us she was called "Goody Two-Shoes" for challenging coworkers directly when they said something racist or inappropriate. At times, Christian workers also felt they were excluded from social events outside of the workplace because of how others perceived them. This dynamic between Christians and their coworkers seems especially salient when Christian workers do not share the religious *or political* views of the majority of their colleagues or superiors.

When They Are in the Minority, Christians May Experience Discrimination

Christians may be more likely to experience religious discrimination in certain occupational contexts. Sociologist and religion scholar John Schmalzbauer sees this kind of discrimination as based, in part, in the cultural tensions some Christians have with the norms and epistemological frameworks that are commonplace in certain types of occupations.[26] For example, as Elaine and Chris found in a study they conducted, academic scientists who are religious—but especially evangelical Christians, who are underrepresented in certain sectors of academic science[27]—report discrimination in the workplace more frequently than their nonreligious colleagues do.[28] Similarly, academic job candidates are viewed more negatively when they identify as conservative Christian or Mormon.[29] Scholar David Hodge finds that Christian social work students are more likely to report religious

discrimination if they are theologically conservative as opposed to theologically liberal.[30] These findings suggest that in some work contexts, where they
are in the minority, devout Christians may experience religious discrimination in ways similar to that experienced by traditional minority groups.[31]

A number of Christians we spoke with who work in occupations where
they are the minority faith, such as science, academia, or technology,
expressed sometimes feeling pressure to defend their theological beliefs or
provide a rationale for their religious views in ways that feel uncomfortable
or invasive.[32] For example, a Black mainline Protestant woman[33] working
as an assistant professor of English described the challenges she has faced
working in academia, and specifically in the humanities, "which tend to not
always be welcoming toward religious people [and Christians specifically],"
she said. She recalled several instances when she was treated differently due
to her religious beliefs and noted that in her work context, "a lot of people
will question the validity of your religion, let alone your faith, and dismiss it
on those rights." Although she was reticent to describe this as religious discrimination, she said her workplace made her feel "unwelcome." Similarly,
a white evangelical woman[34] who used to work at a newspaper, which she
described as a "very liberal, secular environment," said that, in relation to her
faith, the people there were, "Like, 'Why would you believe all that?'"

Geographic location can also influence the experiences Christians have
with religious discrimination at work. In a study Chris conducted with sociologist Katie Corcoran, he found that evangelical Christians in the United
States who are living in the West are more likely to say they have experienced
religious discrimination than are evangelical Christians living in the South.
One explanation for this is that these Southern Christians "perceive themselves as in less conflict with their surroundings than their counterparts in
other regions."[35] On the other hand, the religious culture of the South can
lead those who are not conservative Christians to experience being "othered"
by those in the majority. For example, a white Presbyterian woman[36] in a
rural area of the southern United States described how former colleagues at
the library where she works formed opinions about her due to her religious
affiliation. She explained, "Being Presbyterian, we're kind of known to be a
little more liberal, and I worked with some people that were very conservative and I was viewed as not having the right thinking."

Urban and rural contexts can also influence workers' experience of religious discrimination. An African American evangelical man[37] described
feeling ostracized by colleagues while working at an airport in a major city

due to a "left-right split." While, when asked, he attributed his negative experiences and hostile treatment to political differences rather than religious discrimination per se, he also said his coworkers had "their preconceived notions about Christians, and they just refuse to get along," and "If you weren't in their [liberal] club, then you were singled out for destruction." Because of this "toxic" work environment, he left this job after two years, the shortest work tenure of his career.

Religious Discrimination among Minority Religions

Even though Christians do sometimes perceive workplace discrimination and othering based on their faith, Jewish and Muslim workers report a *much greater frequency and often severity of religious discrimination in the workplace than Christians do*, with Muslims reporting the highest levels of religious discrimination in the workplace. Research shows that Muslim job candidates are less likely to receive callbacks than other applicants,[38] and they consistently report the most overt religious discrimination at all stages in the job pathway. Although less than 1 percent of the US population identifies as Muslim,[39] Muslims account for more than a quarter (28 percent) of all EEOC complaints of religion-related discrimination.[40]

Muslims report higher levels of religious discrimination when they more frequently engage in religious activity and when they believe religion is important to their lives.[41] Again, we also find that geographic location makes a difference. Past research has shown that those who identify as Muslim receive the highest levels of discriminatory behaviors from employers located in the American South, and our own data found that Muslims were more likely to report at least some experience with workplace discrimination in the South (about 80 percent) than in the Northeast (43 percent).[42]

Several Muslim and Jewish workers we spoke with shared that they had often heard colleagues or clients making anti-Semitic or Islamophobic remarks and that they regularly encounter stereotypes in the workplace.[43] For example, a white Jewish woman[44] working in social services recalled being singled out to visit a sick colleague because it was assumed she could prepare chicken soup. Others in her workplace made comments about her being "good at bookkeeping," invoking an anti-Semitic stereotype. A Jewish consultant[45] spoke about a time early in his career when he heard a colleague use the phrase "Jew me down,"[46] though he attributed it to ignorance rather than discrimination. A former Air Force officer[47] recalled how his fellow trainees made "little jokes" about the Holocaust during Officer Training School. At the time, he did not recognize it as anti-Semitism, until a fellow cadet came to him and said, "They're saying this because you're Jewish. Don't you realize it?" An Asian Muslim engineer[48] mentioned hearing coworkers express anti-Islamic views—such as, "Muslims are extremists," or, during the Gulf War, "Send 'em back"—though he did not consider this to be discrimination or directed at him in particular.

Jews and Muslims tended to link their experiences of religious discrimination in the workplace to their religious group membership, or to wearing visible religious identifiers in the workplace.[49] Muslim women, in particular, can face greater religious discrimination—or fear greater religious discrimination—because they are more likely to wear religious items or clothing that visibly marks their group identity, such as head coverings. In another study that Chris and Elaine conducted on experiences of religious discrimination, they found that 36 percent of Muslim women said they "often" wear religious symbols in public, compared with 4 percent of Muslim men.[50] Our research and that of others reveal that discrimination against Muslims in the hiring process has overlapping racial and religious categories, especially for high-status occupations, may be amplified by not only how "Arab-sounding" the applicant's name is, but also the sex of the applicant and the wearing of religious identifiers such as the hijab.

Anticipating mistreatment and hostility from colleagues, several Muslim and Jewish workers we interviewed, especially women, expressed discomfort with wearing religious attire at work or discussed intentionally concealing or downplaying their religious identity in the workplace to preempt discrimination. Aamna,[51] the Muslim gas station owner we interviewed extensively, told us that she doesn't consider her workplace a safe environment to express her faith, even though she owns her business. "There are some people who are so hard to interact with that they will not even think about it, and like if you even try to explain to them, they won't listen," she said of her customers. "They have their own mindset [about Islam], and it's all negative."

A white Jewish project manager[52] at an engineering firm, who also works as a tutor and attends school told us that even though she knows there are policies in place to protect employees from religious discrimination, she does not feel free to express her Judaism in the workplace, stating, "They've always told me, 'You're free to practice your religion.' . . . But because I don't see other people doing it, I don't feel comfortable. And the times that I did have to pray, I actually walked outside into a closed corner in the hallway to do it." As a married woman, she often covered her hair in accordance with Orthodox practices, and she recalled a time when she decided to wear a scarf instead of a wig. "I decided to go in one day [*laughs*] with a head scarf, and I didn't feel comfortable doing it. But I was just so hot and so tired of wearing wigs every day," she said. "And when I walked in, I saw that they did look at me differently, and I felt really uncomfortable. But then, after I wore a scarf, I felt I couldn't just switch back to a wig. So I kept wearing scarves. But every day, I was conscious of people looking at me, conscious of people judging me, and I was so uncomfortable." A Muslim Asian American[53] man working for the federal government summarized navigating these fears of judgment and discrimination in the workplace, concluding that he would not be overt about his religious identity: "If I wear my religion as a badge on my shoulder, it will rub somebody the wrong way. So why do that? Why do I want to get in somebody's face, you know? It's a personal thing and I need to keep it personal."

When the Nonreligious Experience Religious Discrimination

Workers who are not religious reported experiencing marginalization and discrimination in the workplace due to their nonreligion. They tended to link this discrimination to things like people assuming that they are religious or specifically Christian when they are not, being denied work opportunities because of their lack of religion, and a general sense of social isolation in organizations where the management or leadership is Christian.

Shania, a Black woman[54] who considers herself agnostic and now works as an engineer in the Southwest, talked about how religious customers discriminated against her when she waited tables at a restaurant in a predominantly Christian area; she ended up changing how she dressed and presented herself to avoid being read as nonreligious and thus seen as "sinful or satanic," she told us. She said she noticed "a lot of religious people have a very hard time accepting people who don't follow their faith. . . . And even in the workplace, I feel like . . . — it's not something you talk about too much—if I mention, like, directly, like, 'Yes, I'm not religious', then, I might—I will be looked at differently or interacted with differently as well."

One-third of the nonreligious workers we surveyed said they experienced discrimination for having no religion, almost as large a proportion
as evangelical Christians (38 percent) and more than Catholics or mainline
Protestants who reported religious discrimination. Again, location seems to
matter. Given the prominence of religion and that they are in the minority,
nonreligious individuals in the South are the most likely to say they have experienced discrimination due to their nonreligion at 39 percent, compared
with 31 percent of nonreligious individuals in the Midwest and West, and
24 percent in the Northeast.[55] This difference is likely because there are fewer
nonreligious individuals in the South compared, in particular, to the proportion of those in the West and Northeast. Further, evangelical Christians are
concentrated in the southern United States, and nonreligious individuals are
more likely to think that evangelical Christians are prone to othering and
discriminating against the nonreligious.[56]

Religious Discrimination Is Related to Other Types of Discrimination

Our data show that workers who report some experience with religious
discrimination at work are more likely to report experiencing discrimination based on their sex or gender or their race or ethnicity[57] as well. Overall,
50 percent of the individuals we surveyed reported experiencing gender or
sex discrimination, but this percentage increases to 72 percent among those
who say they have experienced religious discrimination.[58] We find a similar
difference in reported discrimination based on race and ethnicity. Overall,
37 percent of the individuals we surveyed reported some experience with
discrimination due to their race or ethnicity, but among those who report religious discrimination, the number increases to 58 percent.[59]

   In part, the connection between religious discrimination and these other
forms of discrimination is a function of the connections between individuals'
identities. Religion is often difficult to separate from race and ethnicity and,
as noted earlier, religious practices can have a gendered dimension—such as
head coverings among women for those who are Muslim or for men for those
who are Sikh—so experiencing discrimination due to those practices can feel
based on faith *and* race or ethnicity or faith *and* gender. It is also likely that
when a person encounters discrimination due to one part of their identity,
it influences their perceptions of other experiences and interactions. Thus,

experiencing religious discrimination might make someone more aware of other biases in the workplace, or experiencing racial discrimination might make someone more focused on how others are treating them due to their religion. It can be difficult to isolate religious discrimination from other forms of discrimination. For example, an African American woman[60] who described herself as a conservative Christian shared that she had felt treated differently in the workplace due to her faith, "such as not being invited to certain things because [my coworkers] would assume, 'Oh, that's not her thing' or, you know, just being omitted basically, but not being outright rude because I never put myself in that position," she said. "But being eliminated and no invitations, and sometimes I've experienced not having close friends in the workplace because I have stood out as a Christian." What is interesting is that this woman also reported past experiences of workplace exclusion, but in those instances, she attributed them to being the only Black person working in her department. In her current workplace, however, there are a large number of Black workers, which may explain why she now attributes social exclusion at work to a religious bias.

Consequences of Religious Discrimination in the Workplace

A large body of research demonstrates that experiences with discrimination of any type tend to have adverse consequences for an individual's physical, mental, and social well-being.[61] Although less research has examined these dynamics in the context of religious discrimination relative to other forms of discrimination, there is evidence—unsurprisingly—that religious discrimination has the same or even more adverse consequences on well-being since there are fewer ways to address religious discrimination in most workplaces when compared to other forms of discrimination.[62] While most research has considered discrimination and its consequences in broad terms, our Faith at Work survey allows us to focus specifically on the negative impacts of *workplace* religious discrimination on an individual's well-being *at work*. One of the questions we asked survey respondents was, "How often do you feel a sense of 'burnout'—meaning physical or mental exhaustion caused by overwork or stress—in your work?" Feelings of burnout in the workplace occur more regularly among individuals who report some experience with religious discrimination.

As seen in Figure 7.2, 13 percent of those who have experienced religious discrimination, for example, say that they "very often" experience a sense of burnout, while 23 percent of this group say they "often" experience burnout. This compares to 8 percent and 18 percent, respectively, among those who have never experienced religious discrimination. We find similar patterns in other questions we asked individuals. For instance, 33 percent of those who say they have experienced religious discrimination strongly agree that they are "very satisfied with [their] current job." This compares to 40 percent of those who have never experienced religious discrimination. And because some religious groups experience workplace religious discrimination at higher rates, this burnout is felt unevenly across religious traditions. Our survey finds, for instance, that 17 percent of Muslim workers report feeling burnout very often, which is almost twice the rate seen among workers overall.

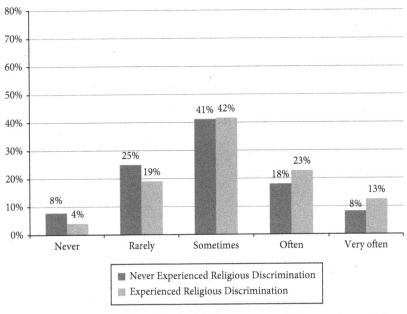

Figure 7.2 Frequency of an individual feeling a sense of "burnout" at work by their experience with religious discrimination

Faith at Work survey. Questions: Burnout: "How often do you feel a sense of 'burnout'—meaning physical or mental exhaustion caused by overwork or stress—in your work?" Religious discrimination: "Throughout your lifetime, how often have you felt that you have been treated unfairly in the context of your work because of the following: Your religion or non-religion?" Percentages represent responses for "rarely," "sometimes," "often," and "very often."

In sum, those who have experienced religious discrimination are less satisfied with their jobs and experience more workplace burnout than those who have not experienced such discrimination. This obviously has consequences for the individuals, but it also has consequences for the organizations in which they work. Dissatisfied and physically or emotionally drained employees usually do not make the best employees, and may be at high risk for leaving their organizations. Research, in fact, supports this logic.[63] This makes tackling religious discrimination not just a morally important issue for organizational leaders but also one that is vital to the health of their organizations.

Leaders Need Tools to Disrupt the Conditions for Religious Discrimination

Religious discrimination can be an especially challenging problem for organizational leaders for many reasons. For one, it can be difficult to prevent religious discrimination in the workplace without suppressing religious expression altogether. Also, if a supervisor directly asks an employee about their religious identity, it could actually be construed as grounds for discrimination.[64] Yet it is important for leaders to know whether any of their workers are being treated differently due to their religious beliefs and practices *and* to provide ways for workers to safely talk about and report religious discrimination—not only to protect the organization legally but also for the health of the workplace. It is wise for managers to pay close attention to differential treatment those from specific religious traditions might experience and to work hard to both address religious discrimination and foster positive conditions where it is less likely to occur. Here are some specific actions they can take.

Make Reporting Procedures Clear

It is important for organizations to clearly identify what religious discrimination is, how it should be reported, and how it will be addressed. These practices are becoming increasingly common for racial and sex discrimination and harassment. They should also be part of organizational procedure for religious discrimination and harassment.

Foster Inclusive Talk and Open Dialogue

Another thing workplace leaders can do is foster an environment where it is safe to have appropriate talk about religion in a way that supports, not undermines, organizational goals. In many workplaces, workers have stereotypes about religion because they have very little experience with people outside their own religious tradition. Current diversity training programs do not often help with this, according to some workers we interviewed. In general, they said that diversity trainings can be the beginning of setting norms and starting conversations, but they never seem to do enough. For one, those trainings generally do not include religion at all. Less than a quarter of the workers we interviewed could point to a portion of a diversity training that included even a mention of religion. When diversity trainings do mention religion, they often do so in such a way that people feel even more uncomfortable or afraid to talk about religion afterward.

For example, Ben,[65] the Black evangelical criminal investigator, told us he was "not a fan" of the mandatory diversity training he had to go through, and he felt it actually prevented meaningful dialogue and didn't result in substantive change, even though it might control some types of speech and actions. "I am a minority myself, and there's hypersensitivity not to offend," he said. The message he's taken away from the diversity trainings he's done at work, he told us, is, "Basically, we need to respect all religions, and we need to make sure we don't discuss religion [ever], because . . . our discussion may offend somebody." He wonders if these diversity trainings as currently constituted really "allow opportunity to explore thoughts and feelings." He said he would prefer diversity trainings be "safe spaces, where people could say, 'OK, hey, I was wondering this. I'm not sure if it's politically correct or if it's going to be offensive, but this is . . . what I always thought and was taught and how I was raised.'"

Foster Inclusive or Multiple Celebrations

Members of minority religious traditions we interviewed said they sometimes felt their colleagues defaulted to excluding them from workplace activities like holiday celebrations, perhaps out of a desire not to transgress perceived religious boundaries. For example, an Indian American Muslim woman[66] working as an optometry technician noted how her colleagues were hesitant to approach her about a gift exchange among the workgroup during the Christmas holiday and were "kind of walking on eggshells around me" until she reassured them that, "Oh, we can definitely do a gift exchange, I'm down for that." Reflecting a similar sense of being treated as "fragile," a white Jewish man[67] working in information technology said that after colleagues learned of his faith, they "don't quite know what to do with me. You're like, all of a sudden, you're like glass, easily breakable or something. And now, we're gonna offend you or something. I'm like, 'Dude, relax. [*laughs*] If I hadn't told you, you probably wouldn't have known.' [*laughs*] . . . It's just new and weird and different, and they don't know what to do with you." While such interactions may be well intentioned or born out of a desire not to offend, for workers from religious minorities in our study, such hesitancy was perceived as socially awkward and created an uncomfortable sense of being singled out in a negative way. Leaders might provide an opportunity for people in their organizations to give feedback about the kind of holiday celebrations they want to see. Indeed, sometimes a simple show of effort on the part of leaders and organizations to support equal treatment can go a long way. If employees perceive their organization and organizational leaders as making efforts to support people from different identity groups and social locations, this goes a long way toward mitigating and even eliminating the negative impacts of discrimination on worker well-being and commitment.[68]

The Bottom Line

- Religious discrimination is present and pervasive in the workplace, and can be experienced by people from all religious groups as well as by those who are not religious.
- Members of minority religious groups (in a region or occupation) experience more religious discrimination than those who belong to the majority religious group.
- Religious discrimination is associated with many negative outcomes at work, including job dissatisfaction, disengagement, and burnout.
- Leaders can take steps to disrupt the conditions for religious discrimination through setting behavioral expectations, providing clear reporting procedures for violations, and fostering conversation and inclusivity.

Notes

1. F@W_ST111, Caucasian, Woman, 63, Retired (Sales), Muslim, conducted August 7, 2019.
2. F@W_ST107, White, Woman, 47, Instructor, Muslim, conducted August 1, 2019.
3. American Psychological Association. n.d. "APA Dictionary of Psychology." Accessed September 1, 2021. https://dictionary.apa.org/two-factor-theory-of-work-motivation.
4. See Gebert, Diether, Sabine Boerner, Eric Kearney, James E. King Jr., K. Zhang, and Lynda Jiwen Song. 2014. "Expressing Religious Identities in the Workplace: Analyzing a Neglected Diversity Dimension." *Human Relations* 67: 543–63. See p. 543 in particular.
5. Ghumman, Sonia, Ann Ryan, Lizabeth Barclay, and Karen Markel. 2013. "Religious Discrimination in the Workplace: A Review and Examination of Current and Future Trends." *Journal of Business and Psychology* 28: 439–54. See p. 449 in particular.
6. See Emerson, Michael O., and Christian Smith. 2000. *Divided by Faith: Evangelical Religion and the Problem of Race in America*. Oxford: Oxford University Press. Not a piece specifically on race and religion, but for more background on the idea of cultural "tool kits" see the seminal Swidler, Ann. 1986. "Culture in Action: Symbols and Strategies." *American Sociological Review* 51(2): 273–86.
7. See the report by Shellnutt, Kate. 2020. "Southern Baptists Keep Quarreling over Critical Race Theory." *Christianity Today*, December 3, and of course the powerful manuscript by Andrew Whitehead and Samuel L. Perry. 2020. *Taking America Back for God: Christian Nationalism in the United States*. New York: Oxford University Press.
8. See Lipka, Michael, and Benjamin Wormald. "Most and Least Religious U.S. States." 2016. Pew Research Center. February 29. https://www.pewresearch.org/fact-tank/2016/02/29/how-religious-is-your-state/.
9. See Scheitle, Christopher P., and Elaine Howard Ecklund. 2020. "Individuals' Experiences with Religious Hostility, Discrimination, and Violence: Findings from a New National Survey." *Socius* 6:2378023120967815.
10. We also asked this question for those who reported being denied employment or being fired due to their religion. We focus on the unfair treatment issue here because it is focused more on the ongoing work experience rather than trying to acquire employment or losing employment.
11. Experiences with Religious Discrimination Survey; respondents could choose multiple reasons, so the percentages are not mutually exclusive.
12. These percentages exclude cases who said that such treatment was "not applicable" to them. If we include this group in the denominator, then the percentages are 61.6 percent never, 14.9 percent rarely, 10.1 percent sometimes, 1.7 percent often, and 1.3 percent very often.
13. It is worth noting that these differences across religious traditions remain even after accounting for a wide range of other characteristics, including religiosity, race, gender, age, education, political ideology, region of residence, organizational position, and type of organization.
14. See Considine, Craig. 2017. "The Racialization of Islam in the United States: Islamophobia, Hate Crimes, and 'Flying While Brown.'" *Religions* 8(9): 165, 1–19.
15. These differences are statistically significant at the $p < .05$ level. The Muslim and Jewish percentages are also statistically significant relative to the evangelical Protestant percentage at the $p < .05$ level. The Buddhist and Hindu percentages do not significantly differ from the evangelical Protestant percentage, though.
16. The no religion group is statistically different from all other groups other than Buddhist and Hindu at the $p < .05$ level.
17. These represent predicted probabilities produced after a logistic regression model controlling for religious tradition, religiosity, age, gender, education, race, region of residence, political ideology, organizational position, and organizational type.
18. These represent predicted probabilities produced after a logistic regression model controlling for religious tradition, religiosity, age, gender, education, race, region of residence, political ideology, organizational position, and organizational type.
19. See Emerson, Michael O. and Christian Smith. 2000. *Divided by Faith: Evangelical Religion and the Problem of Race in America*. New York: Oxford University Press. Note that Emerson and Smith talk specifically about the difference between how Black and white evangelical Christians see race in America.
20. F@W_ST169, Hispanic, Woman, 45, Information Systems Analyst, Catholic, conducted December 5, 2019.

21. F@W_ST42, White, Woman, 31, Art Teacher, Catholic, conducted January 24, 2019.

22. F@W_ST38, Hispanic, Woman, 51, Finance, Evangelical, conducted January 11, 2019.

23. F@W_ST49, Black, Man, 38, Criminal Investigator, Evangelical, conducted February 6, 2019.

24. F@W_ST135, Hispanic, Woman, 27, Packer, Evangelical, conducted September 17, 2019.

25. F@W_ST98, White, Woman, 60, Registered Nurse, Evangelical, conducted July 10, 2019.

26. See Schmalzbauer, John. 2003. *People of Faith: Religious Conviction in American Journalism and Higher Education*. Ithaca: NY: Cornell University Press.

27. There is some evidence of this in our Faith at Work survey. Fifty-eight percent of evangelicals who say they work in the life, physical, or social sciences report some experience with religious discrimination compared to the 38 percent in our survey overall. However, the relatively small numbers (237 in total in that sector, 16 who identify as evangelical) make it difficult to place too much confidence in these differences.

28. Scheitle, Christopher P., and Katie E. Corcoran. 2018. "Religious Tradition and Workplace Religious Discrimination: The Moderating Effects of Regional Context." *Social Currents* 5: 283–300.

29. Yancey, George. 2011. *Compromising Scholarship: Religious and Political Bias in American Higher Education*. Waco, TX: Baylor University Press.

30. Hodge, David R. 2006. "Moving toward a More Inclusive Educational Environment? A Multi-sample Exploration of Religious Discrimination as Seen through the Eyes of Students from Various Faith Traditions." *Journal of Social Work Education* 42(2): 249–67.

31. Yancey, George, Sam Reimer, and Jake O'Connell. 2005. "How Academics View Conservative Protestants." *Sociology of Religion* 76: 315–36.

32. F@W_ST131, Hispanic, Man, 50, Marble Assembly, Catholic, conducted September 11, 2019; F@W_ST49, Black, Man, 38, Criminal Investigator, Evangelical, conducted February 6, 2019; F@W_ST50, Latinx, Man, 48, Co-owner of a Landscape Architect Business, Evangelical, conducted February 6, 2019.

33. F@W_ST102, Black, Woman, 32, Assistant Professor of English, Evangelical, conducted July 17, 2019.

34. F@W_ST45, White, Woman, 48, Tutor, Evangelical, conducted January 30, 2019.

35. Scheitle, Christopher P., and Katie E. Corcoran. 2018. "Religious Tradition and Workplace Religious Discrimination: The Moderating Effects of Regional Context." *Social Currents* 5: 283–300. See p. 297 in particular.

36. F@W_ST161, White, Woman, 62, Sales/Office Work, Mainline, conducted November 20, 2019.

37. F@W_ST80, African American, Man, 43, Law Enforcement, Evangelical, conducted June 4, 2019.

38. See Acquisti, Alessandro, and Christina M. Fong. 2015. "An Experiment in Hiring Discrimination." Online Social Networks. https://ssrn.com/abstract=2031979; Wallace, Michael, Bradley R. E. Wright, and Allen Hyde. 2014. "Religious Affiliation and Hiring Discrimination in the American South: A Field Experiment." *Social Currents* 1: 189–207; Wallace et al., (2014) show that those who identify as Muslims, alongside pagans and atheists, receive the highest levels of discriminatory behaviors from employers located in the American South. See also Wright, Bradley R. E., Michael Wallace, John Bailey, and Allen Hyde. 2013. "Religious Affiliation and Hiring Discrimination in New England: A Field Experiment." *Research in Social Stratification and Mobility* 34: 111–26; Wright et al. (2013) document Muslim candidates to receive only two-thirds of responses from employers compared to their other religious counterparts.

39. Mohammed, Besheer. 2018. "New Estimates Show U.S. Muslim Population Continues to Grow." Pew Research Center. January 3. https://www.pewresearch.org/fact-tank/2018/01/03/new-estimates-show-u-s-muslim-population-continues-to-grow/.

40. U.S. Equal Employment Opportunity Commission. 2023. "Religion-Based Charges Filed from 10/01/2000 through 9/30/2011 Showing Percentage Filed on the Basis of Religion-Muslim." Accessed at www.eeoc.gov.

41. Ghaffari, Azadeh, and Ayşe Çiftçi. 2010. "Religiosity and Self-Esteem of Muslim Immigrants to the United States: The Moderating Role of Perceived Discrimination." *The International Journal for the Psychology of Religion* 20: 14–25; Padela, Aasim I., Huda Adam, Maha Ahmad, Zahra Hosseinian and Farr Curlin. 2015. "Religious Identity and Workplace Discrimination: A National Survey of American Muslim Physicians." *AJOB Empirical Bioethics* 7: 149–59.

42. The regional differences overall are statistically significant at the p < .05 level using a design-based F test (F(2.82, 538.00) = 3.7201).

43. F@W_ST108, White, Man, 52, Consulting, Jewish, conducted August 2, 2019; F@W_ST115, Asian, Man, 53, Engineer, Muslim, conducted August 13, 2019.
44. F@W_ST112, White, Woman, 49, Social Services, Jewish, conducted August 8, 2019.
45. F@W_ST108, White, Man, 52, Consulting, Jewish, conducted August 2, 2019.
46. The term "Jew down" is an anti-Semitic trope that was formed during the Middle Ages about Jews being cheap or prone to hoard money. Oster, Marcy, 2019 (September 25). "What Does 'Jew Down' Mean, and Why Do People Find It Offensive." Jewish Telegraphic Agency. https://www.jta.org/2019/09/25/culture/what-does-jew-down-mean-and-why-do-people-find-it-offensive.
47. F@W_ST151, White, Man, 78, Retired Civil Servant, Jewish, conducted October 23, 2019.
48. F@W_ST115, Asian, Man, 53, Engineer, Muslim, conducted August 13, 2019.
49. See Ghumman, Sonia, and Linda A. Jackson. 2008. "Between a Cross and a Hard Place: Religious Identifiers and Employability." *Journal of Workplace Rights* 13: 259–79. This article identifies sex as a contributing factor in religious discrimination in workplace settings. See also Ghumman, Sonia, and Linda A. Jackson. 2010. "The Downside of Religious Attire: The Muslim Headscarf and Expectations of Obtaining Employment." *Organizational Behavior* 31: 4–23; Ghumman, Sonia, and Ann Marie Ryan. 2013. "Not Welcome Here: Discrimination towards Women Who Wear the Muslim Headscarf." *Human Relations* 66: 671–98; the Ghumman and Jackson (2010) and Ghumman and Ryan (2013) research discusses how religious identifiers like the hijab can increase Muslims' potential for facing discriminatory hiring practices. See Widner, Daniel, and Stephen Chicoine. 2011. "It's All in the Name: Employment Discrimination against Arab Americans." *Sociological Forum* 26: 806–23; this research finds that "Arab-sounding" names can also increase experiences of discriminatory hiring practices for Muslims.
50. In Chris and Elaine's other study discussed in this chapter, 36 percent of Muslim women said that they "often" wear religious head coverings in public. This compared to 4 percent of Muslim men.
51. F@W_ST105, Asian, Woman, 52, Gas Station Owner, Muslim, conducted July 29, 2019.
52. F@W_ST153, White, Woman, 23, Student, Project Manager, and Tutor, Jewish, conducted October 29, 2019.
53. F@W_ST106, Asian, Man, 71, Management in the Department of Justice, Muslim, conducted July 31, 2019.
54. F@W_ST205, Black, Woman, 25, Engineer, Agnostic, conducted May 25, 2021.
55. The Midwest and West percentages are not statistically different from each other, but the others are at the $p < .05$ level. Regions are defined as the four census regions.
56. A study by social psychologists Simpson and Rios found that "atheists . . . distinguish themselves from Christians primarily in terms of how much they value concerns of justice, fairness, equality, and individual rights." See Simpson, Ain, and Kimberly Rios. 2016. "How Do US Christians and Atheists Stereotype One Another's Moral Values?" *The International Journal for the Psychology of Religion* 26(4): 320–36.
57. We also asked about discrimination due to marital status, sexual orientation, national origin, disability, and criminal background.
58. This represents those saying they have at least rarely experienced gender/sex discrimination and religious discrimination. Fifty percent of all individuals surveyed reported gender discrimination. This compares to 72 percent among those who say they have experienced religious discrimination and 39 percent of those who say they have not experienced religious discrimination.
59. This corresponds to other research showing that reporting discrimination on one dimension is often related to reporting discrimination on others. See Scheitle, Christopher P., Taylor Remsburg, and Lisa F. Platt. 2021. "Science Graduate Students' Reports of Discrimination due to Gender, Race, and Religion: Identifying Shared and Unique Predictors." *Socius* 7:23780231211025183.
60. F@W_ST71, African American, Woman, 66, Reimbursement Analyst, Evangelical, conducted May 28, 2019.
61. Schmitt, Michael, Nyla Branscombe, Tom Postmes, and Amber Garcia. 2014. "The Consequences of Perceived Discrimination for Psychological Well-Being: A Meta-analytic Review." *Psychological Bulletin* 140(4): 921–48.
62. Oman, Doug, and Amani M. Nuru-Jeter. 2018. "Social Identity and Discrimination in Religious/Spiritual Influences on Health." In Doug Oman (Ed.). *Why Religion and Spirituality Matter for Public Health.* 111–37. Springer International.

63. Padela, Aasim I., Huda Adam, Maha Ahmad, Zahra Hosseinian, and Farr Curlin. 2016. "Religious Identity and Workplace Discrimination: A National Survey of American Muslim Physicians." *AJOB Empirical Bioethics* 7(3): 149–59; Nunez-Smith, Marcella, Nanlesta Pilgrim, Matthew Wynia, Mayur M. Desai, Cedric Bright, Harlan M. Krumholz, and Elizabeth H. Bradley. 2009. "Health Care Workplace Discrimination and Physician Turnover." *Journal of the National Medical Association* 101(12): 1274–82.

64. "Pre-employment Inquiries and Religious Affiliation or Beliefs." n.d. U.S. Equal Employment Opportunity Commission. Accessed November 30, 2020. https://www.eeoc.gov/pre-employm ent-inquiries-and-religious-affiliation-or-beliefs.

65. F@W_ST49, Black, Man, 38, Criminal Investigator, Evangelical, conducted February 6, 2019.

66. F@W_ST152, Indian-American, Woman, 27, Social Media Manager/Optometry Technician, Muslim, conducted October 23, 2019.

67. F@W_ST121, White, Man, 57, Information Technology, Jewish, conducted August 29, 2019.

68. See Triana, María Del Carmen, María Fernanda García, and Adrienne Colella. 2010. "Managing Diversity: How Organizational Efforts to Support Diversity Moderate the Effects of Perceived Racial Discrimination on Affective Commitment." *Personnel Psychology* 63(4): 817–43. However, we note that the findings depended upon the race of the worker, so in some cases the efforts of organizations to support diversity may have diverging effects on workers.

8

Nuanced Religious Accommodation

As American workplaces become more religiously diverse, new questions, concerns, and difficulties surrounding employer accommodations for religion arise. Under federal law, US organizations are required to accommodate employees' religious beliefs and practices in the workplace, as long as doing so does not cause undue hardship to the employer. This means that, in most circumstances, employers cannot prevent their workers from wearing religious items at work, talking about their religious beliefs in the workplace, or taking reasonable time off from work for religious practice. An employee has legal recourse against an employer if the employee has reported a need for religious accommodation and the employer has not acted cooperatively.

Yet accommodating religious expression in the workplace *only* to follow the law often leads to an overfocus on merely preventing religious discrimination and avoiding lawsuits—important things for sure, but not enough. The word "accommodate" is active. It means to make room for someone or something. Being accommodating connotes an eagerness or willingness to help. True religious accommodation for employees, we believe, is more proactive and nuanced than how it most commonly is implemented. It goes beyond giving employees time off to practice outside the workplace. It involves allowing religious expression and practice *inside* the workplace and helping employees know how to talk about their faith in ways that support a generative work environment for everyone.[1] True religious accommodation includes respect for religious differences in the workplaces, willingness to meet the needs of employees' religious traditions, thoughtful and equitable allowances for religious practices, the right spaces for discussions about religion, intentional care for minority groups that have less power in an organization, and then developing an organizational culture with policies to meet those objectives. All of these are necessary for healthy religious pluralism within a workplace.

Religion in a Changing Workplace. Elaine Howard Ecklund, Denise Daniels, and Christopher P. Scheitle,
Oxford University Press. © Oxford University Press 2024. DOI: 10.1093/oso/9780197675007.003.0008

Tensions around Religious Accommodation

Several workers we spoke with said a workplace should ensure that employees have the freedom to practice their faith *but* should also make sure they do not proselytize or pressure others. An evangelical woman[2] who works as a reimbursement analyst, for example, told us, "Everybody should be free, within reason, to express their faith and feel comfortable as to walking in their faith on a daily workday without any repercussions," which might include having religious symbols on their desk or wearing "Jesus is Lord" T-shirts or caps, she said. She emphasized, though, that "a person should have the right to practice their faith, provided that they don't push it on others."

Workers who are not evangelical Christians often pointed to evangelicals as a group that they are particularly concerned will push their faith on others. In part, this might be because, as we've seen from our study data, evangelicals are especially likely to actively and overtly express their religion at work by talking to others in the workplace about their faith.

While some non-Christian workers don't mind if their Christian coworkers talk about their faith or if their workplace celebrates Christian holidays, other workers are less comfortable with overt expressions of Christian faith at work. "A lot of my coworkers are religious. So, like, Christmas is a big thing to them, and Easter. So, a lot of times, they will project that to you, and they'll say, 'God bless,' and stuff like that. 'Let's pray.' . . . So, they try to incorporate it into the workplace, and it becomes very uneasy for me, uncomfortable," said a nonreligious[3] security guard in California—who says people treat him like the unusual Latino who is nonreligious—whose boss is a Christian. "I feel like they don't see—they don't accept that other people might have different points of view from them. . . . And it could get very uncomfortable at times. It's like they try to force it onto you." He does, however, accept accommodation for their religious expression in the workplace: "I try to learn about them more in depth. . . . I had to turn it into a research-oriented experience, so that I wouldn't be so negative and uncomfortable. I have to respect people. . . . That's their belief, and I have to respect that. And just because I don't believe in that, I can't project any negativity or any disrespect because, in reality, it really has nothing to do with me. So I shouldn't negatively reflect on them because they're doing something that they like, they believe in. It's their belief."

We do find that workplaces are less tolerant of nonreligious workers expressing their beliefs at work, often based on the idea that atheists are trying to push their beliefs (or really nonbelief) on others, according to a series of studies that Chris conducted with other colleagues. They presented individuals with scenarios describing workers who want to express their religion or lack thereof at work, such as a records clerk at a hospital who wants to display a quote from a religious text on their cubicle or a restaurant server who wants to wear a religious pin next to their nametag. They also included scenarios with nonreligious workers who want to display a quote from the prominent atheist scientist Richard Dawkins or wear a pin showing a "Darwin fish."[4] As the researchers predicted, participants said they would be less willing to accommodate the atheist employees' requests. "I think it becomes a very thorny issue when it comes to time off and exceptions to rules in general," a nonreligious consultant[5] in Texas told us, explaining, "American norms and laws are reflected strongly in protection of religious beliefs, but sometimes I feel like that protection is so strong that there is a real terror to question the time and place and validity of those beliefs. . . . I have found myself, for example, being responsible for work because a colleague was on a day of fasting for [a] religious holiday—whereas if I had chosen to engage in said fasting for health benefits, I would not have been afforded the same relief from work."

Knowing the Policies

We asked workers on our Faith at Work Supplemental Survey whether they agree or disagree that their "workplace provides accommodations that allow people to practice their religion." Overall, 19 percent of workers disagreed with this statement.[6] This means that about one in five workers believe that their workplaces do not or would not provide religious accommodations. There are differences across religious traditions in this perception, as seen in Figure 8.1. In particular, Muslim workers are less likely to think that their workplace does or would provide religious accommodations, with 54 percent *disagreeing* that their workplace provides such accommodations. Hindu workers are also somewhat more likely to say that their workplace does not provide religious accommodations.

We also asked workers whether they "know what kinds of religious accommodations the organization [they] work for offers." Overall, only 31 percent agreed that they were aware of what religious accommodations their organization provided. This suggests that relatively few workers are

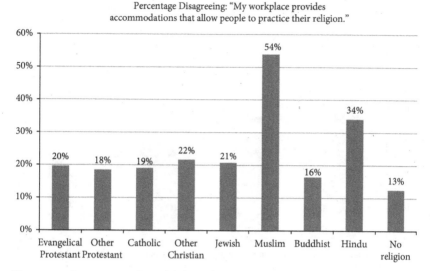

Percentage Disagreeing: "My workplace provides
accommodations that allow people to practice their religion."

Figure 8.1 Perception of Availability of Workplace Accommodations by
Religious Tradition
Faith at Work Supplemental Survey. Percentages in figure combine the "strongly" and "somewhat
disagree" responses.

even aware of what might be possible in terms of religious accommodations
at their workplaces. We might expect—and our data confirm—that more religious workers would have greater awareness of what accommodations are
available as they are likely more invested in knowing such information. As
seen in Figure 8.2, 41 percent of workers who describe themselves as very
religious agree that they know what religious accommodations are available to them. This compares to 34 percent of moderately religious workers,
30 percent of slightly religious workers, and 25 percent of workers who
are not religious at all. Still, this means that over half of the most religious
workers appear to be unaware of what religious accommodations are available to them.

Most of the workers we interviewed described fearing sanctions for talking
too much about religion at work, referencing vague knowledge of policies
that prohibit faith-related discussions and a general idea of what would be
acceptable or not when it comes to expressing religion in the workplace.
Many workers, however, are forced to guess about what kinds of standards
are in place. We found that, very often, workers are not aware of what policies
exist in their workplace regarding religious accommodation and that

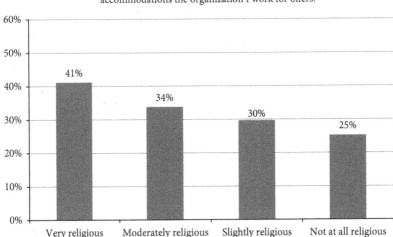

Figure 8.2 Workers' Awareness of Religious Accommodations at Workplace by Religiosity

Faith at Work Supplemental Survey. Percentages in figure combine the "strongly" and "somewhat agree" responses.

managers are often ignorant of what their workplace guidelines say. When we asked nearly two hundred US workers about the policies their workplaces have about expressing faith at work, only a quarter of them were aware of *any* workplace policies about the expression of faith. A minority of those we interviewed guessed that there are policies regarding religious expression in their workplace but were unfamiliar with those policies. "Oh, gosh! I'm sure there are, and I'm sure I should know them, but I don't [*laughs*]," said a woman[7] who works as a corporate trainer for a hospital. An evangelical Christian[8] who works as an admissions evaluator said that she would like to hold religious gatherings during breaks in the workday but is unsure what the policies are or how management would respond. "I think it would be great if it was more out in the open and if we did have opportunities to get together," she said. "I wanted to do either the Bible study or prayer group during lunch times, but I wasn't sure, you know, the policy for that.... If the policies are more, I guess, well known ... I probably would have maybe felt more comfortable." We heard from teachers, engineers, and consultants who did not know how their organizations accommodate religious expression and practice.[9] Yet, while unable to cite the exact policies, they did believe their workplaces have policies on discrimination that touch on religion or sensed that accommodations would or could be made for employees who want to practice their religion during the workday.

For example, when asked about workplace rules on expressions of faith, a woman[10] who works as a survey statistician for her state's government surmised, "It's the government. There must be a policy, somewhere. I just don't know it. I assume that our policy on expressions of faith is something along the lines of, 'You can do what you want to do, in your cube, as long as it's not offensive to other people or other groups, and as long as you don't use any fire!'" When asked about his workplace's policies on religious expression, a physician[11] we spoke with said, "We should look that up, in order to know, for sure. But since I don't know, you know, I don't know. Every now and then, for instance, you'll see someone's desk, and they'll have something [religious], a crucifix or something there. I'm sure that there are [other kinds of] workplaces that would prohibit that. And I see people . . . get away with that." A Christian technical writer[12] told us she has looked up the policies on religious expression in her workplace but found them vague and unclear, leaving her to guess about how to approach religious expression. She knows that workers "cannot be denied the right to practice our religion," she said. "Now, does that mean [we can practice religion] in the office? I don't know," she continued. "Should I kneel down and start praying for two hours a day? No. [I am sure] you can't do that." Because the policies lack any specifications, it seems like "they wrote it as an afterthought or something," she said.

A Culture of Nuanced Religious Accommodation

A Muslim man[13] who works in a technology field told us that his company has broad policies for religious practice, but that the religious makeup and culture of his office make it very hard for him to ask for accommodation. He said there are simply not enough Muslims in his workplace, and among them not enough who would like to practice the daily prayers like he does, to substantiate religious accommodation policies in that regard. While there are multipurpose rooms that his management says Muslims can use for prayers, those rooms are used for many different purposes, which makes it hard to use them as prayer rooms during the workday. A Jewish woman[14] who works in a start-up told us that they have basic policies in place that allow for religious accommodation, but she "just doesn't feel comfortable" expressing her Judaism at work. Workplace policies are one thing, she said, but having an organizational culture in which implementing the policies actually feels OK for the people who work there is another. Sociologists William Ouchi and Alan Wilkins[15] define organizational culture as "the normative bases and the shared understandings that, through subtle and complex expression, regulate social life in organizations." It includes the norms, values, practices, interactions, and expectations that guide employee behavior.

We heard from a number of workers who are unhappy about what they see as the suppression of religion in their workplace. An evangelical Christian woman[16] who works in finance but intends to leave her company said that she has been thinking a lot about what she will say during her exit interview. When they ask why she is leaving, she plans to say, "I just feel like I am spiritually dying." She pointed specifically to how her company treats Christmas, which she sees as symptomatic of much more significant changes. She said the company stopped having a Christmas party and no longer allows decorating for the holiday, citing the fire code, though they still celebrate Halloween. The past holiday season, it "did not feel like Christmas," she said. "You know, it did not even feel like a holiday.... When you looked around overall, at everything... even outside in the parking lot, they used to decorate at least those lamps with something. There was nothing. It was still regular work, an everyday workplace outside.... So I did not feel like I was welcome there anymore, as a Christian." In her view, Christmas decorations had been a symbol that it was OK for employees to celebrate their "Christian-ship," but now it feels like "they just don't want you to really talk about your religion," she said, and "when it comes to talking about your religion, they don't want to hear it," even though there are discussions about ethnicity and sexual orientation. Christians who want to meet need to be secretive about it, she told us. "It is like in the old books, when they said they found each other. Christians would find themselves and start [meeting together]. So you just talk to each other [without letting anyone else know]," she said.

Another evangelical woman who is a teacher[17] in the Midwest wonders if perhaps workplaces are becoming too sensitive about religious differences. In her view, religion is private and doesn't necessarily belong in the workplace, but she believes policies and protections can go too far in suppressing religious expression. "Say you have a Christmas party, and somebody is atheist.... Maybe you've had a Christmas party for twenty-five years, and one person complains about it, and all of a sudden, you don't have a Christmas party anymore," she said by way of example. If an organization responds by accommodating the one person, she believes, then, "you have to make it completely secular. Or can you—can you even mention Christmas?"

Modeling Religious Accommodation

In general, we found that workers want managers to clarify what is acceptable and not in terms of expressing faith in the workplace (especially in relation to holidays). Workers in government and public schools especially gave voice to this desire. "I would like to know what the constraints on religion and [religious expression are]. I would like the lines to be more clearly drawn," one Christian schoolteacher[18] in the South told us. "[The school does] an amazing job of keeping us aware of the norms that are changing, how to address them, how to be professional about it [for other issues] ... but they do not talk about the lines of what's appropriate communication about what religion is and is not."

Workers also want their workplace leaders and employers to create and encourage an environment of equality, respect, and understanding for individuals of all faiths and no faith. We heard again and again from workers that they want their workplace leaders to set the example regarding religious expression and accommodation as part of a commitment to religious pluralism. An atheist[19] who works in an art store in Tennessee, where she suspects most people are religious, for example, explained how after she asked her manager if "anyone was like 'psycho religious' because I will eventually say something that is deeply offensive if they are," her manager had a private conversation with her about how the organization approaches religion, who people are religiously, and how not to offend them.

Model Talking about Religion Where Relevant

In some cases, workers we surveyed and interviewed said they wanted workplace leaders to model appropriate expression of faith in the workplace. For some workers, part of this modeling means that leaders talk about their own religion or spirituality when appropriate and in appropriate ways, and how their religious or spiritual beliefs impact their work. "I appreciate that I have been able to express my faith openly with her and that she has shared some of her personal spiritual struggles with me, that I have learned from," Marla, the evangelical corporate trainer we met earlier,[20] said about her director. "So I appreciate that by having that resource, that I know, to this day, if I am struggling with something, I know I can call her on the phone right now, about personal stuff or work stuff, and she will have a word from the Lord. And I know that. And she has just handled so many things with grace and poise, and she will, like me, she will throw a Scripture in there. And again, if you're not a Christian, you won't even know she just threw a Scripture out there. But I will hear it and recognize it. So I just appreciate her for setting the example that she has."

Another evangelical Christian[21] who works as a paramedic said she would appreciate opportunities to talk with her supervisors about faith: "I think, for myself, I would enjoy it if they were to ever even ask me about it or to have a space of back-and-forth of where they shared their views, and I shared my views, and even how that affected the workplace. I would welcome that. If the doctor I work with or if my boss asked me, 'Hey, how does your faith influence what you do in the workplace?' I feel like I would want to tell them some of what I've told you . . . about how my faith drives me and how it keeps me going. I would welcome that." She said her boss is a Catholic, and they have "talked about it some. And I've shared with her some. And the VP above her is a Christian but our relationship is too formal, where we know kind of each other's religious affiliations, but we don't see each other with that much space. I would like to talk about my faith with her, and I would actually like to know how she, someone with a career background in politics and then, now, is [in a] high-level position . . . how does her faith influence her?"

A Christian program manager[22] in the Midwest talked to us about a place he used to work where leadership set a tone that made people feel they could express their faith. "We should all express what our beliefs are," he told us. Workplace leaders sometimes think that religion does not belong at work and "if we start showing who we are, it's going to cause a legal problem or something," he said, but "they have to set the standard." They need to "come out and say, you know, it's OK for somebody to say that, 'Hey, I'm blessed,'" or for someone to say that they heard an interesting sermon at church and that it has a positive impact on their work. He believes workers ought to have the ability to openly say things like, "'Oh yeah, as a Christian, I go to church,'" he said, and leaders need to "step up and do that as well."

Leaders who share their faith at work must recognize, however, that talking about their beliefs might not be welcome by everyone and can lead to workplace tensions. One man[23] who identifies as Christian told us he thinks religion should be kept out of the workplace "because it's very emotional and it stubs some people's toes and emotions. . . . If the manager is saying something, it may be construed as being that the workers must believe this way or they will leave. So it's nothing to do with work, per se." A Hispanic atheist[24] told us that she failed to connect with her former boss because he is religious and she is not. She felt hurt, she said, when he did not go to bat for her the way she thought he did for her Christian coworkers. One Christian we met who oversees dozens of employees at a wealthy firm mentioned that when his leadership team meets once a week, he reads a Bible passage and has them bow their heads in prayer—even though the team includes Christians, Muslims, and nonreligious individuals. In his view, none of these workers mind his religious expression, but it is also possible that he has so much power in the organization that no worker would say anything about it or challenge his Christian way of doing things even if it makes them feel othered or uncomfortable.

Look Out for Minority Groups

In many workplaces, we find, there is unequal religious accommodation: Those in the religious majority or more powerful roles often feel they have greater religious freedom, and it is often more difficult for workers of minority faiths or in less powerful positions to request the same allowances. We found that workers from religious minorities are often afraid to ask for religious accommodation in the workplace because they fear it might make them subject to religious discrimination.

Workplace leaders should be aware of these differences and help to ensure that workers who are members of religious minorities feel as comfortable expressing their faith as other employees do. They also must strike a balance that ensures religious accommodation is particular to the needs of different religious groups, but also provided in a way that is fair and equitable—so that those who practice minority faiths do not have to jump through extra hoops to justify their need for religious accommodation.

From the workers we spoke with, we heard that acknowledging the various religious holidays of employees can go a long way toward making those of minority religious traditions feel their faith can be accommodated at work. It can also help to give employees distinctive time off for religious observance, rather than bundling religious observance with vacation time.

Work schedules often already accommodate Christians, with days off around Christmas and Easter, and some workers we spoke with said it can be hard to know whether it is acceptable to ask for time off for non-Christian holidays. A Jewish attorney[25] said she likes the policies her workplace, which is a federal government subsidiary, has in place for taking time off for religious services. "There are some policies around religious leave. And actually, they're pretty sweet policies. . . . It's nice because you can have regular comp time, or you can have what's called 'religious-leave comp time,'" she said, and unlike with vacation, she explained, "you can make the comp time up for religious work after the fact" rather than offsetting in advance.

Some workers we spoke with talked about how workplace leaders can and should look out for members of religious minorities. For example, an evangelical Christian nurse[26] in the South said that she believes the Christian faith-based hospital where she works should accommodate employees from other religious traditions and those without religion. "If one of the employee's faith calls them to pray at certain times, we should allow them to do that—if it's safe for the patients—that they're able to step away and pray at the times of day that their religion calls them to do that," she said. She thinks active accommodation for employees of other faiths would "demonstrate an openness for the world, like we're taking a worldview that everyone is welcome, and everyone is safe here." A Muslim woman[27] who works as an optometry technician in a doctor's office told us about how her supervisor made efforts to actively accommodate her religious practice, intentionally seeking her out to tell her that, "'If you ever do prayers or anything, feel free to go to the third room—it can be your space, you can leave your mat in there.'" She said this made her feel like her workplace is "very, very, accommodating." As she explained, "I never felt like I couldn't communicate with them about my religion or what I needed."

In the previous chapter, we introduced psychologist Frederick Herzberg's two-factor theory of worker satisfaction, with organizational factors that motivate and demotivate workers. According to Herzberg, we are motivated to do better work and be more committed to organizations by factors like "achievement, recognition for achievement, the work itself, responsibility, and growth or advancement."[28] Additionally, as workers spend more and more time at work, they are also often now "seeking value, support, and meaning in their lives that find expression not only at home but also on the job." Sometimes, this is achieved by the ability to express and practice their religion in the workplace.

Religious accommodation that keeps all workers motivated and feeling supported requires organizational leaders to develop respect for religious differences in their workplaces, thoughtful and equitable allowances for religious expression and practices, and intentional care for minority groups. They also need to communicate which types of religious expression and practices are acceptable. "I don't think that we need to pretend that [religion] doesn't exist because that's like saying, 'This person doesn't exist,' . . . because sometimes religion and the person are conjoined at the hip," said an evangelical Christian woman[29] working in tech. "I think it also needs to be a balance so that you're not offensive to others who aren't as religious. . . . I feel like you have to find a balance between making sure that no one else is offended and you're not encroaching on anyone else's space."

Companies are beginning to recognize the need to include religion as part of their diversity, equity, and inclusion initiatives, and a growing number of companies now have employee resource groups designed to support people of faith in the workplace, and some have agnostic/atheist support groups as well.[30] Greater religious awareness and accommodation that helps workers reconcile their work life and religious life can appeal to employees. Management scholar Sonia Ghumman and her colleagues have found, for example, a high discrepancy between employers who offer time off for religious observation (56 percent) and employees who expect such accommodation (89 percent).[31] In addition to becoming familiar with the legal landscape, we would encourage organizations to make their policies on religious accommodation more proactive, nuanced, and explicit.

The Bottom Line

- Nuanced religious accommodation is part of a thriving workplace.
- Organizations are often more accommodating of religious expression and practice by those in the religious majority or positions of power.
- Research shows that those who are in the religious minority can have difficulty asking for religious accommodations at work.
- Leaders need to help their employees understand and interpret policies related to religion in the workplace and feel comfortable asking for accommodations.
- Leaders need to model how religion and nonreligion can and should be expressed and accommodated in the workplace and establish a workplace culture that supports religious diversity.

Notes

1. See Cash, Karen C., and George R. Gray. 2000. "A Framework for Accommodating Religion and Spirituality in the Workplace." *Academy of Management Perspectives* 14(3): 124–33.
2. See F@W_ST71, African American, Woman, 66, Reimbursement Analyst, Evangelical, conducted May 28, 2019.
3. F@W_ST200, Latino, Man, 42, Security Guard, Nonreligious, conducted May 3, 2021.
4. Rios, Kimberly, Leah R. Halper, and Christopher P. Scheitle. 2021. "Explaining Anti-atheist Discrimination in the Workplace: The Role of Intergroup Threat." *Psychology of Religion and Spirituality* 14(3): 371–80.
5. F@W_ST206, South Asian, Man, 29, Consultant, Nonreligious, conducted June 2, 2021.
6. Faith at Work Supplemental Survey. Forty-seven percent neither agree nor disagree that their workplace provides religious accommodations, while 34 percent agree that their workplace provides religious accommodations.
7. F@W_ST17, Black, Woman, 40, Corporate Trainer, Evangelical/Assemblies of God, conducted November 27, 2018.
8. F@W_ST170, Asian, Woman, 32, Admissions Evaluator, Evangelical, conducted December 5, 2019.
9. F@W_ST144, Mixed Race (Black/White), Man, 36, Teacher, Mainline, conducted October 10, 2019; F@W_ST75, White, Man, 69, Reliability and Quality Engineer, Evangelical, conducted May 30, 2019; F@W_ST46, White/Hispanic, Man, 57, Consultant/Manager, Mainline, conducted January 30, 2019.
10. F@W_ST155, White, Woman, 41, Survey Statistician, Jewish, conducted November 1, 2019.
11. F@W_ST129, Black, Man, 65, Physician, Catholic, conducted September 10, 2019.
12. F@W_ST164, White, Woman, 63, Technical Writer, Mainline, conducted November 25, 2019.
13. F@W_ST148, Indian-American, Man, 42, Technical Staff, Muslim, conducted October 17, 2019.
14. See F@W_ST153, White, Woman, 23, Student, Jewish, conducted October 29, 2019.
15. See Ouchi, William, and Alan Wilkins. 1985. "Organizational Culture." *Annual Review of Sociology* 11: 457–83. Quote comes from p. 458. See also Martin, JoAnne. 2002. *Organizational Culture: Mapping the Terrain*. New York: Sage. See also Thorngate, Warren. 2002. "Organizational Culture: Mapping the Terrain by Joanne, Martin." *Journal of Comparative Policy Analysis* 4: 217–21. See, for example, Lindsay, D. Michael. 2021. *Hinge Moments: Making the Most of Life's Transitions*. Downers Grove, IL: InterVarsity Press.
16. F@W_ST38, Hispanic, Woman, 51, Finance, Evangelical, conducted January 11, 2019.
17. F@W_ST19, White, Woman, 55, Spanish Teacher, Evangelical, conducted November 28, 2018.
18. F@W_ ST144, Mixed Race (Black/White), Man, 36, Teacher, Mainline, conducted October 10, 2019.
19. F@W ST195, Hispanic White, Woman, 39, Freelance Artist/Art Store Clerk, Atheist, conducted April 8, 2019.
20. See F@W_ST17, Black, Woman, 40, Corporate Trainer, Evangelical/Assemblies of God, conducted November 27, 2018.
21. F@W_ST142, White, Woman, 35, Paramedic, Evangelical, conducted October 7, 2019.
22. F@W_ST09, African American, Man, 50, Program Manager, Evangelical, conducted November 2, 2018.
23. F@W_ST46, White, Man, 57, Consultant/Manager, Mainline, conducted January 30, 2019.
24. F@W ST195, Hispanic White, Woman, 39, Freelance Artist/Art Store Clerk, Atheist, conducted April 8, 2019.
25. F@W_ST152, White, Woman, 39, Attorney, Conservative Jewish, conducted October 18, 2019.
26. F@W_ST86, White, Woman, 21, Nurse, Evangelical, conducted June 13, 2019.
27. F@W_ST152, Indian American, Woman, 27, Social Media Manager/Optometry Technician, Muslim, conducted October 23, 2019.
28. Cash, Karen C., and George R. Gray. 2000. "A Framework for Accommodating Religion and Spirituality in the Workplace." *Academy of Management Perspectives* 14(3): 124–33.

29. F@W_ST66, African American, Woman, 50, Tech Consultant, Evangelical, conducted May 16, 2019.

30. Peel, Bill. n.d. "Faith-Based Employee Resource Groups on the Rise." Center for Faith and Work at LeTorneau University. Accessed November 30, 2020. https://centerforfaithandwork.com/article/faith-based-employee-resource-groups-rise.

31. Ghumman, Sonia, Anne Marie Ryan, Lizabeth A. Barclay, and Karen S. Markel. 2013. "Religious Discrimination in the Workplace: A Review and Examination of Current and Future Trends." *Journal of Business and Psychology* 28(4): 439–54.

9

Faith, Family, and Work

Thus far, we have looked at how faith influences workers *inside* of the workplace. Here we broaden the picture to examine how religion can influence attitudes toward work *outside* of the workplace, specifically how faith can have an impact on the relationship between work and family and how workers approach the work-family relationship. The boundaries between work and family—and the demands presented by each—are neither solid nor static. Our work and family lives often spill into each other, each fighting for more of our devotion and time. Both work and family have been called "greedy institutions" that try to claim a person's full temporal and cognitive attention. We should not be surprised then that tension and conflict often result from attempts to balance the respective demands of family life and work life. A man who works as a legislative assistant and belongs to a Black Protestant church[1] told us that family responsibilities lead to "a lot" of stress. "You know, I have four kids. [And work makes it sometimes] so like I can't pick my kids up or, you know, I don't have all the time to help them with their homework and they rely on their mother to do that stuff, so sometimes that creates stress, especially because we [have] a newborn." A Muslim man[2] talked about how in his early work life he had to go through "hell and high waters for several years, and things fell apart both places, work and home. You know, besides great emotional stress . . . there was a huge financial stress also." The challenges of balancing the demands of work and family life were discussed by many of the workers we interviewed, who talked about how those demands sometimes overlap or clash, and how work responsibilities can interfere with family life and vice versa.

In these circumstances, religious communities can provide a helpful balm or, in many cases, contribute to work-family tensions, especially those felt by women. Yet to date, much of the scholarly research that has tried to help people find a work-life balance has not included the role of religion. We found that religion can shape workers' attitudes and behaviors toward family, and faith-influenced visions of family life can sometimes lead to greater conflict with work. Like the other facets of faith at work we have explored, these

Religion in a Changing Workplace. Elaine Howard Ecklund, Denise Daniels, and Christopher P. Scheitle,
Oxford University Press. © Oxford University Press 2024. DOI: 10.1093/oso/9780197675007.003.0009

dynamics are deeply shaped by a worker's religious tradition, racial background, and gender, all factors that only became more salient during the pandemic.

Religion and Family Are Linked

Religious institutions often stress the importance of family, and many religions focus heavily on the creation, regulation, and maintenance of family life. Religious organizations usually set up their programming around families and also provide family advice and guidance.[3] In many instances, religious traditions define appropriate family forms. Religious lives tend to be grounded in families, both in the sense that we are often socialized into a particular faith tradition within our family of origin and in the sense that we typically practice faith alongside our family of creation. Religion and family are what the sociologist Penny Edgell has called "linked institutions."[4]

In a recent analysis of nearly fifty years of data from the General Social Survey, a long-running survey of US adults, sociologist Ryan Burge found that evangelical Protestants have consistently had more children than members of the broader US public. In recent years, Protestants have had about 2.1 children on average, while religiously unaffiliated individuals have had an average of about 1.3 children. When compared with the average US adult forty years of age or older, the religiously unaffiliated are more likely to report that they have never had children. There are similar patterns with regard to marriage, with evangelical Christians more likely than the average American to have ever been married and the religiously unaffiliated less likely to have ever been married.[5] Studies also show that adolescents who grow up in more religious families tend to place more importance on getting married and having kids when they grow up, and adolescents who say they are more religious or were raised in certain faith traditions, such as conservative Protestantism or Mormonism, are more likely to get married, get married at a younger age, have kids, and have more kids than those who were raised less religious or without a religious tradition at all.[6]

Our own national survey only reinforces the links among faith, marriage, and children. We asked individuals if they currently have children living in their household. Obviously, the likelihood of having children is going to be affected by several factors beyond religion, such as age, education, and marital status. If we statistically eliminate the role of those other factors, however, we find that individuals who say they are not at all religious are significantly less likely than those who are slightly, moderately, or very religious to say they have children in their household. As seen in Figure 9.1, those who are not at all religious have about a 47 percent chance of having a child in the household, while those who are very religious have about a 56 percent chance.[7] Note that these differences are *independent* of religious tradition. This means that just identifying as more religious, regardless of the religious tradition they belong to, is associated with an increased likelihood of having a child in the household. We do find religious tradition differences as well, though. Our data show, for instance, that evangelical Protestants are significantly more likely to have children in the household than are more moderate or liberal Protestants *regardless of their personal religiosity.* When it comes to family formation, progressive Protestants are a bit more like the nonreligious, and all of the other religious categories are more like one another.

These religion-related effects, we find, add onto other group-level differences. For instance, our survey data show differences across racial and ethnic groups, with Black individuals and those who identify as Hispanic more likely than white and non-Hispanic individuals to have a child in the household. On the other hand, all else being equal, Asian individuals are less likely to have a child in the household. There are also significant gender differences, with women significantly more likely than men to have a child

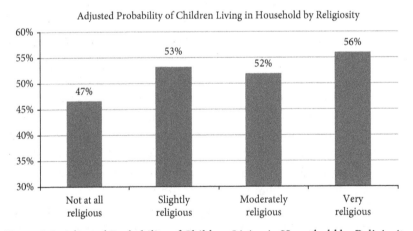

Adjusted Probability of Children Living in Household by Religiosity

Figure 9.1 Adjusted Probability of Children Living in Household by Religiosity

Note: Faith at Work Main Survey. Probabilities produced after estimating logistic regression model controlling for religious tradition, gender, age, age squared, race, ethnicity, marital status, and education. The not at all religious category is statistically different from the three other categories at $p < .05$.

in their household regardless of their other social and demographic characteristics. As a result, Black women who consider themselves very religious are among the most likely to have a child in the household. After we take out other factors like age and income, we find that very religious Black women have a 70 percent chance of having a child in the household compared with a 52 percent chance for very religious white men.

We find a similar pattern when looking at religiosity and the probability of being partnered—that is, currently married or living with a partner. As seen in Figure 9.2, independent of other social and demographic factors, individuals who are not at all religious are less likely to be currently partnered than are those who are moderately or very religious.[8] Specifically, those who are not at all religious have about a 64 percent chance of currently being partnered, while those who are very religious have about a 69 percent chance.

Workers who are married and have children have a harder time balancing work life and their family life—so it's important to note that religious workers are more likely to be married and have children in their household than are nonreligious workers. Children, in particular, can make managing work more arduous, as parents must navigate the challenges of their children's care, education, and general well-being while simultaneously meeting the

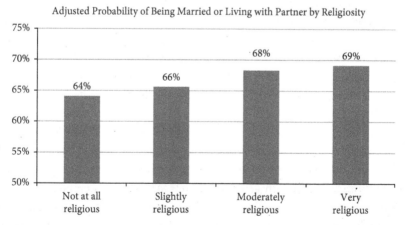

Adjusted Probability of Being Married or Living with Partner by Religiosity

Figure 9.2 Percent married or living with partner by religiosity (adjusted for other factors)

Note: Faith at Work Main Survey; Probabilities produced after estimating logistic regression model controlling for religious tradition, gender, age, age squared, race, ethnicity, and education. The not at all religious category is statistically different from moderately and very religious categories at p<.05.

expectations of their job. Such responsibilities tend to be disproportionately felt by certain groups of workers, such as women and those with lower incomes.

Work and Family Often Conflict

The General Social Survey asks working individuals, "How often do the demands of your job interfere with your family life?" In recent years, about 14 percent of full-time workers have said that such interference occurs "often," while another 34 percent said it occurs "sometimes."[9] The survey has also asked individuals, "How often do the demands of your family interfere with your work on the job?" About 4 percent of full-time workers said this happens often, and 23 percent said this happens sometimes.[10] When we delve further into these responses, we are not surprised to find that individuals who work more hours are more likely to feel their work interferes with their family life.[11] This is independent of a wide range of other social and demographic factors, meaning that if we compare individuals who are otherwise identical we would expect those working more hours to feel more work-family conflict. Also, as we might expect, individuals with more children are more likely to say that work interferes with their family life. The data also show that married individuals are more likely than those who have never been married to feel their work interferes with their family life. To be clear, this is not simply a function of age or the presence of children. Rather, the presence of a partner itself seems to increase feelings of work-family conflict, possibly because it introduces another individual's needs and schedules into the mix. We also find that more highly educated workers are more likely to say that work interferes with their family life (possibly because these more highly educated workers have more demanding jobs that require effort outside of a typical nine-to-five schedule, but also perhaps because these workers have higher expectations of "having it all," assuming they will be able both to engage fully at work and engage fully with their families), and white workers are more likely than Black workers to say that work interferes with their family life. In some ways being able to ponder how work interferes with family life may be a preserve of the privileged. Those who have fewer resources may not have the expectation of resolving such tensions.

Yet when we looked at how religion shapes workers' feelings of work-family interference, we found almost no *direct* effect. That is, independent of other social and demographic factors, workers who are more religious workers and those who are less religious do not differ in how they feel about how much work interferes with their family life and vice versa. We also find no differences across religious traditions. To be clear, this does not mean that religion is irrelevant to feelings of work-family conflict. As we noted, the presence of children does increase feelings of work-family interference, as does the presence of a marriage partner, and religious workers are more likely to be married and have a child in their household. Thus, religion does shape work-family conflict *indirectly* by increasing the likelihood of certain factors that lead to that conflict.

Work-Family Conflicts Are Gendered

Despite all the changes in the labor force and family structure over the past fifty years—including those encouraging women to work outside the home and men to be more involved in family life—household activities and childcare are still believed to be more the domain of women than men.[12] Women are disproportionately responsible for childcare, and other family responsibilities generally tend to fall on women more than men as well.[13] These gender norms and disparities are directly linked to work-family conflict for women, especially for women in time-demanding professions that allow for few responsibilities and commitments outside of work.[14] "I mean, just because we're at work so much, right? You get to that point where all you can think about is how long you haven't put your laundry away," said a woman who works as an attorney.[15] Among elite professionals, long hours are even seen as a badge of courage, signaling a primary commitment to the workforce.[16]

Men in professional occupations, researchers find, have strong devotion to the world of paid work,[17] and among middle-class men, this devotion demands long hours and a strong identification with career, which is often expressed as an all-consuming commitment to their employer.[18] Yet in both heterosexual and same-sex couples raising children, it is increasingly likely that both parents are part of the paid labor force, and norms for "ideal" fatherhood are changing, demanding men spend more time with their children. As a result, we are seeing much greater work-family conflict for men than in the past. Today, men feel compelled not only to be their family's primary breadwinner but also to be highly involved with their kids—what psychologist Kerstin Aumann and colleagues call the "new male mystique."[19] They claim that men are pressured to "do it all in order to have it all," in a way that is similar to the pressures felt by women in the workforce. One research study found that in 1965, fathers reported 42 hours of paid work per week, compared with 37 hours in 2011, while their hours spent on housework increased from 4 to 10. In 1965, men reported spending an average of 2.5 hours per week on childcare, while in 2011 they reported spending 7 hours per week. This number has not changed appreciably since then, as the 2021 American Time Use Survey also found that men spent an average of 7 hours per week on childcare. Yet tellingly, another study found that 95 percent of men would like to spend more time with their families.[20] While childcare hours have increased for men over the years, childcare hours for mothers have also increased, from 10 to 14 hours per week, revealing that women still provide the majority of childcare hours.[21]

Faith Communities Can Hurt Working Women by Fostering Gender Traditionalism

A woman we spoke with who attends a Black conservative Protestant congregation[22] talked about how professional working women in her church can sometimes feel marginalized and encumbered by gender norms. She told us, for example, that when a man in her congregation talked about his work as a regional manager of a Burger King, people in the church would try to listen intently to help him, but when she talked about her work at a bank, the congregation members seemed to feel she was thinking too highly of herself. "So when I got up and said something to the congregation about the church's financial position and offered what I knew because I actually do work at a bank too," she said, "they were like, 'Well, you think you know something,' or 'She's just talking.' . . . I forgot how it was phrased."

Religion is responsible for some of the traditional gender norms surrounding work and family in US culture. Religious traditions, conservative and progressive, often connect family-related beliefs to gender-related beliefs, especially regarding work. To assess the relationship between religion and gender role attitudes, we asked workers whether they agreed with the statement "It is much better for everyone involved if the man is the achiever outside the home and the woman takes care of the home and family."[23] Figure 9.3 shows individuals' agreement with this statement overall

Full-Time Employees' Agreement with Statement "It is much better for everyone involved if the man earns the money and the woman takes care of the home and children" by Gender and Religious Tradition

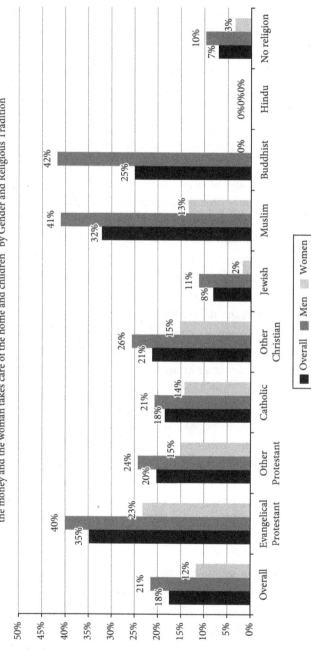

Figure 9.3 Full-Time employees' agreement with statement "It is much better for everyone involved if the man earns the money and the woman takes care of the home and children" by gender and religious tradition

Note: Faith at Work Main Survey: Analysis limited to those employed full-time; Percentages represent combined somewhat agree and strongly agree categories; No Hindu respondent and no Buddhist woman agreed with this statement, hence why the bars are not visible for those categories.

and broken out by religious tradition and gender. Overall, we see that about 21 percent of men agree with this traditional breadwinner-homemaker statement compared to 12 percent of women. Although not shown in this figure, our analyses also find that more religious individuals are more likely to agree with this statement, regardless of their specific religious tradition. What's more, people of color (Black, Asian, and Native individuals) are significantly less likely than white individuals to agree with the statement, independent of their religion or other factors.[24]

Looking across the religious traditions in Figure 9.3, we see that evangelicals and Muslims are more likely than individuals belonging to other religious traditions to express agreement with this breadwinner-homemaker ideal, although evangelical and Muslim women are still less likely than men in these traditions to agree with this statement.[25] One Muslim woman[26] explained that her religious community both explicitly and implicitly encourages women to raise kids and be at home, "kind of like they always like look to you when it comes to, like, being someone that is really involved with the children and, like, more so [than] the husband or the men in their lives."

While there is a significant difference between evangelical men's and women's views on this question, working evangelical women are nonetheless more likely than women in any other religious tradition to say that the gendered breadwinner-homemaker approach is much better for everyone. Almost a quarter of evangelical women employed full time agreed that it would be better if instead of working they were home to take care of the house and family. This might be because these women have a more conservative view of gender roles that has been cultivated by their faith tradition. As one woman who described her church as conservative[27] framed it, "There are definitely separate roles for men and women, but that doesn't make any role more important or less deserving." Interestingly, this particular woman was a business owner herself, but she didn't seem to see any contradiction between her view of different roles for men and women and her own role in the business world.

Other women might be more likely to feel ambivalent about their employment status when their churches elevate traditional gender norms or devalue work outside the home for women. Evangelical men were often aware of the impact of these gender expectations for women within the church, although they did not express the same degree or frequency of personal frustration about it as did the women we interviewed. When we asked a white evangelical man[28] whether his pastor has ever discussed issues of gender equality in the workplace, he stated bluntly about his church, "I've heard the opposite of that. 'Barefoot and pregnant' is the best way I can describe it." Another evangelical man[29] said his church "is still struggling to figure out how to support two-worker households. I think it's more of a challenge for women in general just because of all the cultural expectations."

Several evangelical women we spoke with in our interviews mentioned encountering and negotiating the gendered work expectations of their religious tradition and community. Evangelical working women also spoke to us about feeling frustrated at times with a lack of awareness or concern for working women in their religious community. One evangelical woman who works as a nurse practitioner,[30] for example, said she "gets annoyed that the [church's] mom's group meets during the week, so I can't really go." Another evangelical woman who works as a real estate agent[31] said she has observed that men in her church community "aren't asked as often to teach Sunday school or to do AWANAs [Bible-based youth programs] and take care of the little kids and volunteer in the nursery. And, God forbid, if a woman has to work and misses Bible study . . . but for a man that's expected." We did not hear these same concerns voiced by men. They were unlikely to criticize their faith community for lacking attention to the demands of their work. They were also less likely than women to recognize the differential ways their faith community attends to the needs of working women.

The support for women who work outside the home is not necessarily greater in progressive congregations. A woman who is a teacher and librarian[32] said her mainline congregation is still "struggling with some deeply ingrained sexism that says that men's work is more important." She is on the parish council, she said, and if at a meeting, "one of the male members of the parish council says, 'Oh, I have a work thing, I can't meet then,' everybody just says, 'Oh, of course, uh-huh,'" she told us. "But if a woman says, 'Oh, I have a work thing, I can't meet then,' it's almost just an atmosphere. It's not—there's nothing verbal. It's not stated, but there's just this little bit of judgmental atmosphere like, 'Oh well, you are not managing your time well,' or 'Your priorities aren't straight,' or, you know, 'Do you really have something important at work, how important is that?' I guess when I think about it, when a man says that, people around the room, around the table will go, 'Uh-huh, um-hum.' They will get that nonverbal validation. And a woman will not. A woman will not. I've felt it myself . . . and God knows I've been guilty of it toward other women around the table as well."

How Religion Supported Working Women
during the Pandemic

For many of the individuals we interviewed, the challenges of trying to balance work and family life became even more difficult during the COVID-19 pandemic, as the boundaries between work and home life blurred or disappeared altogether. The early phase of the pandemic also highlighted the deeply ingrained gendered dynamics at the intersection of work and family, making it an especially challenging time for working women. "In the first few months of the pandemic, my daughter was in kindergarten. Kindergarten shut down. We had kids in daycare. Daycare shut down. . . . So, for like three or four months, everybody was home all the time. That was really crazy," recalled a white Jewish woman who works as a data analyst and whose husband also works in a computer-based job.[33] "So we did a lot of juggling meetings and responsibilities. And I would work some during the day, and then the kids would go to bed, and I'd work for several hours at night." An evangelical woman[34] described to us how, on the one hand, she and her husband were "in the same boat" in dealing with the pandemic, but on the other hand, "I still feel like I'm the one mostly running around and dealing with all of the kids' tasks while also balancing my own work," she said. The pandemic was particularly challenging for working parents who no longer had external activities in which their children could participate, and again, this load was felt disproportionately by women. "Typically, the women were already in the caregiving role, in addition to working. And I mean, even if they weren't working, part of their relief was when the children went to school or were engaged in some activity. So once that was completely removed, then there was no relief. There was no place to go for your own mental health," another evangelical woman who works as a life coach[35] noted.

"Women have always held the bigger burden in families," a Catholic woman who works as a middle school teacher[36] said plainly. "This kind of just came to the forefront in the pandemic. For too long, women had strived to 'have it all,' without necessarily passing on some of those traditionally female roles to their counterparts or to their spouses. And so I think definitely the childcare component of it kind of came to the forefront. When childcare facilities closed, it wasn't men that decided to stay home most of the time. It was women."

We asked individuals who said they attended religious services at least some time during the pandemic, either virtually or in person, whether their "faith community looked for ways to support those who had increased demands on their time due to school or daycare closures." As seen in Figure 9.4, 48 percent of these individuals somewhat or strongly agreed that their faith community engaged in such efforts. In our national survey, Catholics were significantly less likely than evangelicals to say they saw their faith community support individuals facing school or daycare closures during the pandemic. Muslims, on the other hand, were significantly more likely than evangelicals to say they saw their faith community step up in this way. Because Muslims in the United States are a minority religious group, and the religious group most likely to be discriminated against in most domains, it is possible that the threat of the pandemic made this group even more tight knit. Members of other religious traditions did not significantly differ from evangelicals in their reports of their congregations helping with school and daycare closures.[37]

A white mainline Protestant woman who works in information technology[38] described how she observed her congregation "rally behind whoever needed them to rally behind, whether it was a family or a single mom or a single dad or even people who are sort of peripherally connected to the community." She said they "have an extensive ministry around caring for people when something happens in their life. A baby is being born [and we

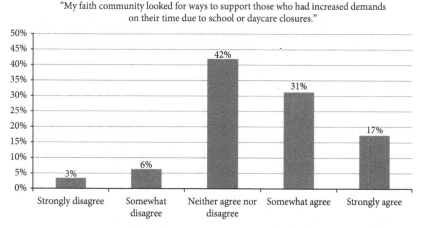

Figure 9.4 Percent agreeing "My faith community looked for ways to support those who had increased demands on their time due to school or daycare closures."

Note: Faith at Work Supplement Data; Question only asked of those who attended religious services more than "never" during the pandemic, either online or in-person.

as a community provide resources]. We will have people cleaning your house and walking your dog or taking your kids to school and feeding you, right, and we just know how to care for each other that way and just expect to." A Black Protestant woman who works as a public health executive[39] said her relationships with members of her faith community were most important in helping her cope with the difficulties of balancing work and family during the pandemic. For example, she recounted, if she "was just feeling uneasy about something or the high stress levels during COVID, being able to talk to others in the congregation or even just through prayer or even just through the messages that I heard, it would be . . . an encouragement to be able to still do the work that I do."

In most cases, women we spoke with said the support provided by their faith community was emotional or spiritual. An evangelical woman,[40] for instance, said her faith helped her be less afraid for her family and her own personal well-being during the pandemic and allowed her to keep substitute teaching in the local schools. "Like, there were substitutes who said, 'Well, I'm not doing it, because I don't need the money, and I don't wanna get sick.' And I felt like, well . . . I'm not gonna be afraid. God—you know, our times are in His hands, and I enjoy [the substitute teaching work] so I just kept on going because of that." Due to her faith, she said, "The COVID did not impact that." When asked how her faith helped her manage the challenges associated with the pandemic, a mainline Protestant woman who owns a garden shop[41] referred to her faith as her "backbone," saying that "it provides you that inner strength."

Some workers talked about ways they wished their religious community would have been more supportive of workers during the pandemic. One evangelical woman,[42] for example, reflected on her experiences at church prior to the pandemic where, she said, "they had like a daycare. . . . If they had the capacity, they will allow childcare. I know they took care of children while families went to work." She suggested this was a way churches could have provided more support to families during the early phases of the pandemic, particularly for parents who could not work from home: "Maybe that would help people that don't have that remote option and don't have other options, so that they can live easier." A Catholic woman[43] seemed frustrated that her church hadn't done more to organize more structural support for working parents during the pandemic. "Like, I don't understand. They have a list of the congregation. It's not that many people. So, they could've [asked] does anyone need help or does anyone need assistance? Does anybody need help with grocery shopping or does anybody need this or that?" she said.

"But," she added, "there was none of that." While these desires for support were undoubtedly complicated by the public health messaging regarding social distancing during the pandemic, it was notable that a number of women in particular expressed a desire for more tangible support from their faith communities to manage their roles as working parents during that stressful and challenging time.

We find that religious communities can offer support and resources to help their members balance work and the demands of family life. Sometimes, this is via individual, internalized, spiritual comfort, and sometimes the support is more structural and material. Structural and material supports, however, come less readily to congregations, even those that are more progressive, because of longstanding views on the family that influence their attitudes on gender and work. Religions often promote the traditional family structure and the idea that motherhood is the proper, most important, and most noble role for women—preferring women to stay at home and care for the house and children while men go off to work. By upholding these gender norms, religion can be a source of work-family conflict, especially for women. We believe religious communities can better serve both working men and women by providing a new vision of the family and work-life dynamics— recognizing that women can have a calling outside the home, acknowledging that working women are essential and appreciated, and celebrating men who take a more active role in the household and childcare.

The Bottom Line

- Highly religious workers are more likely than their less religious counterparts to be partnered and to have children at home.
- Work-family conflict is more prevalent for women than for men, but as men's roles in the family change, balancing work and family is becoming increasingly challenging for men as well.
- Workplace leaders might benefit from recognizing that many employees experience significant work-family tension, and that this tension may be more significant for some employees (women and those high in religiosity, particularly) than for others.
- Religious communities can sometimes be a resource and support for workers, but at other times exacerbate experiences of work-life conflict, especially for working women.

- In addition to spiritual support, faith communities may want to consider ways they can provide tangible support to working parents.
- Religious leaders can help workers in their congregations by communicating the value of women who work and men who contribute to household and childcare responsibilities.

Notes

1. F@W_ST176, Black, Man, 32, Legislative Assistant, Evangelical, conducted November 11, 2019.
2. F@W_ST106, Asian American, Man, 71, Management in Department of Justice, Muslim, conducted January 31, 2019.
3. See Petts, Richard. 2019. "Introduction to the Special Issue of Religions: Religion and Family Life." *Religions* 10(4): 1.
4. Edgell, Penny. 2006. *Religion and Family in a Changing Society.* Princeton, NJ: Princeton University Press.
5. Burge, Ryan. 2022 (September 8). "'God-Denying' Women and Self-Replacing Christians: How Religion Changes Birthrates." Ahead of the Trend (blog) http://blogs.thearda.com/trend/featured/god-denying-women-and-self-replacing-christians-how-religion-changes-birthrates/.
6. Hayford, Sarah R., and S. Philip Morgan. 2008. "Religiosity and Fertility in the United States: The Role of Fertility Intentions." *Social Forces* 86(3): 1163–88; Uecker, Jeremy E., and Charles E. Stokes. 2008. "Early Marriage in the United States." *Journal of Marriage and Family* 70(4): 835–46; Uecker, Jeremy E. 2014. "Religion and Early Marriage in the United States: Evidence from the Add Health Study." *Journal for the Scientific Study of Religion* 53(2): 392–415; Ellison, Christopher G., Amy M. Burdette, and Norval D. Glenn. 2011. "Praying for Mr. Right? Religion, Family Background, and Marital Expectations among College Women." *Journal of Family Issues* 32(7): 906–31.
7. This is setting all other measures at their respective means.
8. They do not statistically differ from those who are only slightly religious.
9. 2018 General Social Survey. Thirty-one percent responded "rarely" and 22 percent responded "never."
10. 2018 General Social Survey. Forty-four percent responded "rarely" and 30 percent responded "never."
11. Ordinary least squares regression analysis of the General Social Survey question (wkfsfam), "How often do the demands of your job interfere with your family life?" Predictors include religiosity, religious tradition, employment status (full- vs. part-time), hours worked in previous week, gender, marital status, number of children, age, race, and highest educational degree. N = 5,596. Data were weighted using variable wtssnr.
12. Folbre, Nancy. 2007. *Valuing Children: Rethinking the Economics of Family.* Cambridge, MA: Harvard University Press; Kan, M.-Y., M. Zhou, K. Kolpashnikova, E. Hertog, S. Yoda, and J. Jun. 2022. "Revisiting the Gender Revolution: Time on Paid Work, Domestic Work, and Total Work in East Asian and Western Societies 1985–2016." *Gender & Society* 36(3): 368–96; Carlson, Daniel L., Richard J. Petts, and Joanna R. Pepin. 2022. "Changes in US Parents' Domestic Labor During the Early Days of the COVID-19 Pandemic." *Sociological Inquiry* 92(3): 1217–44; Molina, José Alberto. 2021. "The Work–family Conflict: Evidence from the Recent Decade and Lines of Future Research." *Journal of Family and Economic Issues* 42(1): 4–10.
13. See Gerson, Kathleen. 2010. *The Unfinished Revolution: How a New Generation Is Reshaping Family, Work, and Gender in America.* New York: Oxford University Press. See also Hochschild, Arlie. 1989. *The Second Shift: Working Parents and the Revolution at Home.* New York: Viking. Also Williams, Joan C. 2000. *Unbending Gender: Why Family and Work Conflict and What to Do about It.* New York: Oxford University Press.

14. See Fox, Mary Frank. 1995. "Women and Scientific Careers." In Sheila Jasanoff, Gerald E. Markle, James C. Petersen, and Trevor Pinch (Eds.), *Handbook of Science and Technology Studies*. 205–24. New York: Sage. See also Shapin, Steven. 2008. *The Scientific Life: A Moral History of a Late Modern Vocation*. Chicago: University of Chicago Press.

15. F@W_ST150, White, Woman, 39, Attorney, Jewish, conducted October 18, 2019.

16. See Del Vento Bielby, Denise, and William T. Bielby. 1984. "Work Commitment, Sex-Role Attitudes, and Women's Employment." *American Sociological Review* 49(2): 234–47. See also Blair-Loy, Mary. 2003. *Competing Devotions: Career and Family among Women Executives*. Cambridge, MA: Harvard University Press; Cooper, Maria. 2000. "Being the 'Go-To Guy': Fatherhood, Masculinity, and the Organization of Work in Silicon Valley." *Qualitative Sociology* 23: 379–405; and Epstein, Cynthia Fuchs, Carroll Seron, Bonnie Oglensky, and Robert Sauté. 1999. *The Part-Time Paradox: Time Norms, Professional Life, Family and Gender*. New York: Routledge.

17. Blair-Loy, *Competing Devotions*. Vuga, Janja, and Jelena Juvan. 2013. "Work-Family Conflict between Two Greedy Institutions: The Family and the Military." *Current Sociology* 61(7): 1058–77.

18. See also Whyte, William. 1956. *The Organization Man*. New York: Simon and Schuster.

19. Aumann, Kerstin, Ellen Galinsky, and Kenneth Matos. 2011. *The New Male Mystique*. New York: Families and Work Institute.

20. See Gornick, Janet C., and Marcia Meyers. 2003. *Families That Work: Policies for Reconciling Parenthood and Employment*. New York: Russell Sage Foundation.

21. Parker, Kim, and Wendy Wang. 2013. "Modern Parenthood," Pew Research Center's Social & Demographic Trends Project. March 14. http://www.pewsocialtrends.org/2013/03/14/mod ern-parenthood-roles-of-moms-and-dads-converge-as-they-balance-work-and-family/.

22. F@W_ST18, African American, Woman, 45, Financial Analyst, Mainline, conducted November 28, 2018.

23. See, for example, Shu, Xiaoling, and Kelsey D. Meagher. 2018. "Beyond the Stalled Gender Revolution: Historical and Cohort Dynamics in Gender Attitudes from 1977 to 2016." *Social Forces* 96(3): 1243–74.

24. Our analysis also finds that older individuals and those not engaged in the workforce are more likely to endorse this gender idea, while those with more education are less likely to endorse it.

25. Ordinary least squares regression model predicting gender traditional attitude with personal religiosity, religious tradition, gender, age, education, employment status, and race and ethnicity. Relative to evangelical Protestants, every religious tradition with the exception of Muslims is significantly less likely to endorse the traditional gendered breadwinner-homemaker idea.

26. F@W_ST119, African American, Woman, 26, Case Manager, Muslim, conducted August 28, 2019.

27. F@W_ST65, Alaskan Native, Woman, 35, Small Business Owner, Evangelical, conducted May 16, 2019.

28. F@W_ST16, White, Man, 32, Engineering Consulting, Evangelical, conducted November 26, 2018.

29. F@W_ST96, Caucasian, Man, 50, Actuary, Evangelical, conducted July 3, 2019.

30. F@W_ST54, White, Woman, 36, Nurse Practitioner, Evangelical, conducted February 13, 2019.

31. F@W_ST130, Caucasian American Indian, Woman, 44, Realtor, Evangelical, conducted September 11, 2019.

32. F@W_ST103, White, Woman, 57, Teacher and Librarian, Mainline, conducted July 18, 2019.

33. F@WSUP_27, White, Woman, 33, Data Analyst, Jewish, conducted February 3, 2022.

34. F@W SUP_19, Hispanic, Woman, 26, Associate Commercial Underwriter for Insurance, Evangelical, conducted December 15, 2021.

35. F@WSUP_6, Hispanic, Woman, 40, Life Coach, Evangelical, conducted October 25, 2021.

36. F@WSUP_15, Hispanic, Woman, 35, Middle School Teacher, Catholic, conducted December 2, 2021.

37. Ordinary least squares regression controlling for religious tradition, frequency of religious service attendance during the pandemic (online or in person), children in household, gender, age, education, race, marital status, and income. Other than the noted religious tradition differences, our analysis found no real differences across any of the other predictors in individuals' reports of their faith community helping with school and childcare closures during the pandemic.

38. F@W_ST07, White, Woman, 49, Senior Communications Specialist/University IT, Mainline, conducted October 31, 2018.
39. F@WSUP_12, Black, Woman, 47, Public Health Executive, Black Protestant, conducted November 12, 2021.
40. F@WSUP_14, Asian, Woman, 64, Caregiver/Substitute Teacher, Evangelical, conducted November 30, 2021.
41. F@WSUP_11, Asian, Woman, 68, Business Owner Garden Shop, Mainline, conducted November 10, 2021.
42. F@WSUP_19, Hispanic, Woman, 26, Associate Commercial Underwriter for Insurance, Evangelical, conducted December 15, 2021.
43. F@WSUP_16, Hispanic, Woman, 34, Film Director, Catholic, conducted October 25, 2021.

10

Ways Forward for Religion at Work

We started our research five years ago with three big questions: What criteria
do individuals and organizations use to determine the place of faith in the
workplace? How do social factors and group identities intersect with organizational culture and practice to shape the ways workers express their faith
in the workplace? How can organizational leaders and workers foster intelligent engagement of faith in the workplace in a way that supports healthy
religious pluralism more broadly?

We found that how individuals express their faith at work is shaped, unsurprisingly, by their religious identity, but much more importantly by how
central their faith is to their lives. People who say they are very religious are
much more likely to want to engage their faith at work. We also found that
how workers express and experience religion at work is shaped by their racial and gender identities, their profession, their industry, and their organizational role and rank. For example, Black workers are more likely than
those of other racial groups to feel motivated to talk about their faith at
work. Workers in caretaking industries are more likely to express their religious identity than are those in science and technology fields. Workers in
smaller organizations are more likely than those in larger organizations to
talk about faith or display religious symbols at work, and those at the top of
their organization—particularly men—are more likely to talk about faith at
work than are those at the bottom. These and other findings from our studies
can help organizational leaders begin to understand how different groups of
individuals, from different backgrounds and religious perspectives, in different kinds of organizations, feel about religion at work.

While organizational leaders are beginning to realize that many employees
want to bring their "whole self" to work, they still worry about employees
bringing religion into the workplace, fearing that expressions of faith or religious identity will create conflict, cause offense, or lead to marginalization.
Thus, they often respond by suppressing faith at work, subtly or explicitly encouraging their employees to keep their faith private. When organizational

Religion in a Changing Workplace. Elaine Howard Ecklund, Denise Daniels, and Christopher P. Scheitle,
Oxford University Press. © Oxford University Press 2024. DOI: 10.1093/oso/9780197675007.003.0010

leaders try to keep faith out of the workplace, it can have several unintended consequences. Many workers feel their organization is indifferent or even hostile to their religious or spiritual beliefs and commitments, which can be a key part of their identity. It can minimize a potential source of coping for employees who might otherwise use their faith to deal with difficult work situations. In addition, it can marginalize members of groups that are more likely to take their faith especially seriously, such as nonwhite Christians, Muslims of all races, and women. Failing to include religion as part of diversity and inclusion efforts can also further alienate workers of minority faith traditions, a growing part of the workforce.

In the midst of our research, the COVID-19 pandemic began, creating a natural experiment for reckoning with faith in a changing workplace. The distinctions between work and home were blurred, and workers were less able to separate their work life from their private life. Working from home at least some of the time became the new normal in many organizations. When we looked at the intersection of religion and work during the early months of the pandemic, again we saw both positive and negative consequences. We found that religious communities provided invaluable support in helping families navigate and mitigate work-family conflicts. At the same time, religious ideologies and belief systems that value traditional family and gender roles put more pressure on working women, who felt they should be taking on more responsibilities at home and faced greater feelings of work-life conflict as a result.

Next Steps for a Positive Approach to Religion at Work

Our years of research on this topic lead us to conclude that shutting out religion from the workplace is not only impractical, if not impossible, but also not the best way forward. While it may be difficult to establish an approach to religious expression in the workplace that is useful, productive, healthy, and does not marginalize those who are not adherents, we think it is important for organizational leaders to address religion in the workplace rather than to avoid it. When workplaces are not thoughtful about how to approach religion, inappropriate suppression of religious identity, religious discrimination, and lack of suitable religious accommodation can result. Yet while we are arguing for the benefits that accrue to individuals and workplaces when workers feel they can appropriately express their faith at work, some potential downsides must be reckoned with as well. We have some recommendations for what organizational leaders should look out for and focus on.

Focus on Workers Who Belong to Minority Faith Traditions

US workplaces are changing. In most regions of the country and in most industries the majority of workers are Christians or nonreligious. But there are growing numbers of those of minority faith traditions—primarily Muslim and Jewish workers, but also Buddhists, Hindus, Sikhs, and others. While we have demonstrated that many workers experience positive outcomes when they engage their religious identity at work, we also found that there is particular concern among religious minority workers over whether they have equal opportunity to express their beliefs in the workplace. In response to concerns about how their faith perspectives might be received, many of the workers from minority religious traditions we spoke with talked about compartmentalizing their faith at work. Organizational leaders can begin to address religion in the workplace by taking stock of faith-based policies, dismantling biased practices, and building an inclusive environment in which all workers feel equally comfortable and safe sharing their religious identities.

Understand Workers Who Do Not See Their Work as a Calling—and Those Who Do

Regardless of their organizational position or salary, workers who view their work as a spiritual calling have higher levels of life and work satisfaction than those who do not feel spiritually called to their work.[1] Our national survey shows that 53 percent of those who feel called to their work strongly agree that they are "very satisfied" with their current job, compared with 39 percent of those who do not feel called to their work.[2] Seeing their work as a calling is also connected with better job performance and stronger commitment to their jobs. Organizational leaders can foster a sense of calling among their workers by emphasizing the purpose and value of their work, reminding them how their work helps others, or focusing on how the organization contributes to the common good. For those at the bottom of an organization—who are less likely than those at the top to see their work as a calling—organizational leaders can help these employees reframe or recraft their jobs where possible to make work feel more meaningful. We found that when an individual attaches meaning and purpose to work that is hard or unappealing, it can significantly impact their short- and long-term well-being, reducing the stress they experience in difficult workplace situations.

Organizational leaders should also be on the lookout, however, for workers who are feeling burned out due to their sense of calling. As research has shown, because workers who feel called to their work have a high level of commitment to their jobs, they tend to be more likely to suffer through or ignore work situations that are unfair, overwhelming, unreasonable, or exploitative. We also found that workers who see their job as a spiritual calling may be less able to empathize with those who are unhappy or unfulfilled in their work, and thus might not recognize or care when their fellow workers are suffering or discontent in their roles.

Understand How Workers Use Religion to Cope

Many workers said feeling spiritually called to their work helps them get through the extraordinarily difficult or mundane aspects of their job, and religious and spiritual ideas and behaviors help workers cope with a variety of stressors and their effects—which affords obvious benefits at work. Yet workers who use religion to cope can inadvertently mask toxic aspects of their work, making it difficult for organizational leaders to see when the workplace is creating unhealthy stress or likely to cause burnout. This in turn puts the onus on workers to rely even more on their personal religious beliefs and practices to help them cope with the challenges of their job. Organizational leaders will want to make sure that workers who use religion to cope with stress at work are not allowing systemic workplace issues to be swept under the rug. Allowing structural problems to go unaddressed could lead to workers struggling due to stress, frustration, or other negative feelings, and may ultimately lead to increased turnover.

Workers Who Prioritize Religious Ethics

According to our findings, most employees believe they act ethically in the workplace. However, the more religious a person is, the more they want their day-to-day ethical decisions to be shaped by their religiously informed moral frameworks.[3] While this can lead to positive outcomes, it can also lead to workplace conflict. For one, religious ethics in the workplace most often operates at the personal level rather than the structural level, and religious workers often find that the moral codes and expectations of their religion outweigh the role expectations of their workplace or profession, causing tension or unease. Workplace leaders might look out for places where religious workers could feel discord between the moral and ethical codes of their religion and the "occupational rules-in-use"[4] so that they can address such situations as they arise.

Know That Younger Workers Will Change the Dynamics

Younger workers are both less likely to be part of a traditional religion *and* want to be able to express their faith and values in the workplace. And for many, diversity, equity, and inclusion efforts are extremely important. Early-career workers told us they wrestled with how to express their faith at work and said they wanted clear direction from their organization on how to do so in ways that are acceptable and appropriate, and demonstrate respect for others in the workplace. We are reminded of the twenty-three-year-old Catholic engineer,[5] for example, who said he wants people to be better equipped to have "a rational conversation" with those of different religions in ways that encourage openness and curiosity.

Know That Perceived Religious Discrimination Involves Minority and Majority Groups

We found that religious discrimination and harassment are present, pervasive, and on the rise in US workplaces, and members of all religious groups who observe religious holidays or display religious symbols in the workplace think they experience verbal microaggressions, stereotyping, and social exclusion as a result. Individuals who express their faith at work perceive more religious discrimination than those who do not. Christian, Muslim, Jewish, and nonreligious workers all talked about feeling they have to be careful in how they express their beliefs at work due to fear of mistreatment or judgment. It might surprise organizational leaders to discover that Christian workers say they can feel discriminated against in the workplace, with a significant proportion of Black Christians saying they perceive religious discrimination at work. Christian workers tend to feel that the discrimination they perceive against them results from them taking a moral stand or expressing piety in the workplace. Evangelical Christians are especially likely to report discrimination in the western United States, which should be of particular interest to organizational leaders in that region of the country.

Muslim and Jewish workers, however, report experiencing religious discrimination in the workplace much more often than Christians do. Workers from these religious groups describe feeling they are seen as religiously foreign and tend to link perceived discrimination against them to group-based identities—just being Muslim or Jewish. Among the religious workers we surveyed, Muslims reported the highest levels of religious discrimination in the workplace, and they are much more likely to report at least some experience with workplace discrimination in the South and West when compared to Muslims in the Northeast. Workplace leaders in these regions should marshal more of their energies toward thinking about how to protect workers who are members of these religious groups. It is also important to pay special attention to workers who experience religious discrimination in the workplace because our data show that workers who report some experience with religious discrimination at work are more likely to also report experiencing discrimination based on their sex or gender or their race or ethnicity. Whether this is because of structural elements in the workplace or because these workers are more attuned to discrimination and thus more likely to perceive it, organizational leaders can benefit from being aware of the connection, looking out for these workers particularly, and making efforts to counteract workplace discrimination of any kind.

Our Final Bottom Line

We believe that workplaces should be faith friendly. We have found that employees can express their faith at work in ways that are important and valuable to them, show consideration for coworkers with different belief systems, and foster a sense of community and belonging in the workplace.[6] In some cases, talking about faith at work can help workers develop understanding and respect for (or at least tolerance of) those of other faiths. Trying to ignore or suppress religion in the workplace is misguided and not consequence free. Creating a faith-friendly workplace includes making sure that workers feel that they can be their true selves, creating a culture in which workers feel safe to express their beliefs, meeting the needs of all religious individuals, addressing biases and discrimination, protecting those—including the nonreligious—who may experience others' sincerely held beliefs as dismissive or denigrating, and promoting religious diversity and inclusion. Supporting religious workers in the workplace is not just a requirement to avoid lawsuits or a bitter pill to be swallowed. Sincere and informed efforts can help ensure that the positive side of this double-edged sword is experienced. In the end, workplaces can benefit from organizational leaders who take the time to understand and attend to the impacts and outcomes of religion at work, making the workplace more supportive for all.

Notes

1. Wrzesniewski, Amy, Clark McCauley, Paul Rozin, and Barry Schwartz. 1997. "Jobs, Careers, and Callings: People's Relations to Their Work." *Journal of Research in Personality* 31(1): 21–33; Dobrow, Shoshana R., Hannah Weisman, Daniel Heller, and Jennifer Tosti-Kharas. 2023. "Calling and the Good Life: A Meta-Analysis and Theoretical Extension." *Administrative Science Quarterly*, 68(2): 508–50.
2. This cross-tabulation is statistically significant at $p < .001$ (design-based F test). This difference remains even if we look at only very religious individuals.
3. Bader, Christopher D., and Roger Finke. 2010. "What Does God Require? Understanding Religious Context and Morality." In Steven Hitlin and Stephen Vaisey (Eds.). *Handbook of the Sociology of Morality*. 241–54 New York: Springer.
4. Jackall, Robert. 2010. "Morality in Organizations." In Steven Hitlin and Stephen Vaisey (Eds.), *Handbook of the Sociology of Morality*. 203–10. New York: Springer.
5. F@W_ST72, White, Man, 23, Engineer, Catholic, conducted May 29, 2019.
6. Ecklund, Elaine Howard, Denise Daniels, Daniel Bolger, and Laura Johnson. 2020. "A Nationally Representative Survey of Faith and Work: Demographic Subgroup Differences around Calling and Conflict." *Religions* 11(6): 287, 1–18; Ecklund, Elaine Howard, Denise Daniels, and Rachel C. Schneider. 2020. "From Secular to Sacred: Bringing Work to Church." *Religions* 11(9): 442, 1–24.

Appendices

Appendix A

Methodology

This book is based on data from two connected studies: the Faith at Work Study and the Faith at Work Supplement Study, the latter of which specifically examines faith at work during the COVID-19 pandemic.

Faith at Work Study

The Faith at Work Study was a groundbreaking and comprehensive study of how people integrate faith and work through a broad-based general US population survey as well as in-depth, follow-up interviews.

Survey

The survey was fielded from October 2, 2018, to December 15, 2018, using the Gallup Panel, a probability-based panel of US adults that are recruited using random-digit-dial (RDD) phone interviews that cover landlines and cell phones and address-based sampling methods (ABS). A stratified sample of 29,345 US adults were drawn from the Gallup Panel. The demographic distribution of the sample matched the US population targets for US adults obtained from the 2017 Current Population Survey. Additionally, the stratified sample included oversamples of 752 preidentified Muslim and 882 preidentified Jewish respondents. By mode, 24,534 web and 4,811 mail Panel members were sampled. By language, 27,766 English and 1,579 Spanish Panel members were sampled.

A total of 13,270 people completed the survey. This equates to an overall completion rate of 45.2 percent. This completion rate was higher among the Jewish subsample (65 percent) and lower among the Muslim subsample (27 percent). Response rates for panel surveys must also take into account all stages of selection into the sample, which occurs in several stages. Panel recruiting begins on the Gallup Daily tracking survey, which has an average American Association for Public Opinion Research (AAPOR) Response Rate 3 (RR3) of 12 percent. An average of 77 percent of respondents agreed to recontact, and the average response rate (RR3) for the panel recruitment is 28 percent. The overall final response rate for the survey, accounting for all stages of the survey, is 1.2 percent (.12 * .77 * .28 * .452).

Interviews

Interviews occurred during project years two and three. In total, we interviewed 205 workers from our survey who—based on their survey responses—stated that they were working full-time, part-time, or not currently working but looking for work; identified with a religious tradition; and were at least somewhat active in a religious community based on their frequency of religious service attendance. We also interviewed 12 nonreligious workers from our survey. We selected all interview subjects with the goal of ensuring a representative distribution across gender and race and ethnicity. However, twelve interviews with workers were ultimately excluded from our analyses because the subject had infrequent religious service attendance or because they did not identify as Christian, Muslim, or Jewish. In the end, we analyzed 182 worker interviews consisting of 159 Christians, 10 Muslims, and 13 Jewish subjects.

Additionally, we interviewed 29 Christian religious leaders. All 29 interviews with religious leaders were included in the final pastor interview sample.

Pandemic, Faith, and Work Study

The Pandemic, Faith, and Work Study was conceived as a supplement to the Faith at Work Study as the latter was in progress to assess how two emergent crises—the COVID-19 pandemic and racial conflict in the United States—were shaping the relationship between faith and work for US adults. This supplemental project included a population survey and in-depth interviews to explore the nuanced implications—including the social, economic, and spiritual realities—of these crises in the lives of workers and the faith leaders who work and serve among them, with a particular focus on the lives of Black and brown workers.

Survey

The survey for the Pandemic, Faith, and Work Study was fielded from September 7, 2021, to October 4, 2021, via a web survey. US adults were selected from the Gallup Panel, a probability-based panel of US adults that is recruited using random-digit-dial (RDD) phone interviews that cover landlines and cell phones and address-based sampling methods (ABS). Gallup statisticians in total drew a sample of 9,299 adults, ages eighteen and older.

First, a sample of 4,933 was drawn. Of these, 250 cases were randomly assigned to the pilot, and 4,683 were assigned to the full survey launch. However, during the main field period, participation fell behind anticipated response rates, and additional reminders resulted in very few new completes. Therefore, to meet the required number of completes, additional sample was pulled (4,366) and sent the survey on October 1, 2021. The number of additional required completes could only be achieved through the addition of new sample. Other strategies, such as increased incentives, would not have improved response rates enough to reach the required number of completes. The demographic distribution of the sample matched the US population targets for US adults obtained from the 2019 Current Population Survey based on age, race, ethnicity, and education level.

A total of 2,486 people completed the survey. This equates to an overall completion rate of 26.7 percent. Response rates for panel surveys must also take into account all stages of selection into the sample, which occurs in several stages. Panel recruiting begins on the Gallup Daily tracking survey, which has an average AAPOR RR3 of 8 percent. The overall final response rate for the survey, accounting for all stages of the survey, is 2.1 percent (.08 * .267).

Interviews

At the end of the survey, respondents were asked if they would be willing to be recontacted for a follow-up interview, and 1,405 agreed to be recontacted. Gallup provided the contact information for any survey takers who agreed to be contacted. Generally, first name, email address, and phone number were provided. Contact began while the survey was still taking place, based on information provided in weekly recontact files. We contacted 107 survey takers to participate in follow-up interviews with the goal of generating a racially and religiously diverse sample of interview subjects. Fifty-one respondents completed interviews.

Appendix B

Faith at Work Main Survey Guide

Q1. Which of the following best describes your current employment status?
  1. Employed full-time
  2. Employed part-time
  3. Not employed but looking for work
  4. Not employed and not currently looking for work
Q2. How many jobs do you have? [Only asked of those who code 1 or 2 in Q1]
Q3. Do any of the following categories currently apply to you? Mark all that apply.
  1. Self-employed
  2. Homemaker
  3. Student
  4. Volunteer
  5. Retired
  6. Unable to work
  7. None of these apply to me
Q4. How many hours a week do you usually work (if you have more than one job, please include all hours you spend working). [Only asked of those who code 1 or 2 in Q1]
Q5. How many hours a week do you usually provide caretaking without pay (e.g., caring for children or elders)?
  As you answer the remaining questions in this survey, please think about your typical experience at work. If you have multiple jobs, think about your experience across all of your jobs. If you are retired, think about how you would have responded in your most recent job.
  Please indicate your level of agreement or disagreement with each of the following items.
Q6. The primary reason I work is to make money. [Only asked of those who code 1 in Q1, code 2 in Q1, code 1 in Q3, or code 5 in Q3]
  1. Strongly agree
  2. Somewhat agree
  3. Neither disagree nor agree
  4. Somewhat disagree
  5. Strongly disagree

Q7. It would be easy for me to get another job if I wanted to. [Only asked of those who code 1 in Q1, code 2 in Q1, code 1 in Q3, or code 5 in Q3]
1. Strongly agree
2. Somewhat agree
3. Neither disagree nor agree
4. Somewhat disagree
5. Strongly disagree

Q8. I have a lot of freedom to make decisions in my work. [Only asked of those who code 1 in Q1, code 2 in Q1, code 1 in Q3, or code 5 in Q3]
1. Strongly agree
2. Somewhat agree
3. Neither disagree nor agree
4. Somewhat disagree
5. Strongly disagree

Q9. Overall, I am very satisfied with my current job. [Only asked of those who code 1 in Q1, code 2 in Q1, code 1 in Q3, or code 5 in Q3]
1. Strongly agree
2. Somewhat agree
3. Neither disagree nor agree
4. Somewhat disagree
5. Strongly disagree

Q10. I feel a strong sense of commitment to the organization I work for. [Only asked of those who code 1 in Q1, code 2 in Q1, code 1 in Q3, or code 5 in Q3]
1. Strongly agree
2. Somewhat agree
3. Neither disagree nor agree
4. Somewhat disagree
5. Strongly disagree

Q11. How often do you feel a sense of "burnout"—meaning physical or mental exhaustion caused by overwork or stress—in your work? [Only asked of those who code 1 in Q1, code 2 in Q1, code 1 in Q3, or code 5 in Q3]
1. Strongly agree
2. Somewhat agree
3. Neither disagree nor agree
4. Somewhat disagree
5. Strongly disagree

Q12. Anyone can find a good job if they try hard enough. [Only asked of those who code 1 in Q1, code 2 in Q1, code 1 in Q3, or code 5 in Q3]
1. Strongly agree
2. Somewhat agree
3. Neither disagree nor agree
4. Somewhat disagree
5. Strongly disagree

Q13. It is much better for everyone involved if the man earns the money and the woman takes care of the home and children. [Only asked of those who code 1 in Q1, code 2 in Q1, code 1 in Q3, or code 5 in Q3]
1. Strongly agree
2. Somewhat agree
3. Neither disagree nor agree

4. Somewhat disagree
5. Strongly disagree

Q14. Currently, what is your religious identity?
1. Protestant
2. Catholic
3. Other Christian
4. Jewish
5. Muslim
6. Buddhist
7. Hindu
8. Other
9. No religion

Q15. Which of the following best describes your religious congregation? Mark all that apply. [Only asked of those who code 1, 2, or 3 in Q14]
1. Fundamentalist
2. Evangelical
3. Mainline
4. Liberal
5. Charismatic
6. None
7. Don't know

Q16. How often do you attend religious services?
1. Never
2. Less than once a year
3. Once a year
4. Several times a year
5. Once a month
6. 2 to 3 times a month
7. Nearly every week
8. Every week
9. More than once a week

Q17. About how often do you pray?
1. Never
2. Less than once a week
3. Once a week
4. Several times a week
5. Once a day
6. Several times a day

Q18. Independently of whether you attend religious services or not, would you say you are...?
1. Not at all religious
2. Slightly religious
3. Moderately religious
4. Very religious

Q19. To what extent do you consider yourself a spiritual person?
1. Not at all spiritual
2. Slightly spiritual
3. Moderately spiritual
4. Very spiritual

Q20. Please indicate which statement below comes closest to expressing what you believe about God.
1. I don't believe in God
2. I don't know whether there is a God, and I don't believe there is any way to find out.
3. I don't believe in a personal God, but I do believe in a Higher Power of some kind
4. I find myself believing in God some of the time, but not at others
5. While I have doubts, I feel that I do believe in God
6. I know God really exists and I have no doubts about it

Q21. Which of these statements comes closest to describing your feelings about the Bible?
1. The Bible is the actual word of God and is to be taken literally, word for word
2. The Bible is the inspired word of God but not everything should be taken literally, word for word
3. The Bible is an ancient book of fables, legends, history, and moral precepts recorded by Man
4. Don't know

Q22. Please indicate which statement below comes closest to expressing what you believed about God at age 16.
1. I didn't believe in God
2. I didn't know whether there was a God and I didn't believe there was any way to find out
3. I didn't believe in a personal God, but I did believe in a Higher Power of some kind
4. I found myself believing in God some of the time, but not at others
5. While I had doubts, I felt that I did believe in God
6. I knew God really existed and I had no doubts about it

Q23. Please indicate the extent to which you agree or disagree with the following statements. If you are retired, think about how you would have responded in your most recent job. For some people these items will not feel applicable. If you do not feel a question is relevant for you, select "Not applicable." [Only asked of those who code 1 in Q1, code 2 in Q1, code 1 in Q3, or code 5 in Q3]
a) Even if it does not benefit me, I always act with integrity at work.
b) I express my view when I observe unfair work practices that conflict with my faith/spirituality.
c) I feel motivated to talk about my faith/spirituality with people at work.
d) At work, I display or wear items that represent my faith/spirituality.
e) I benefit from praying or meditating privately at work.
f) I value participating with others in a faith/spiritual group or activity to help me better deal with work-related issues.
g) My faith/spirituality helps me experience meaning and purpose in my daily work tasks.
h) The end product or service itself produced by my organization is highly meaningful to me.
1. Strongly disagree
2. Somewhat disagree
3. Neither disagree nor agree

  4. Somewhat agree
  5. Strongly agree
  6. Not applicable

Q24. My faith or spirituality influenced the choice of my current job(s). Do you . . . [Only asked of those who code 1 in Q1, code 2 in Q1, code 1 in Q3, or code 5 in Q3]
  1. Strongly agree
  2. Somewhat agree
  3. Neither disagree nor agree
  4. Somewhat disagree
  5. Strongly disagree
  6. This does not apply to me

Q25. I see my work as a spiritual calling. [Only asked of those who code 1 in Q1, code 2 in Q1, code 1 in Q3, or code 5 in Q3]
  1. Strongly agree
  2. Somewhat agree
  3. Neither disagree nor agree
  4. Somewhat disagree
  5. Strongly disagree

Q26. Skills and habits that I have learned from my faith community help me succeed at work. [Only asked of those who code 1 in Q1, code 2 in Q1, code 1 in Q3, or code 5 in Q3]
  1. Strongly agree
  2. Somewhat agree
  3. Neither disagree nor agree
  4. Somewhat disagree
  5. Strongly disagree
  6. I do not have a faith community

Q27. At work, I am expected to act in ways that contradict my religious beliefs. [Only asked of those who code 1 in Q1, code 2 in Q1, code 1 in Q3, or code 5 in Q3]
  1. Never
  2. Rarely
  3. Sometimes
  4. Often
  5. Very often
  6. I do not have religious beliefs

Q28. I feel comfortable talking about my faith at work. [Only asked of those who code 1 in Q1, code 2 in Q1, code 1 in Q3, or code 5 in Q3]
  1. Strongly agree
  2. Somewhat agree
  3. Neither disagree nor agree
  4. Somewhat disagree
  5. Strongly disagree
  6. This does not apply to me

Q29. My faith guides me through stressful times in my work-life. [Only asked of those who code 1 in Q1, code 2 in Q1, code 1 in Q3, or code 5 in Q3]
  1. Strongly agree
  2. Somewhat agree

3. Neither disagree nor agree
4. Somewhat disagree
5. Strongly disagree
6. This does not apply to me

Q30. My faith community supports me in my work or career. [Only asked of those who code 1 in Q1, code 2 in Q1, code 1 in Q3, or code 5 in Q3]

1. Strongly agree
2. Somewhat agree
3. Neither disagree nor agree
4. Somewhat disagree
5. Strongly disagree
6. I do not have a faith community

Q31. The people I work with have influenced my thoughts about faith. [Only asked of those who code 1 in Q1, code 2 in Q1, code 1 in Q3, or code 5 in Q3]

1. Strongly agree
2. Somewhat agree
3. Neither disagree nor agree
4. Somewhat disagree
5. Strongly disagree

Turning now to some questions about your personal experiences.

Q32. Throughout your lifetime, how often have you felt that you have been treated unfairly in the context of your work because of the following:

a) Your religion or non-religion
b) Your sex or gender
c) Your marital status (e.g., married, divorced, separated, single)
d) Your race or ethnicity
e) Your sexual orientation (e.g., heterosexual, homosexual, bisexual)
f) Your national origin
g) Your disability
h) Your criminal background

   1. Never
   2. Rarely
   3. Sometimes
   4. Often
   5. Very often
   6. Not applicable

Q33. How often do you participate in discussion groups about faith and work?

1. Not at all
2. Less than once per month
3. 1–2 times per month
4. 3–4 times per month
5. 5 or more times per month

Q34. My faith leader teaches about the meaning of work.

1. Never
2. Rarely
3. Sometimes
4. Often
5. Very often
6. I do not have a faith leader

Q35. My faith leader discusses how we should behave at work.
1. Never
2. Rarely
3. Sometimes
4. Often
5. Very often
6. I do not have a faith leader

Q36. How often do you talk with a faith leader about workplace issues?
1. Never
2. Rarely
3. Sometimes
4. Often
5. Very often

Q37. Now we'd like to ask you some questions about how you perceive yourself and your background. Here are a number of personality traits that may or may not apply to you. Please indicate the extent to which you agree or disagree with each statement. You should rate the extent to which the pair of traits applies to you, even if one characteristic applies more strongly than the other.
I see myself as:
a. Extroverted, enthusiastic
b. Critical, quarrelsome
c. Dependable, self-disciplined
d. Anxious, easily upset
e. Open to new experiences, complex
f. Reserved, quiet
g. Sympathetic, warm
h. Disorganized, careless
i. Calm, emotionally stable
j. Conventional, uncreative
  1. Disagree strongly
  2. Disagree moderately
  3. Disagree a little
  4. Neither agree or disagree
  5. Agree a little
  6. Agree moderately
  7. Agree strongly

Q38. Which of the following categories best describe the industry you primarily work/worked in? Mark all that apply. [Only asked of those who code 1 in Q1, code 2 in Q1, code 1 in Q3, or code 5 in Q3]
1. Architecture or engineering
2. Arts, design, entertainment, or media
3. Business or finance
4. Caretaking (e.g., child care or elder care)
5. Community or social services
6. Computer or mathematical
7. Construction or mining
8. Education, training, or library

     9. Farming, fishing, or forestry

    10. Food service or hospitality

    11. Healthcare

    12. Installation, maintenance, or repair

    13. Legal

    14. Life, physical, and social sciences

    15. Manufacturing or production

    16. Military

    17. Religion

    18. Retail or sales

    19. Transportation

    20. Other

Q39. Think about the organization of job roles in your industry, where the leaders are at the top of the organization and employees are at the bottom of the organization. Would you say that you are toward the top of the organization, middle, or at the bottom? [Only asked of those who code 1 in Q1, code 2 in Q1, code 1 in Q3, or code 5 in Q3]

    1. Top

    2. Middle

    3. Bottom

Q40. About how many people work at the location where you work? (Please include part-time and full-time employees in all areas, departments, and buildings.) [Only asked of those who code 1 in Q1, code 2 in Q1, code 1 in Q3, or code 5 in Q3]

    1. 1 to 9

    2. 10 to 49

    3. 50 to 99

    4. 100 to 499

    5. 500 to 999

    6. 1,000 to 1,999

    7. 2,000 or more

    8. Don't know

Q41. About how long have you worked for your current organization? [Only asked of those who code 1 in Q1, code 2 in Q1, code 1 in Q3, or code 5 in Q3]

    1. Less than a year

    2. 1 to 5 years

    3. 6 to 10 years

    4. 11 to 20 years

    5. 21 to 30 years

    6. More than 30 years

Q42. Are you a manager? A manager is someone whose primary role is to manage or supervise others. [Only asked of those who code 1 in Q1, code 2 in Q1, code 1 in Q3, or code 5 in Q3]

    1. Yes

    2. No

Q43. What best describes the type of organization you work for? [Only asked of those who code 1 in Q1, code 2 in Q1, code 1 in Q3, or code 5 in Q3]

    1. For-profit

2. Non-profit

3. Hybrid—both for-profit and non-profit

4. Government

5. Other

Q44. Does your organization have a religious mission? [Only asked of those who code 1 in Q1, code 2 in Q1, code 1 in Q3, or code 5 in Q3]

1. Yes

2. No

3. Don't know

Q45. In the past three years, were you ever unemployed and looking for a job for more than one month?

1. Yes

2. No

3. Don't know

Q46. What was the sex on your original birth certificate?

1. Male

2. Female

3. Prefer not to say

Q47. What is your current gender?

1. Man

2. Woman

3. Prefer to self-describe

4. Prefer not to say

Q48. Which of the following best describes you?

a. Heterosexual or straight

b. Gay, lesbian, or homosexual

c. Bisexual

d. Prefer to self-describe

e. Prefer not to say

f. Don't know

Q49. What is the highest level of school that your mother (or your female primary care-giver during childhood) completed or the highest degree they have received?

1. Less than a high school diploma

2. High school graduate or GED

3. Technical, trade, or vocational

4. Some college but no degree

5. Two-year associate degree

6. Four-year bachelor's degree

7. Some postgraduate or professional schooling

8. Postgraduate or professional degree

9. This does not apply to me

Q50. What is the highest level of education that your father (or your male primary care-giver during childhood) completed or the highest degree they have received?

1. Less than a high school diploma

2. High school graduate or GED

3. Technical, trade, or vocational

4. Some college but no degree
5. Two-year associate degree
6. Four-year bachelor's degree
7. Some postgraduate or professional schooling
8. Postgraduate or professional degree
9. This does not apply to me

Q51. Are you currently . . .
1. Married
2. Living with a partner
3. Divorced
4. Separated
5. Widowed
6. Single

Q52. What is your total ANNUAL household income, before taxes? Please include income from wages and salaries, remittances from family members living elsewhere, farming, and all other sources.
1. Less than $12,000
2. $12,000 to $23,999
3. $24,000 to $35,999
4. $36,000 to $47,999
5. $48,000 to $59,999
6. $60,000 to $89,999
7. $90,000 to $119,999
8. $120,000 to $179,999
9. $180,000 to $239,999
10. $240,000 to $1,000,000
11. More than $1,000,000
12. Don't know

Q53. How many children are currently living in your household?

Q54. There is a lot of talk these days about liberals and conservatives. On a scale of extremely liberal to extremely conservative, where would you place yourself?
1. Extremely liberal
2. Liberal
3. Slightly liberal
4. Moderate
5. Slightly conservative
6. Conservative
7. Extremely conservative

Q55. Is English your first language?
1. Yes
2. No

Q56. Did one or both of your parents immigrate to the United States?
1. Yes
2. No

Q57. Did you immigrate to the United States?
1. Yes
2. No

Q58. In what year did you immigrate to the United States? [Only asked of those who code 1 in Q57]

Q59. Thank you very much for answering all of these questions. Researchers at Rice University and Seattle Pacific University (SPU) would like to invite some people who completed this survey to take part in a follow-up interview about the topics discussed in this survey. People who participate in the follow-up interview will receive a $30 incentive for your participation. Do you want to be considered for this opportunity? If you select "yes" Gallup will provide researchers at Rice and SPU with your name and contact information. They will only be allowed to contact you regarding the follow-up interview. If you select "no" or leave this question blank, your personal contact information will not be provided to Rice and SPU.

    1. Yes

    2. No

This is the end of the survey. Thank you very much for taking part. We are very grateful to you for contributing your time to this academic research. Please place your completed questionnaire in the postage-paid envelope provided and return it to Gallup. If you have any comments about this survey, you can enclose them on a separate piece of paper.

Appendix C

Faith at Work Main Interview Guide

Background Information

1. Why don't we start with you telling me—in just a few sentences—a little bit about what you do for a living? What's your job title, if you don't mind me asking?
2. Could you walk me through some of the tasks or responsibilities you have as part of your work?
3. Specifically, do you have responsibility for others and for their work as part of your job?
4. Could you help me understand your workplace a bit better just in terms of diversity? PROBES: To what extent is your workplace a diverse environment? [*Interviewer should probe to get a sense of how respondent thinks about diversity*] Are most of your colleagues women/men? What about race? Is there any religious diversity that you are aware of?
5. In terms of your day-to-day work, some people say they feel pressed for time in their work. Does that kind of statement resonate with you? If so, what kind of time pressures do you have?
6. How about something else? Some people tell us that they feel bored at work. Is that something that you identify with? Tell me a bit more.
7. Some people say the demands of work interfere with other areas of life (i.e., relationships, leisure, sleep, etc.). Does that statement ring true for you? Tell me a bit about how this is true for you.
8. Do you attend church? Could you tell me a bit about your church? For example, what tradition or denomination is the church? [For Jewish and Muslim respondents] Are you a part of a [synagogue/masjid]? Could you tell me a bit about it? For example, what tradition is it?
9. About how long have you been attending this particular church? And what activities are you most involved in? [For Jewish and Muslim respondents] About how

long have you been a part of this particular community? And what activities are you most involved in?

10. And some other specific questions about your church: about how many people do you think attend on a weekly basis?

11. Do you have any feel about what percentage are male versus female, as well as the percentage of different racial groups?

Faith and Work

As you know, part of what I am interested in studying is how you understand the relationship between your faith and your work.

12. Think for a moment about the work you do. To what extent do you see your work as a spiritual calling, for example? Could you say more about why? [for Jewish and Muslim respondents] PROBE: Do you view your work as a form of tikkun olam / Zakat? Tell me a little about why you do or do not see this concept as being aligned with your work.

13. There are a number of factors that motivate people to accept jobs. What made you decide to take your current job?

14. In what ways, specifically, did your faith influence your decision to take your job?

15. Some people say that certain jobs are more valuable than other jobs, specifically in terms of serving God. How would you respond to that kind of thinking?

16. In what ways do you think your faith affects the work you do at your job? PROBE: To what extent does your faith affect how you interact with others, manage stress, or approach your work responsibilities?

17. To what extent does your faith compel you to create change at your workplace?

18. Do you have a boss or manager? What would you like to say to your boss or management about the issue of religion in the workplace?

Expressing Faith in the Workplace

I also have some questions about how you express faith in the workplace.

19. To what extent do you think people ought to openly express faith in workplaces? PROBE: Do you consider your workplace a generally safe place to express yourself in this way, or have you ever experienced difficulties?

20. And how about you? Do you express your faith openly in your workplace? Tell me a little bit about why you do or why you hesitate to express your faith in this way.

21. To your knowledge, are there any policies in place regarding expressions of faith in the workplace? If so, what are they?

22. To what extent does your workplace accommodate employees who want to pray during work hours (i.e., access to prayer rooms)?

23. Can you tell me a little bit about any restrictions your workplace has regarding religious attire?

24. How does your workplace handle holiday celebrations?

25. Do you know any of your colleagues for whom faith is very important? How do you know faith is important to these colleagues? PROBE: Do they wear religious symbols or keep any in their office space? Do you know through conversation?

26. Thinking more generally, to what extent do you see your religious colleagues as different from your nonreligious colleagues? PROBE: Have you noticed that your

religious colleagues view work differently than your nonreligious colleagues? Is the quality of their work different in any way? Do they handle stress differently?

Faith and Conflict in the Workplace

I'd like to turn now to some additional issues related to religious conflict in the workplace.

27. Have you ever been treated differently in your place of work due to your religious identity or religious beliefs? If so, how would you describe that experience?
28. Have you personally experienced any religious discrimination in your workplace? PROBE: Do you think you've been treated differently in the workplace because of religious symbols or articles of faith you wear?
29. And related, have you noticed anyone else experiencing any religious discrimination in your workplace? PROBE: It would be helpful if you could tell me a little bit more about what happened.
30. Do you have any experience participating in diversity trainings/workshops in your workplace? If so, describe the nature of the training session and what kind of issues were discussed. Did religion ever come up? PROBE: Did you find these training sessions beneficial personally? [*Try to get a sense broadly of whether they think that diversity training is at all useful*] How about in terms of the overall workplace dynamic? In your sense of things, what would make these training sessions more useful?
31. Some people have told us that they feel uneasy about a task related to their job because of their religious faith. Does that ring true for you? PROBE: Can you describe any particular situations where this was the case? How did you manage that situation?
32. People have also said that they feel ethically uncomfortable about the products or services their organization provides. Is anything like that relevant to you?
33. To what extent have you been treated unfairly or differently at work because of your sex or gender?
34. Some people say that they are treated unfairly or differently at work because of their race or ethnicity. For you personally, is this the case? PROBE: If so, could you tell me a bit more about that?
35. IF YOU HAVE BEEN TREATED UNFAIRLY AT WORK, to what extent has your faith helped you to deal with that situation? PROBE: How specifically did it help or not help?
36. Do you have a boss or manager? What would you like to say to your boss or management about the issue of religion in the workplace?

Churches and Work

Switching now to how work might come up in your local church.

37. Does your pastor/priest or other leader in your church ever bring up faith in the workplace specifically? What does that look like?
38. Do you ever participate in religious groups (i.e., *small group, life group, or house church*) where faith in the workplace is discussed? PROBE: What was the setting for this group, and what did you discuss?
39. What other settings does talk about work come up in your church or faith community?

40. Are there any skills you have learned through church that you find also help you at work? Could you tell me a bit more about that?
41. Have you ever had a conversation with your religious leader or other members of your church community about difficulties you have experienced at work? What were those discussions like? Did they help?
42. What resources, if any, from your church have you found to be most helpful in dealing with work-related issues? PROBE: Have you found any other religious or spiritual resources to be helpful in dealing with work issues? What were they? How did they help you?
43. To what extent do you think people in your particular kind of job are supported in their work at your church? [*Quickly summarize the work the respondent does in a phrase.*]
44. Is your church's support for people who work different for women than for men? What makes you say this? PROBE: Can you give me a story or an example of this?
45. To what extent do you feel your responsibilities at home create additional stress for your work
46. We are also interested in helping faith communities to better address the topic of faith and work. If you could have the world any way you want it, what suggestions would you make about how faith leaders can better support people in their work?

Concluding Questions

47. How about issues of gender equality in the workplace? Has your pastor or church leader ever brought up anything related to these issues?
48. How about sexual harassment or #METOO type issues; has your pastor or church leader brought up things related to those?
49. How about things related to racism in the workplace? Has your pastor or really anyone in your church brought up things like that?
50. Are there any other issues related to faith and work that I didn't mention that you think are important?

Demographic Questions
Just for bookkeeping, I'd now like to ask you some questions to help me situate you among other individuals I have talked with. Again, all this information will be strictly confidential.

51. How old are you?
52. How would you describe yourself racially or ethnically?
53. Are you currently married or in a long-term committed relationship? [*Discern which one.*]
54. What is the best religious label for you?
55. Do you have any children?
    a. IF YES, how many?
    b. What are their ages?
56. What level of schooling have you been through?
57. What is your occupation?
58. IF MARRIED OR PARTNERED, what is your spouse's occupation?
59. What state do you live in?
60. What is your country of origin?
    a. How many years have you lived in the US?

Appendix D

Faith at Work Supplemental Survey Guide

Gallup is conducting this study on behalf of researchers at Rice University and Wheaton College. The survey will cover a variety of issues, reflecting our broad interest in studying how people understand their work.

In this survey, we are interested in your experiences with and opinions about faith and work, especially changes to your work and the workplace in light of the pandemic and national conversations about race. You do not need to be religious in any way to complete this survey as we are interested in understanding how everyone in the United States feels about these topics.

Please note that your participation in this survey is optional. If you complete this questionnaire, your information will be kept private and combined with responses of other people for research purposes only. All data are reported so that individuals cannot be identified. Gallup, Inc., will share the data from this survey with the project research teams at Rice University and Wheaton College. All individual responses will be kept strictly confidential by Gallup, Rice University, and Wheaton College. Your identity will not be disclosed in any findings disseminated from this study.

Unless otherwise specified, please select only one response per question.

Q1. Which of the following best describes your current employment status?
1. Employed full-time
2. Employed part-time
3. Not employed but looking for work
4. Not employed and not currently looking for work

Q2. How many jobs do you have? [Ask if Q1 = 1 or 2]
1. Employed in a single job
2. Employed in multiple jobs

Q3. Do any of the following categories currently apply to you? Mark all that apply.
Self-employed
Entrepreneur
Homemaker
Student
Volunteer
Retired
Unable to work
None of these apply to me.

Q4. How many hours a week do you usually work (If you have more than one job, please include all hours you spend working)? [Ask if Q1 = 1 or 2 or Q3 = 1 or 2]

Q5. How many hours a week do you usually provide care for others without pay (e.g., childcare or eldercare)?

Q6. Did the number of hours you spent providing unpaid childcare or eldercare change as a result of the pandemic?
1. No, my unpaid caretaking hours did not change
2. Yes, my unpaid caretaking hours increased
3. Yes, my unpaid caretaking hours decreased

Q7. Do you have any children under 18 currently living in your household?
1. Yes
2. No

Q8. I have had to help more with my child(ren)'s schooling during the pandemic. [Ask if Q7 = 1]
1. Strongly disagree
2. Somewhat disagree
3. Neither disagree nor agree
4. Somewhat agree
5. Strongly agree

Q9. Currently, what is your religious identity?
1. Protestant
2. Catholic
3. Other Christian
4. Jewish
5. Muslim
6. Buddhist
7. Hindu
8. Other
9. No religion
10. Don't know

Q10. During the pandemic, how often did you attend religious services either in person or online?
1. Never
2. Less than once a year
3. Once a year
4. Several times a year
5. Once a month
6. 2 to 3 times a month
7. Nearly every week
8. Every week
9. More than once a week

Q11. Which of the following best describes your religious congregation? Select all that apply. [Ask if Q9 = 1 or 2 or 3 and Q10 > 1]
1. Fundamentalist
2. Evangelical
3. Mainline
4. Liberal
5. Charismatic
6. None of the above
7. Don't know

Q12. Which of the following best describes the racial composition of your religious congregation? Please select one. [Ask if Q10 > 1]
1. More than half white
2. More than half Black
3. More than half Asian
4. More than half Hispanic
5. No single racial group is more than half of the congregation
6. Other, please specify:

Q13. About how often do you pray?
1. Never
2. Less than once a week
3. Once a week

4. Several times a week
5. Once a day
6. Several times a day

Q14. Regardless of whether you attend religious services or not, would you say you are ...?
1. Very religious
2. Moderately religious
3. Slightly religious
4. Not at all religious

Q15. To what extent do you consider yourself a spiritual person?
1. Very spiritual
2. Moderately spiritual
3. Slightly spiritual
4. Not at all spiritual

Q16. Please indicate which statement below comes closest to expressing what you believe about God.
1. I don't believe in God
2. I don't know whether there is a God, and I don't believe there is any way to find out
3. I don't believe in a personal God, but I do believe in a Higher Power of some kind
4. I find myself believing in God some of the time, but not at others
5. While I have doubts, I feel that I do believe in God
6. I know God really exists and I have no doubts about it

Q17. As you answer the remaining questions in this survey, please think about your typical experience at work. If you have multiple jobs, think about your experience across all of your jobs. If you are retired, think about how you would have responded in your most recent job.

Please share the extent to which you agree or disagree with the following statements. [Ask if Q1 = 1 or 2 or Q3 = 1 or 2 or 6]

a. The goods or services my organization provides have a positive impact on others in the world
b. My work gives me the ability to support others outside of work (e.g., providing for family, religious community, charitable giving, etc.).
c. I have a positive impact on those I encounter in the workplace (e.g., colleagues, customers, clients).
d. I find my work meaningful.
e. I have kept my religious beliefs from others at work for fear of how others would view me.
f. I feel comfortable talking about my religious beliefs at work.
g. I can really be myself at my job.
h. Overall, I am very satisfied with my current job.
i. I feel a strong sense of commitment to the organization I work for.
j. I turn to faith for support through stressful times in my work life.
k. My workplace provides accommodations that allow people to practice their religion.
l. I know what kinds of religious accommodations the organization I work for offers.
m. The organization I work for cares about the spiritual well-being of its employees.

    n. I see my work as a spiritual calling.

    o. I have been guided to my work by God or a higher power.

        1. Strongly disagree
        2. Somewhat disagree
        3. Neither disagree nor agree
        4. Somewhat agree
        5. Strongly agree

    Turning now to some questions about your personal experiences.

Q18. Throughout your lifetime, how often have you felt like you have been treated unfairly in the context of your work because of the following:

    a. Your religion or non-religion
    b. Your sex or gender
    c. Your marital status (e.g., married, divorced, separated, single)
    d. Your race or ethnicity
    e. Your sexual orientation (e.g., heterosexual, homosexual, bisexual)
    f. Your national origin
    g. Your disability
    h. Your criminal background

        1. Never
        2. Rarely
        3. Sometimes
        4. Often
        5. Very often
        6. Not applicable [Display for items g and h only]

    As you answer the remaining questions in this survey, please think about your typical experience at work during the pandemic. If you have multiple jobs, think about your experience across all of your jobs. If you are retired, think about how you would have responded in your most recent job.

    Please indicate your level of agreement or disagreement with each of the following items.

Q19. Many people experienced significant changes to their work during the pandemic. Select any of the following that apply to you: [Ask if Q1 = 1 or 2 or Q3 = 1 or 2 or 6]

    1. My work hours did not change
    2. My work hours increased
    3. My work hours decreased
    4. I worked from home part of the time
    5. I worked from home all of the time
    6. I changed jobs

Q20. During the pandemic I was considered an essential worker. [Ask if Q1 = 1 or 2 or Q3 = 1 or 2 or 6]

    1. Yes, I worked in healthcare or public health
    2. Yes, I provided critical services or functions outside of healthcare
    3. No

Q21. Compared with before the pandemic, do you now have: [Ask if Q1 = 1 or 2 or Q3 = 1 or 2 or 6]

    1. More flexibility to choose the location where you put in your work hours
    2. Less flexibility to choose the location where you put in your work hours
    3. About the same flexibility as before

Q22. During the pandemic, how often have you felt a sense of "burnout"—meaning physical or mental exhaustion caused by overwork or stress—in your work? [Ask if Q1 = 1 or 2 or Q3 = 1 or 2 or 6]

1. Never
2. Rarely
3. Sometimes
4. Often
5. Very often

Q23. Please tell us the extent to which you agree or disagree with the following: [Ask if Q1 = 1 or 2 or Q3 = 1 or 2 or 6]

a. Since the beginning of the pandemic, I have experienced increased racial discrimination at work.
b. Since the beginning of the pandemic, I have experienced increased religious discrimination at work.
c. Since the beginning of the pandemic, I have experienced increased sex or gender discrimination at work.
d. My faith helps me cope with racial discrimination at work.
e. My faith helps me cope with religious discrimination at work.
f. My faith helps me cope with sex or gender discrimination at work.
   1. Strongly disagree
   2. Somewhat disagree
   3. Neither disagree nor agree
   4. Somewhat agree
   5. Strongly agree

Q24. Consider how individuals in your workplace experienced various aspects of life during the pandemic. To what extent do you agree or disagree with the following: [Ask if Q1 = 1 or 2 or Q3 = 1 or 2 or 6]

a. People in my workplace were personally affected by racial injustice
b. People in my workplace were personally affected by loss or reduction of employment
c. People in my workplace had increased demands on their time due to school or daycare closures
d. People in my workplace experienced the impact of COVID19 on their own or their family members' physical health.
e. People in my workplace experienced the impact of COVID19 on their own or their family members' mental health.
   1. Strongly disagree
   2. Somewhat disagree
   3. Neither disagree nor agree
   4. Somewhat agree
   5. Strongly agree

Q25. The following questions refer to your workplace's response to events during the pandemic. [Ask if Q1 = 1 or 2 or Q3 = 1 or 2 or 6]

a. My workplace addressed issues of racial justice.
b. My workplace looked for ways to support those whose jobs were negatively affected because of COVID19.
c. My workplace looked for ways to support those who had increased demands on their time due to school or daycare closures.
d. My workplace looked for ways to support those whose physical health was negatively affected because of COVID19.

    e. My workplace looked for ways to support those whose mental health was negatively affected because of COVID19.

    f. My workplace looked for ways to support those who were negatively affected by racial injustice
      1. Strongly disagree
      2. Somewhat disagree
      3. Neither disagree nor agree
      4. Somewhat agree
      5. Strongly agree

Q27. Now we are going to turn to some specific questions about the experiences of people in your faith community during the pandemic. To what extent do you agree or disagree with the following: [Ask if Q10 > 1]

    a. People in my faith community were personally affected by racial injustice.

    b. People in my faith community were personally affected by loss or reduction of employment.

    c. People in my faith community had increased demands on their time due to school or daycare closures.

    d. People in my faith community experienced the impact of COVID19 on their own or their family members' physical health.

    e. People in my faith community experienced the impact of COVID19 on their own or their family members' mental health.
      1. Strongly disagree
      2. Somewhat disagree
      3. Neither disagree nor agree
      4. Somewhat agree
      5. Strongly agree

Q28. The following questions refer to your faith community's response to events during the pandemic. [Ask if Q10 > 1]

    a. My faith community addressed issues of racial justice.

    b. My faith community looked for ways to support those whose jobs were negatively affected because of COVID19.

    c. My faith community looked for ways to support those who had increased demands on their time due to school or daycare closures.

    d. My faith community looked for ways to support those whose physical health was negatively affected because of COVID19.

    e. My faith community looked for ways to support those whose mental health was negatively affected because of COVID19.

    f. My faith community looked for ways to support those who were negatively affected by racial injustice.
      1. Strongly disagree
      2. Somewhat disagree
      3. Neither disagree nor agree
      4. Somewhat agree
      5. Strongly agree

Q29. During the pandemic have you heard any messages from your faith community that expressed any of the following? [Ask if Q10 > 1]

    a. Support for racial justice

b. Opposition to divisive discussions about race

c. The importance of taking steps to limit the spread of the coronavirus

d. Opposition to government restrictions elated to masks or in-person gatherings

  1. Yes, have heard this

  2. No, have not heard this

Q30. Since you reached the age of 16, how often do you suspect that you have experienced the following kinds of incidents at work because of your race or ethnicity?

a. Been denied employment

b. Been fired from a job

c. Received an unfair work evaluation

d. Missed out on a promotion or raise opportunity

e. Been called names or insulted

f. Been threatened or harassed

g. Been treated poorly by co-workers

h. Been asked to lead efforts to address racial inequality

  1. Never

  2. Once

  3. Twice or more

Q31. Since you reached the age of 16, how often do you suspect that you have experienced the following kinds of incidents at work because of your religion?

a. Been denied employment

b. Been fired from a job

c. Received an unfair work evaluation

d. Missed out on a promotion or raise opportunity

e. Been called names or insulted

f. Been threatened or harassed

g. Been treated poorly by co-workers

h. Been asked to lead efforts to address religious inequality.

  1. Never

  2. Once

  3. Twice or more

Q32. Since you reached the age of 16, how often do you suspect that you have experienced the following kinds of incidents at work because of your sex or gender?

a. Been denied employment

b. Been fired from a job

c. Received an unfair work evaluation

d. Missed out on a promotion or raise opportunity

e. Been called names or insulted

f. Been threatened or harassed

g. Been treated poorly by co-workers

h. Been asked to lead efforts to address sex or gender inequality

  1. Never

  2. Once

  3. Twice or more

Q33. During the pandemic have you heard any communication at work that expressed any of the following? [Ask if Q1 = 1 or 2 or Q3 = 1 or 2 or 6]
  a. Support for racial justice
  b. Opposition to divisive racial rhetoric
  c. The importance of taking steps to limit the spread of the coronavirus
  d. Opposition to government mandates related to masks or in-person gatherings
    1. Yes, have heard this
    2. No, have not heard this

Q34. Which of the following best describes your COVID vaccination status:
  1. I have been vaccinated (select this item even if you have only gotten one vaccine dose)
  2. I plan to be vaccinated
  3. I will only get vaccinated if my concerns about the vaccine are fully addressed
  4. I am not able to be vaccinated for medical or health reasons
  5. I am not planning to be vaccinated for religious or philosophical reasons
  6. Other: please specify:

Q35. I felt pressured by my employer to get the COVID19 vaccine.
  1. Strongly disagree
  2. Somewhat disagree
  3. Neither disagree nor agree
  4. Somewhat agree
  5. Strongly agree

Q36. Which of the following categories best describe the industry you primarily work/worked in? [Ask if Q1 = 1 or 2 or Q3 = 1 or 2 or 6]
  1. Architecture or engineering
  2. Arts, design, entertainment, sports, or media
  3. Business or finance
  4. Caretaking (e.g., childcare or elder care)
  5. Community or social services
  6. Computer or mathematical
  7. Construction or mining
  8. Education, training, or library
  9. Farming, fishing, or forestry
  10. Food service or hospitality
  11. Healthcare
  12. Installation, maintenance, or repair
  13. Legal
  14. Life, physical, and social sciences
  15. Manufacturing or production
  16. Military
  17. Religion
  18. Retail or sales
  19. Transportation
  20. Other, please specify:

Q37. Think about the organization of job roles in your industry, where the leaders are at the top of the organization and employees are at the bottom of the organization. Would you say that you are toward the top of the organization, middle or at the bottom? [Ask if Q1 = 1 or 2 or Q3 = 1 or 2 or 6]

1. Top
2. Middle
3. Bottom

Q38. About how many people work at the location where you work? (Please include part-time and full-time employees in all areas, departments, and buildings.) [Ask if Q1 = 1 or 2 or Q3 = 1 or 2 or 6]

1. 1 to 9
2. 10 to 49
3. 50 to 99
4. 100 to 499
5. 500 to 999
6. 1,000 to 1,999
7. 2,000 or more
8. Don't know

Q39. About how long have you worked for your current organization? [Ask if Q1 = 1 or 2 or Q3 = 1 or 2 or 6]

1. Less than a year
2. 1 to 5 years
3. 6 to 10 years
4. 11 to 20 years
5. 21 to 30 years
6. More than 30 years

Q40. Are you a manager? A manager is someone whose primary role is to manage or supervise others. [Ask if Q1 = 1 or 2 or Q3 = 1 or 2 or 6]

1. Yes
2. No

Q41. What best describes the type of organization you work for? [Ask if Q1 = 1 or 2 or Q3 = 1 or 2 or 6]

1. For-profit
2. Nonprofit
3. Hybrid—both for-profit and nonprofit
4. Government
5. Don't know

Q42. Does your organization have a religious mission? [Ask if Q1 = 1 or 2 or Q3 = 1 or 2 or 6]

1. Yes
2. No
3. Don't know

Q43. During the coronavirus pandemic were you ever unemployed and looking for a job for more than one month?

1. Yes
2. No

Q44. What was the sex on your original birth certificate?
    1. Male
    2. Female
    3. Prefer not to say

Q45. What is your current gender?
    1. Man
    2. Woman
    3. Prefer to self-describe: please describe here
    4. Prefer not to say

Q46. Which of the following best describes you?
    1. Heterosexual or straight
    2. Gay, lesbian, or homosexual
    3. Bisexual
    4. Prefer to self-describe:
    5. Prefer not to say
    6. Don't know

Q47. What is the highest level of school that you completed or the highest degree you have received?
    1. Less than a high school diploma
    2. High school graduate or GED
    3. Technical, trade, or vocational
    4. Some college but no degree
    5. Two-year associate degree
    6. Four-year bachelor's degree
    7. Some postgraduate or professional schooling
    8. Postgraduate or professional degree

Q48. Are you currently...
    1. Married
    2. Living with a partner
    3. Divorced
    4. Separated
    5. Widowed
    6. Single

Q49. What is your total ANNUAL household income, before taxes? Please include income from wages and salaries, remittances from family members living elsewhere, farming, and all other sources.
    1. Less than $12,000
    2. $12,000 to $23,999
    3. $24,000 to $35,999
    4. $36,000 to $47,999
    5. $48,000 to $59,999
    6. $60,000 to $89,999
    7. $90,000 to $119,999
    8. $120,000 to $179,999
    9. $180,000 to $239,999
    10. $240,000 to $1,000,000
    11. More than $1,000,000

Q50. How many children under the age of 18 are currently living in your household?

Q51. There is a lot of talk these days about liberals and conservatives. On a scale of extremely liberal to extremely conservative, where would you place yourself?
1. Extremely liberal
2. Liberal
3. Slightly liberal
4. Moderate
5. Slightly conservative
6. Conservative
7. Extremely conservative

Q52. Is English your first language?
1. Yes
2. No

Q53. Did one or both of your parents immigrate to the United States?
1. Yes
2. No

Q54. Did you immigrate to the United States?
1. Yes
2. No

Q55. In what year did you immigrate to the United States? [Ask if 54 = 1]

Q56. Thank you very much for answering all of these questions. Researchers at Rice University and Wheaton College would like to invite some people who completed this survey to take part in a follow-up interview about the topics discussed in this survey. People who participate in the follow-up interview will receive a $30 incentive for their participation. Do you want to be considered for this opportunity? If you select "yes" Gallup will provide researchers at Rice and Wheaton with your name and contact information. They will only be allowed to contact you regarding the follow-up interview. If you select "no" or leave this question blank, your personal contact information will not be provided to Rice and Wheaton.
1. Yes
2. No

That is the end of the survey. Thank you very much for taking part. We are very grateful to you for contributing your time to this academic research.

Appendix E

Faith at Work Supplemental Interview Guide

Background Information

1. Why don't we start with you telling me—in just a few sentences—a little bit about what you do for a living? What's your job title, if you don't mind me asking?
2. Could you walk me through some of the tasks or responsibilities you have as part of your work?
3. Could you help me understand the makeup of your workplace (keep in mind here that not everyone will be working in an office)? Are most of your colleagues women/men? What about race? How about the makeup of religious groups?

4. [FOR ESSENTIAL WORKERS] I see from the survey you filled out for us that you were considered an essential worker during the pandemic? Can you tell me as much as you are able a little bit about what this was like for you?

Faith and Work

Now some questions about your work broadly

5. There are a number of factors that motivate people to accept jobs. What made you decide to take your current job?
6. Given the type of work you do, how does what you do at work impact the people you work with? (e.g., How do your interactions with colleagues or customers impact them?)
7. How does what you do at work impact people outside of work? (e.g., To what extent does your organization make things or provide services that benefit others?)
8. Some people see their work as meaningful because it provides ways of meeting other needs or goals in life. To what extent is this the case for you?
9. In what ways do you think your faith or religion affects the work you do at your job? Specifically, to what extent does your tradition [or faith, depending on what is most appropriate for each person] affect how you interact with others, manage stress, or approach your work responsibilities?
10. In general, to what extent do you see your work as a spiritual calling? Could you say more about why or why not?

Pandemic and the Workplace

I am also interested in figuring out how people's work was and is impacted by the pandemic.

11. Could you tell me broadly how your work experience was and is impacted by the pandemic?
12. Do you have any children in your household? IF YES: How has the pandemic shaped how you balanced your work and childcare? Were or are there tensions between work and caretaking responsibilities?
13. Did you or any of your family members get sick with COVID? If yes, how did this impact your work?
14. To what extent did your [understanding of your faith / your religious tradition] shape how you responded to any challenges associated with your work during the pandemic?
15. Are there any other resources that have been helpful to you in dealing with stress associated with your work during the pandemic?

Gender and Workplace

16. We have been hearing that the pandemic has had a greater impact on the work lives of women when compared to men. What's your own sense of this? What has your own experience been like?

17. Throughout the pandemic, has your job performance been consistent with your typical standards? (If better or worse) Why do you think that is? How has your performance affected your relationship with your boss/supervisor? Your coworkers?

18. As a result of the pandemic do you think you have been expected to care for others more in the workplace (for example, helping to solve people's difficulties, listening to personal problems, mentoring others, and so on)? What did that look like?

19. Throughout the pandemic, what has your job performance been like, especially compared with others at your work? (If better or worse) Why do you think that is? How do you think it will impact your future?

20. How understanding has your boss/supervisor been when your work was impacted by the pandemic?

Race and Workplace

21. During this past year and a half, there has been increased national attention on race and racial injustice. Can you tell me a little bit about how a focus on race and racial injustice has shaped your own experiences at work?

22. How has your workplace responded to increased national calls for racial justice?

23. How satisfied have you been with your workplace's response or lack of response? If not satisfied, what would you like to see done differently?

24. Have you personally been involved with your workplace response to calls for racial justice? If so, how did that involvement come about? How does this involvement relate to your core work responsibilities?

25. Do you think things are getting better or worse with respect to race in the US? What do you think would make things improve?

Faith and Discrimination in the Workplace

I'd like to turn now to some additional issues related to unfairness in the workplace.

26. Have you personally experienced being treated unfairly or differently at work because of your sex or gender, race or ethnicity?

27. How about for your religion or non-religion? PROBE: Do you think you've been treated differently in the workplace because of religious symbols or articles of faith you wear?

28. IF YOU HAVE BEEN TREATED UNFAIRLY AT WORK, to what extent has your faith / religious tradition / understanding of spirituality helped you to deal with that situation? PROBE: How specifically did it help or not help?

29. Do you have any experience participating in diversity trainings/workshops in your workplace? If so, describe the nature of the training session and what kind of issues were discussed. Did religion ever come up? PROBE: Did you think these sessions were helpful for preventing unfairness in the workplace? Did you find these training sessions beneficial personally?

Pandemic and Religious Organizations

30. [FOR CHRISTIAN RESPONDENTS / OTHER RELIGIOUS RESPONDENTS]
Do you attend church/mosque/gurdwara/ashram . . . ? Could you tell me a bit
about your church/OTHER? For example, what tradition or denomination is the
church?
31. About how long have you been attending this particular church / CHOOSE
OTHER? And what activities are you most involved in?
32. And some other specific questions about your church / CHOOSE OTHER;
about how many people do you think attend on a weekly basis?
33. Do you have any feel about what percentage are male versus female, as well as the
percentage of different racial groups?
34. IF ATTEND A RELIGIOUS ORGANIZATION—We also want to know how
the pandemic had an impact on your [church / other org as appropriate]. Can
you tell me a little bit about how the pandemic has impacted your church OR
RELIGIOUS ORGANIZATION?
35. And how has your RELIGIOUS ORGANIZATION responded to the pandemic? Were there things that your congregation in particular did to help church
members during the pandemic?
36. How similar or different were the things you heard in your church about the pandemic compared to what you heard in your workplace?
37. IF ATTEND A RELIGIOUS ORGANIZATION—How about increased national
calls for racial justice? How has your church responded to these?
38. How similar or different were the things you heard in your church about racial
justice compared to what you heard in your workplace?

Churches and Work

Switching now to how work might come up in your local church.

39. During the pandemic, to what extent did you feel like your church was a place
you could turn to for support or encouragement in your work? Tell me more
about that if you would.
40. Is your church's support for people who work different for women than for men?
What makes you say this? PROBE: Can you give me a story or an example of this?
41. We are also interested in knowing how faith communities might be able to do a
better job of supporting people at work? Especially considering all the changes
to people's work lives because of the pandemic, are there things you would want
your faith community to do to support you in this new work world?
42. Are there any other issues that I didn't mention that you think are important?

Demographic Questions

*Just for bookkeeping, I'd now like to ask you some questions to help me situate you among
other individuals I have talked with. Again, all this information will be strictly confidential.*

43. How old are you?
44. How would you describe yourself racially or ethnically?

45. Are you currently married or in a long-term committed relationship? [Discern which one.]
46. What is the best religious label for you?
47. Do you have any children?
    a. IF YES, how many?
    b. What are their ages?
48. What level of schooling have you been through?
49. What is your occupation?
50. IF MARRIED OR PARTNERED, what is your spouse's occupation?
51. What state do you live in?
52. What is your country of origin?
    a. How many years have you lived in the US?

References

Acquisti, Alessandro, and Christina M. Fong. 2015. "An Experiment in Hiring Discrimination." Online Social Networks. https://ssrn.com/abstract=2031979.

Ali, Abbas J., and Abdullah Al-Owaihan. 2008. "Islamic Work Ethic: A Critical Review." *Cross Cultural Management* 15(1): 5–19.

Allan, Blake A., Cassandra Batz-Barbarich, Haley M. Sterling, and Louis Tay. 2019. "Outcomes of Meaningful Work: A Meta-analysis." *Journal of Management Studies* 56(3): 500–528.

Aumann, Kerstin, Ellen Galinsky, and Kenneth Matos. 2011. *The New Male Mystique.* New York: Families and Work Institute.

Bacchus, Denise N. A. 2008. "Coping with Work-Related Stress: A Study of the Use of Coping Resources among Professional Black Women." *Journal of Ethnic Cultural Diversity in Social Work* 17(1): 60–81.

Bader, Christopher D., and Roger Finke. 2010. "What Does God Require? Understanding Religious Context and Morality." In *Handbook of the Sociology of Morality*, edited by Steven Hitlin and Stephen Vaisey. 241–54. New York: Springer.

Baker, Joseph O'Brian, and Buster Smith. 2009. "None Too Simple: Examining Issues of Religious Nonbelief and Nonbelonging in the United States." *Journal for the Scientific Study of Religion* 48(4): 719–33.

Bakibinga, Pauline, Hege Forbech Vinje, and Maurice Mittelmark. 2014. "The Role of Religion in the Work Lives and Coping Strategies of Ugandan Nurses." *Journal of Religion and Health* 53(5): 1342–52.

Beder, Sharon. 2000. *Selling the Work Ethic: From Puritan Pulpit to Corporate PR.* London: Zed Books.

Best, Kenneth. 2018. "Know Thyself: The Philosophy of Self-Knowledge." Uconn Today. August 7. https://today.uconn.edu/2018/08/know-thyself-philosophy-self-knowledge/#.

Bielby, D. D. V., and W. T. Bielby. 1984. "Work Commitment, Sex-Role Attitudes, and Women's Employment." *American Sociological Review* 49(2): 234–47.

Bierman, Alex. 2006. "Does Religion Buffer the Effects of Discrimination on Mental Health? Differing Effects by Race." *Journal for the Scientific Study of Religion* 45: 551–65.

Blair-Loy, Mary. 2003. *Competing Devotions: Career and Family among Women Executives.* Cambridge, MA: Harvard University Press.

Bunderson, J. Stuart, and Jeffrey A. Thompson. 2009. "The Call of the Wild: Zookeepers, Callings, and the Double-Edged Sword of Deeply Meaningful Work." *Administrative Science Quarterly* 54(1): 32–57.

Burge, Ryan. 2022. "God-Denying Women and Self-Replacing Christians: How Religion Changes Birthrates." Religion News Service. September 8. https://religionnews.com/2022/09/08/god-denying-women-and-self-replacing-christians-how-religion-changes-birthrates/.

Cash, K. C., and G. R. Gray. 2000. "A Framework for Accommodating Religion and Spirituality in the Workplace." *Academy of Management Perspectives* 14(3): 124–33.

Charoensap-Kelly, Piyawan, Colleen L. Mestayer, and G. Brandon Knight. 2020. "To Come Out or Not to Come Out: Minority Religious Identity Self-Disclosure in the United States Workplace." *Management Communication Quarterly* 34(2): 213–50.

Chen, Carolyn. 2022. *Work, Pray, Code: When Work Becomes Religion in Silicon Valley.* Princeton, NJ: Princeton University Press.

Collins, Randall. 1980. "Weber's Last Theory of Capitalism: A Systematization." *American Sociological Review* 45(6): 924–42.

Considine, Craig. 2017. "The Racialization of Islam in the United States: Islamophobia, Hate Crimes, and 'Flying While Brown.'" *Religions* 8(9): 165.

Cooper, Maria. 2000. "Being the 'Go-to Guy': Fatherhood, Masculinity, and the Organization of Work in Silicon Valley." *Qualitative Sociology* 23: 379–405.

Cox, Daniel, and Robert P. Jones. 2017. "America's Changing Religious Identity." PRRI. https://www.prri.org/research/american-religious-landscape-christian-religiously-unaffiliated/.

Cummings, Jeremy P., and Kenneth I. Pargament. 2012. "Religious Coping with Workplace Stress." In *Psychology of Religion and Workplace Spirituality,* edited by Peter C. Hill and Bryan J. Hik. 157–77. Charlotte, NC: Information Age Publishing.

Cunningham, George B. 2010. "The Influence of Religious Personal Identity on the Relationships among Religious Dissimilarity, Value Dissimilarity, and Job Satisfaction." *Social Justice Research* 23(1): 60–76.

Davidson, James C., and David P. Caddell. 1994. "Religion and the Meaning of Work." *Journal for the Scientific Study of Religion* 33: 135–47.

Dawson, J. 2005. "A History of Vocation: Tracing a Keyword of Work, Meaning, and Moral Purpose." *Adult Education Quarterly* 55(3): 220–31.

De Bock, Veerle. 2014. "Building Cathedrals, the Secret of Meaningful Work! Chances to Change." October 28. https://www.chancestochange.com/building-cathedrals-the-secret-of-meaningful-work/.

Deci, E. L. 1971. "Effects of Externally Mediated Rewards on Intrinsic Motivation." *Journal of Personality and Social Psychology* 18: 105–15.

Deci, E. L., R. Koestner, and R. M. Ryan. 1999. "A Meta-analytic Review of Experiments Examining the Effects of Extrinsic Rewards on Intrinsic Motivation." *Psychological Bulletin* 125(6): 627–68.

Del Vento Bielby, Denise, and William T. Bielby. 1984. "Work Commitment, Sex-Role Attitudes, and Women's Employment." *American Sociological Review* 49(2): 234–47.

Dik, Bryan. J., and Ryan D. Duffy. 2009. "Calling and Vocation at Work: Definitions and Prospects for Research and Practice." *Counseling Psychology* 37: 424–50.

Dougherty, Kevin D., and Michael O. Emerson. 2018. "The Changing Complexion of American Congregations." *Journal for the Scientific Study of Religion* 57(1): 24–38.

Duffy, Ryan D., Blake A. Allan, Kelsey L. Autin, and Richard P. Douglass. 2014. "Living a Calling and Work Well-Being: A Longitudinal Study." *Journal of Counseling Psychology* 61(4): 605–15.

Duffy, Ryan D., and Bryan J. Dik. 2013. "Research on Calling: What Have We Learned and Where Are We Going?" *Journal of Vocational Behavior* 83(3): 428–36.

Duffy, Ryan D., Laura Reid, and Bryan J. Dik. 2010. "Spirituality, Religion, and Career Development: Implications for the Workplace." *Journal of Management, Spirituality and Religion* 7: 209–21.

Ecklund, Elaine Howard, Denise Daniels, Daniel Bolger, and Laura Johnson. 2020. "A Nationally Representative Survey of Faith and Work: Demographic Subgroup Differences around Calling and Conflict." *Religions* 11(6): 287.

Ecklund, Elaine Howard, Denise Daniels, and Rachel C. Schneider. 2020. "From Secular to Sacred: Bringing Work to Church." *Religions* 11(9): 442.

Ecklund, Elaine Howard, and Anne E. Lincoln. 2016. *Failing Families, Failing Science: Work-Family Conflict in Academic Science.* New York: New York University Press.

Edgell, P. 2006. *Religion and Family in a Changing Society.* Princeton, NJ: Princeton University Press.

Ellison, Christopher, G., Amy M. Burdette, and Norval D. Glenn. 2011. "Praying for Mr. Right? Religion, Family Background, and Marital Expectations among College Women." *Journal of Family Issues* 32(7): 906–31.

Ellison, Christopher G., Reed T. DeAngelis, and Metin Güven. 2017. "Does Religious Involvement Mitigate the Effects of Major Discrimination on the Mental Health of African Americans? Findings from the Nashville Stress and Health Study." *Religions* 8(9): 195.

Emerson, Michael O., and Glenn E. Bracey. Forthcoming. *The Grand Betrayal: The Agonizing Story of Religion, Race, and Rejection in American Life*. New York: Oxford University Press.

Emerson, Michael O. and Christian Smith. 2000. *Divided by Faith: Evangelical Religion and the Problem of Race in America*. New York: Oxford University Press.

Epstein, Cynthia Fuchs, Carroll Seron, Bonnie Oglensky, and Robert Sauté. 1999. *The Part-Time Paradox: Time Norms, Professional Life, Family and Gender*. New York: Routledge.

Folbre, N. 2008. *Valuing Children: Rethinking the Economics of the Family*. Cambridge, MA: Harvard University Press.

Fotohabadi, Mark, and Louise Kelly. 2018. "Making Conflict Work: Authentic Leadership and Reactive and Reflective Management Styles." *Journal of General Management* 43(2): 70–78.

Fox, Mary Frank. 1995. "Women and Scientific Careers." In *Handbook of Science and Technology Studies*, edited by Sheila Jasanoff, Gerald E. Markle, James C. Petersen, and Trevor Pinch. 205–24. New York: Sage.

Gebert, Diether, Sabine Boerner, Eric Kearney, James E. King Jr., K. Zhang, and Lynda Jiwen Song. 2014. "Expressing Religious Identities in the Workplace: Analyzing a Neglected Diversity Dimension." *Human Relations* 67: 543–63.

General Social Survey. 1972–2021. Accessed at GSS Data Explorer | NORC at the University of Chicago.

Gerson, Kathleen. 2010. *The Unfinished Revolution: How a New Generation Is Reshaping Family, Work, and Gender in America*. Oxford: Oxford University Press.

Ghaffari, Azadeh, and Ayşe Çiftçi. 2010. "Religiosity and Self-Esteem of Muslim Immigrants to the United States: The Moderating Role of Perceived Discrimination." *The International Journal for the Psychology of Religion* 20: 14–25.

Ghumman, Sonia, and Linda A. Jackson. 2008. "Between a Cross and a Hard Place: Religious Identifiers and Employability." *Journal of Workplace Rights* 13: 259–79.

Ghumman, Sonia, Ann Ryan, Lizabeth Barclay, and Karen Markel. 2013. "Religious Discrimination in the Workplace: A Review and Examination of Current and Future Trends." *Journal of Business and Psychology* 28: 439–54.

Gornick, Janet C., and Marcia Meyers. 2003. *Families That Work: Policies for Reconciling Parenthood and Employment*. New York: Russell Sage Foundation.

Graham, Jesse, and Jonathan Haidt. 2010. "Beyond Beliefs: Religions Bind Individuals in Moral Communities." *Personality and Social Psychology Review* 14(1): 140–50.

Grandey, Alicia, Su Chuen Foo, Markus Groth, and Robyn E. Goodwin. 2012. "Free to Be You and Me: A Climate of Authenticity Alleviates Burnout from Emotional Labor." *Journal of Occupational Health Psychology* 17(1): 1–14.

Hall, Douglas T., and Dawn E. Chandler. 2005. "Psychological Success: When the Career Is a Calling." *Journal of Organizational Behavior* 26(2): 155–76.

Hall, J. Camille, Johnnie Hamilton-Mason, and Joyce E. Everett. 2012. "Black Women Talk about Workplace Stress and How They Cope." *Journal of Black Studies* 43(2): 207–26.

Hastwell, Claire. 2019. "How the Best Companies Ensure People Can Bring Their Whole Selves to Work." Great Place to Work. September 13. https://www.greatplacetowork.com/resources/blog/4-ideas-to-encourage-people-to-bring-their-whole-self-to-work.

Hayford, S. R., and S. P. Morgan. 2008. "Religiosity and Fertility in the United States: The Role of Fertility Intentions." *Social Forces* 86(3): 1163–88.

Hochschild, A., and A. Machung. 1989. *Working Parents and the Revolution at Home*. New York: Viking.

Hodge, David R. 2006. "Moving toward a More Inclusive Educational Environment? A Multi-sample Exploration of Religious Discrimination as Seen through the Eyes of Students from Various Faith Traditions." *Journal of Social Work Education* 42(2): 249–67.

Jackall, Robert. 2010. "Morality in Organizations." In *Handbook of the Sociology of Morality*, edited by Steven Hitlin and Stephen Vaisey. 203–10. New York: Springer.

Keller, Timothy, and John D. Inazu. 2020. *Uncommon Ground: Living Faithfully in a World of Difference*. Nashville: Thomas Nelson.

Khazan, Olga. 2022. "I Gave Myself Three Months to Change My Personality. The Results Were Mixed." *The Atlantic*. February 10. https://www.theatlantic.com/magazine/archive/2022/03/how-to-change-your-personality-happiness/621306/.

Koenig, Harold G., and David B. Larson. 2001. "Religion and Mental Health: Evidence for an Association." *International Review of Psychiatry* 13(2): 67–78.

Lawrence, Ericka R., and James E. King Jr. 2008. "Determinants of Religious Expression in the Workplace." *Culture and Religion: An Interdisciplinary Journal* 9(3): 251–65.

Lee, Daniel B., Melissa K. Peckins, Alison L. Miller, Meredith O. Hope, Enrique W. Neblett, Shervin Assari, Jaime Muñoz-Velázquez, and Marc A. Zimmerman. 2021. "Pathways from Racial Discrimination to Cortisol/DHEA Imbalance: Protective Role of Religious Involvement." *Ethnicity & Health* 26(3): 413–30.

Lindsay, D. Michael. 2008. *Faith in the Halls of Power: How Evangelicals Joined the American Elite*. New York: Oxford University Press.

Lindsay, D. Michael, 2021. *Hinge Moments: Making the Most of Life's Transitions*. Downers Grove, IL: InterVarsity Press.

Lindsay, D. Michael, and Bradley Smith. 2010. "Accounting by Faith: The Negotiated Logic of Elite Evangelicals' Workplace Decision-Making." *Journal of the American Academy of Religion* 78(3): 721–49.

Lipka, Michael, and Benjamin Wormald. 2016. "Most and Least Religious U.S. States." Pew Research Center. February 29. https://www.pewresearch.org/fact-tank/2016/02/29/how-religious-is-your-state/.

Lyons, Brent, Jennifer Wessel, Sonia Ghumman, Annie Marie Ryan, and Sooyeol Kim. 2014. "Applying Models of Employee Identity Management across Cultures: Christianity in the USA and South Korea." *Journal of Organizational Behavior* 35(5): 678–704.

Martin, Joanne. 2002. *Organizational Culture: Mapping the Terrain*. Thousand Oaks, CA: Sage.

Marx, Karl. 1978. "The German Ideology." In *The Marx-Engels Reader*, 2nd ed, edited by Robert C. Tucker. 146–200. New York: Norton.

Mattis, Jacqueline S. 2002. "Religion and Spirituality in the Meaning-Making and Coping Experiences of African American Women: A Qualitative Analysis." *Psychology of Women Quarterly* 26(4): 309–21.

McKinsey & Company. 2020. "Diversity Wins: How Inclusion Matters." https://www.mckinsey.com/featured-insights/diversity-and-inclusion/diversity-wins-how-inclusion-matters.

Mehta, Sharan Kaur, Rachel C. Schneider, and Elaine Howard Ecklund. 2022. "'God Sees No Color' So Why Should I? How Racial Ignorance and Inequality Are Produced by White Christians." *Sociological Inquiry* 92(2): 623–46.

Mohammed, Besheer. 2018. "New Estimates Show U.S. Muslim Population Continues to Grow." Pew Research Center. January 3. https://www.pewresearch.org/fact-tank/2018/01/03/new-estimates-show-u-s-muslim-population-continues-to-grow/.

Morris, Aldon D. 1986. *The Origins of the Civil Rights Movement: Black Communities Organizing for Change*. New York: Free Press.

Neal, Judi. 2013. *Handbook of Faith and Spirituality in the Workplace: Emerging Research and Practice*. New York: Springer.

Neubert, Mitchell J., and Katie Halbesleben. 2015. "Called to Commitment: An Examination of Relationships between Spiritual Calling, Job Satisfaction, and Organizational Commitment." *Journal of Business Ethics* 132: 859–72.

Ní Raghallaigh, Muireann. 2011. "Religion in the Lives of Unaccompanied Minors: An Available and Compelling Coping Resource." *British Journal of Social Work* 41(3): 539–56.

Nunez-Smith, Marcella, Nanlesta Pilgrim, Matthew Wynia, Mayur M. Desai, Cedric Bright, Harlan M. Krumholz, and Elizabeth H. Bradley. 2009. "Health Care Workplace Discrimination and Physician Turnover." *Journal of the National Medical Association* 101(12): 1274–82.

Oman, Doug, and Amani M. Nuru-Jeter. 2018. "Social Identity and Discrimination in Religious/Spiritual Influences on Health." In *Why Religion and Spirituality Matter for Public Health*, edited by Doug Oman. 111–37. Cham, Switzerland: Springer International.

Ouchi, W. G., and Alan L. Wilkins. 1985. "Organizational Culture." *Annual Review of Sociology* 11(1): 457–83.

Padela, Aasim I., Huda Adam, Maha Ahmad, Zahra Hosseinian, and Farr Curlin. 2015. "Religious Identity and Workplace Discrimination: A National Survey of American Muslim Physicians." *AJOB Empirical Bioethics* 7: 149–59.

Pandey, Jatin, and Manjari Singh. 2019. "Positive Religious Coping as a Mechanism for Enhancing Job Satisfaction and Reducing Work-Family Conflict: A Moderated Mediation Analysis." *Journal of Management, Spirituality & Religion* 16(3): 314–38.

Pargament, Kenneth. I. 2011. "Religion and Coping: The Current State of Knowledge." In *The Oxford Handbook of Stress, Health, and Coping*, edited by Susan Folkman. 269–88. New York: Oxford University Press.

Parker, Kim, and Wendy Wang. 2013. "Modern Parenthood." Pew Research Center's Social & Demographic Trends Project. March 14. http://www.pewsocialtrends.org/2013/03/14/modern-parenthood-roles-of-moms-and-dads-converge-as-they-balance-work-and-family/.

Peel, Bill. 2020. "Faith-Based Employee Resource Groups on the Rise." Center for Faith and Work St. Louis. December 5. https://www.faithandworkstl.org/blog/faith-based-emplo yee-resource-groups-on-the-rise/.

Peres, Julio F. P., Alexander Moreira-Almeida, Antonia Gladys Nasello, and Harold G. Koenig. 2007. "Spirituality and Resilience in Trauma Victims." *Journal of Religion and Health* 46(3): 343–50.

Perry, Samuel L., and Andrew L. Whitehead. 2019. "Christian America in Black and White: Racial Identity, Religious-National Group Boundaries, and Explanations for Racial Inequality." *Sociology of Religion* 80(3): 277–98.

Petts, R. J. 2019. Introduction to the Special Issue of *Religions*. "Religion and Family Life." *Religion and Family Life* 10(4): 265.

Religious Freedom and Business Foundation. 2020. "Corporate Religious Equity, Diversity, and Inclusion (REDI) Index." https://religiousfreedomandbusiness.org/redi.

Rios, K., L. R. Halper, and C. P. Scheitle. 2021. "Explaining Anti-atheist Discrimination in the Workplace: The Role of Intergroup Threat. *Psychology of Religion and Spirituality* 14(3): 371–80.

Rosa, Anna Dalla, Michelangelo Vianello, and Pasquale Anselmi. 2019. "Longitudinal Predictors of the Development of a Calling: New Evidence for the A Posteriori Hypothesis." *Journal of Vocational Behavior* 114: 44–56.

Sabat, Isaac E., Alex P. Lindsey, Kristen P. Jones, Eden B. King, Carolyn Winslow, Ashley Membere, and Nicholas A. Smith. 2019. "Stigma Expression Outcome and Boundary Conditions: A Meta-analysis." *Journal of Business and Psychology* 35: 171–86.

Scheitle, Christopher P., and Katie E. Corcoran. 2018. "Religious Tradition and Workplace Religious Discrimination: The Moderating Effects of Regional Context." *Social Currents* 5: 283–300.

Scheitle, Christopher P., and Elaine Howard Ecklund. 2020. "Individuals' Experiences with Religious Hostility, Discrimination, and Violence: Findings from a New National Survey." *Socius* 6: 2378023120967815.

Scheitle, Christopher P., and Elaine Howard Ecklund. 2018. "Perceptions of Religious Discrimination among U.S. Scientists." *Journal for the Scientific Study of Religion* 57(1): 139–55.

Scheitle, Christopher P., and Elaine Howard Ecklund. 2017. "Examining the Effects of Exposure to Religion in the Workplace on Perceptions of Religious Discrimination." *Review of Religious Research* 59(1): 1–20.

Scheitle, Christopher P., Taylor Remsburg, and Lisa F. Platt. 2021. "Science Graduate Students' Reports of Discrimination due to Gender, Race, and Religion: Identifying Shared and Unique Predictors." *Socius* 7: 23780231211025183.

Scheitle, Christopher P., and Jeffery T. Ulmer. 2018. "Profane Concerns in Sacred Spaces: The Challenges and Consequences of Implementing Security Measures in Religious Congregations." *Journal of Applied Security Research* 13(1): 29–44.

Schmalzbauer, John. 2003. *People of Faith: Religious Conviction in American Journalism and Higher Education.* Ithaca, NY: Cornell University Press.

Schmitt, Michael, Nyla Branscombe, Tom Postmes, and Amber Garcia. 2014. "The Consequences of Perceived Discrimination for Psychological Well-Being: A Meta-analytic Review." *Psychological Bulletin* 140(4): 921–48.

Schnabel, Landon, and Scott Schieman. 2021. "Religion Protected Mental Health but Constrained Crisis Response during Crucial Early Days of the COVID-19 Pandemic." *Journal for the Scientific Study of Religion* 66(2): 530–43.

Shapin, Steven. 2008. *The Scientific Life: A Moral History of a Late Modern Vocation.* Chicago: University of Chicago Press.

Shellnutt, Kate. 2020. "Southern Baptists Keep Quarreling over Critical Race Theory." *Christianity Today.* December 3.

Shu, Xiaoling, and Kelsey D. Meagher. 2018. "Beyond the Stalled Gender Revolution: Historical and Cohort Dynamics in Gender Attitudes from 1977 to 2016." *Social Forces* 96(3): 1243–74.

Simpson, Ain, and Kimberly Rios. 2016. "How Do US Christians and Atheists Stereotype One Another's Moral Values?" *The International Journal for the Psychology of Religion* 26(4): 320–36.

Swart, Lisanne. 2019. "From the Short Stories Series: Three Brick Layers." November 30. https://www.lisanneswart.com/2019/11/30/from-the-short-stories-series-three-bric klayers/.

Tam, Ruth, and Sylvie Douglis. 2022. "It's OK to Not Be Passionate about Your Job." NPR— Houston Public Media. February 1. https://www.npr.org/2022/01/31/1076978534/the-trouble-with-passion-when-it-comes-to-your-career.

Tayan, Brian. 2016. "The Wells Fargo Cross-Selling Scandal." Harvard Law School Forum on Corporate Governance. https://corpgov.law.harvard.edu/2016/12/19/the-wells-fargo-cross-selling-scandal/.

Treadgold, Richard. 1999. "Transcendent Vocations: Their Relationship to Stress, Depression, and Clarity of Self-Concept." *Journal of Humanistic Psychology* 39(1): 81–105.

Triana, María Del Carmen, María Fernanda García, and Adrienne Colella. 2010. "Managing Diversity: How Organizational Efforts to Support Diversity Moderate the Effects of Perceived Racial Discrimination on Affective Commitment." *Personnel Psychology* 63(4): 817–43.

Topgolf Blog. 2013. "The Freedom to Be Your Whole Self at Work." July 3. https://topgolf.com/blog/post/2013/07/the-freedom-to-be-your-whole-self-at-work/.

Uecker, J. E. 2014. "Religion and Early Marriage in the United States: Evidence from the Add Health Study." *Journal for the Scientific Study of Religion* 53(2): 392–415.

Uecker, J. E., and C. E. Stokes. 2008. "Early Marriage in the United States." *Journal of Marriage and Family* 70(4): 835–46.

Vuga, Janja, and Jelena Juvan. 2013. "Work-Family Conflict between Two Greedy Institutions: The Family and the Military." *Current Sociology* 61(7): 1058–77.

Wachholtz, Amy B., Michelle J. Pearce, and Harold Koenig. 2007. "Exploring the Relationship between Spirituality, Coping, and Pain." *Journal of Behavioral Medicine* 30(4): 311–18.

Wallace, Michael, Bradley R. E. Wright, and Allen Hyde. 2014. "Religious Affiliation and Hiring Discrimination in the American South: A Field Experiment." *Social Currents* 1: 189–207.

Weaver, Gary. 2006. "Virtue in Organizations: Moral Identity as a Foundation for Moral Agency." *Organization Studies* 27(3: 341–68.

Weaver, Gary, and Bradley Agle. 2002. "Religiosity and Ethical Behavior in Organizations: A Symbolic Interactionist Perspective." *Academy of Management Review* 27(1): 77–97.

Weaver, Gary, and Jason Stansbury. 2014. "Religion in Organizations: Cognition and Behavior." *Research in the Sociology of Organizations* 41: 65–110.

Weber, Max. 1930. *The Protestant Ethic and the Spirit of Capitalism*. New York: Scribners.

Weber, Max. 2006 [1930]. *The Protestant Ethic and the Spirit of Capitalism*. New York: Routledge.

Whitehead, Andrew L., and Samuel L. Perry. 2020. *Taking America Back for God: Christian Nationalism in the United States*. Oxford: Oxford University Press.

Whyte, William. 1956. *The Organization Man*. New York: Simon and Schuster.

Widner, Daniel, and Stephen Chicoine. 2011. "It's All in the Name: Employment Discrimination against Arab Americans." *Sociological Forum* 26: 806–23.

Williams, J. 2001. *Unbending Gender: Why Family and Work Conflict and What to Do about It*. New York: Oxford University Press.

Wright, Bradley R. E., Michael Wallace, John Bailey, and Allen Hyde. 2013. "Religious Affiliation and Hiring Discrimination in New England: A Field Experiment." *Research in Social Stratification and Mobility* 34: 111–26.

Wrzesniewski, Amy, Clark McCauley, Paul Rozin, and Barry Schwartz. 1997. "Jobs, Careers, and Callings: People's Relations to Their Work." *Journal of Research in Personality* 31(1): 21–33.

Wuthnow, Robert. 1994. *God and Mammon in America*. New York: Free Press.

Wuthnow, Robert. 1993. "Pious Materialism: How Americans View Faith and Money." *Christian Century*. March 3.

Yancey, George. 2011. *Compromising Scholarship: Religious and Political Bias in American Higher Education*. Waco, TX: Baylor University Press.

Yancey, George, Sam Reimer, and Jake O. Connell. 2005. "How Academics View Conservative Protestants." *Sociology of Religion* 76: 315–36.

Index

For the benefit of digital users, indexed terms that span two pages (e.g., 52–53) may, on occasion, appear on only one of those pages.

Figures are indicated by an italic *f*, following the page number.